ABORIGINAL WELL-BEING

Canada's Continuing Challenge

ABORIGINAL WELL-BEING

Canada's Continuing Challenge

Edited by

Jerry White, Dan Beavon, and Nicholas Spence

THOMPSON EDUCATIONAL PUBLISHING, INC.
Toronto, Ontario

Information on how to obtain copies of this book is available at:

Website:	http://www.thompsonbooks.com
E-mail:	publisher@thompsonbooks.com
Telephone:	(416) 766–2763
Fax:	(416) 766–0398

Library and Archives Canada Cataloguing in Publication

Aboriginal well-being : Canada's continuing challenge / edited by Jerry White, Daniel Beavon, Nicholas Spence.

Includes bibliographical references.
ISBN 978-1-55077-177-0

1. Native peoples--Canada--Social conditions. 2. Native peoples--Canada--Economic conditions. 3. Native peoples--Canada--Health and hygiene. I. Beavon, Daniel J. K. II. Spence, Nicholas III. White, Jerry, 1951-

E78.C2A36 2007   305.897′071   C2007-905797-7

Production Editor:	Katy Harrison
Cover Design:	Christine Kwan
Copy Editor:	Rachel Stuckey
Proofreader:	Crystal J. Hall
Cover Illustration:	Daphne Odjig *A Comparing of Experiences*, 1982 acrylic on canvas 105cm x 85cm Reproduced by permission of Daphne Odjig Courtesy of Indian and Inuit Art Centres, Indian and Northern Affairs Canada

Every reasonable effort has been made to acquire permission for copyrighted materials used in this book and to acknowledge such permissions accurately. Any errors or omissions called to the publisher's attention will be corrected for future printings

Statistics Canada information is used with the permission of Statistics Canada. Users are forbidden to copy the data and redisseminate them, in an original or modified form, for commercial purposes, without permission from Statistics Canada. Information on the availability of the wide range of data from Statistics Canada can be obtained from Statistics Canada's Regional Offices, its World Wide Web site at http://www.statcan.ca, and its toll-free access number 1-800-263-1136.

We acknowledge the support of the Government of Canada through the Book Publishing Industry Development Program for our publishing activities.

Printed in Canada. 1 2 3 4 5 6 11 10 09 08 07

Table of Contents

Preface
The Importance of Indicators

This address was invited by Dan Beavon, Jerry White, and Peter Dinsdale, Co-Chairs for the Aboriginal Policy Research Conference in Ottawa on March 23, 2006. At this conference the United Nations held a consultative forum on the issues of indicators. In this closing address Elsa Stamatopoulou outlines her views on the importance of developing research on well-being indicators.

Address of Ms. Elsa Stamatopoulou, Chief, Secretariat of the UN Permanent Forum on Indigenous Issues, Division for Social Policy and Development, UN Department for Economic and Social Affairs

[...]

Indicators are a difficult issue, they take long to develop and they are a so-called sensitive matter, at the UN and elsewhere. They raise the issue of the definition of no more and no less than what is happiness, or what Socrates called "the highest good."

Some years back, when I was working in OHCHR, I was very involved with our team in trying to integrate human rights in the UN system's development work and we had a really difficult time with indicators: our colleagues from the development agencies thought that our language was from another planet! Such conceptual differences are not unfamiliar to Indigenous peoples when they try to put forward their visions of their own development—and it is sure that one of the challenges is one of communication, of cultural translation between Indigenous development visions and non-Indigenous development visions.

One day a seminar was organized in NY on good governance indicators by high level experts of an important state: they said they had been working on good governance indicators for 13 years, with inconclusive results ... In our work during this conference, on Indigenous peoples and indicators of well-being I am thinking: the states can wait, the intergovernmental organizations can wait, but Indigenous peoples cannot wait.

A. The Work of the UNPFII

The development of data and indicators that capture the situation of Indigenous peoples based on their own perceptions and aspirations is a methodological priority of the UN Permanent Forum on Indigenous Issues. This priority is due to the overwhelming invisibility of Indigenous peoples in national censuses and other surveys which measure progress and inform policy initiatives in a large number of countries. We understand from certain global estimates that Indigenous peoples in most parts of the world are marginalized and disproportionately constitute a significant number of the world's most impoverished people. We also know from statistical data that many Indigenous peoples in the developed world are living in conditions of the so called 'Fourth World.' The Permanent Forum therefore believes that disaggregation of data is an essential strategy to bring more visibility to the disparities and address the situation of Indigenous peoples. Without such data, or relevant indicators for measuring Indigenous peoples' well-being, mainstream models of development intervention are often thrust upon Indigenous peoples based on assumptions that they work, thereby resulting in inappropriate development policies, forcible assimilation, and dependency on certain welfare-oriented service delivery models.

In response to these issues, the Permanent Forum organized a workshop on data collection and disaggregation in January 2004. The workshop noted a number of important conclusions and recommendations which were consequently adopted by the Permanent Forum. Some of the key observations of the workshop included: that data collection and disaggregation should help "detect discrimination, inequality, and exclusion of Indigenous peoples, both individually and as a group" and it should be 'culturally specific' and relevant to the problems identified by Indigenous peoples.[1] The workshop also noted the necessity of qualitative and human rights indicators to assess the true social situation of Indigenous peoples.

Some of the key recommendations of the workshop included: the free, prior, and informed consent of Indigenous peoples in data collection; the involvement of Indigenous peoples themselves in data collection, analysis and reporting; and the desirability of long-term standardized data based on multiple identification criteria developed with the full participation of local Indigenous peoples. The workshop also noted that data collection exercises should be conducted in local languages and employ local Indigenous interviewers.

Based on this work, last year, the Permanent Forum stated that "… Poverty indicators based on Indigenous peoples' own perception of their situation and experiences should be developed jointly with Indigenous peoples."[2]

B. The Ottawa Conference in a Global Perspective

Let me explain how this conference, including the international expert meeting we conducted, fits within a global process and effort that will feed into the Permanent Forum and the international system.

In fact, during this year, in addition to the meeting in Ottawa which focused on Indigenous peoples in developed countries and indicators of well-being, we will hold three more regional meetings on participatory indicator-setting, in Latin America and the Caribbean, in Africa and in Asia. Parallel to this effort, the Interagency Support Group on Indigenous Issues, which brings together 29 UN and other intergovernmental organizations, has prepared and submitted to the Forum's session this coming May its own paper and survey of Indigenous-related indicators that already exist and also identifying the gaps. The results of all the regional meetings and the UN survey will then be synthesized, so that a number of core global and regional indicators can be proposed, through the Permanent Forum to the UN system, and other intergovernmental organizations, including IFIs, governments, the private sector and other civil society actors, as for example conservationist organizations. They can also be used by Indigenous peoples themselves.

I am pleased that our international expert group meeting on Indigenous Peoples and Indicators of Well-being—the first in the series we are planning—has come to a successful conclusion. And we are grateful to Indian and Northern Affairs Canada, and the co-hosts [The University of Western Ontario and the National Association of Friendship Centres], for co-sponsoring this workshop. The workshop brought in Indigenous experts from the Russian Federation, the Arctic, First Nations of Canada, Native America, Australia, and New Zealand to discuss work done on indicators of relevance to Indigenous peoples within their respective regions with the following objectives in mind:

1) Identify gaps in existing indicators at the global, regional, and national levels that assess the situation of Indigenous peoples and impact policy making, governance, and program development, including from a gender perspective.

2) Examine work being done to improve indicators so that they take into account Indigenous peoples and their concerns and assess them according to qualitative and quantitative criteria, including a gender perspective.

3) Examine linkages between quantitative and qualitative indicators, particularly indicators that look at processes affecting Indigenous peoples

4) Propose the formulation of core global and regional indicators that address the specific concerns and situations of Indigenous peoples, including Indigenous women and can also be used by international financial institutions, the UN system and other intergovernmental organizations, including regional ones.

C. The Main Results of the International Workshop on Indigenous Peoples and Indicators of Well-being

(A) Our meeting highlighted **the necessity and importance of indicators for understanding and measuring the quality of life of Indigenous peoples-according to their own perceptions**. In particular, the meeting addressed the **question of measurement**, i.e. **what is being measured**

and according to whose standards and whose visions—is it government or Indigenous peoples themselves? Existing international and national indicator frameworks developed by governments and international institutions in many parts of the world often times do not capture the situation or inadequately capture the situation of Indigenous peoples. For example, an indicator such as the proportion of population below $1/day may not capture Indigenous peoples' perception of poverty. Indigenous peoples may perceive their own poverty in terms of lack of access to and integrity of their traditional lands, forests, scarcity and threats to traditional seeds, plant medicines, food animals, or integrity of and access to sacred sites.

(B) A second focus of the discussions was **the gap in determinants of well-being amidst Indigenous peoples relative to the general population**.

(C) Thirdly, **indicators were highlighted as a means for supporting data development, policy, and program responses**. In many countries, collection techniques often overlook or are unable to determine the quality of life and well-being of Indigenous peoples. Inappropriate techniques or the lack of disaggregated data often place us in a quandary in terms of further data development in Indigenous communities. **One method for breaking the cycle of data gaps is to develop indicators that are both statistically relevant and culturally appropriate as a means of capturing more precise and relevant information**. When public policies are top-down, they result in improper and culturally irrelevant statistical information. And we all know that indicator and statistical frameworks inform debates and decision-making amongst Indigenous peoples themselves as much as government

An important issue to capture in indicator setting is the particular situation of Indigenous women and gender more comprehensively—and also the situation of IPs though the whole span of their life: children, youth, and elders.

We were encouraged to hear about some important efforts of Indigenous peoples themselves and others to capture culturally sensitive and relevant indicators of well-being, showing that good work is really possible if the will is there. As one of our Maori participants from New Zealand repeatedly stressed, in doing this work on indicators and statistics "we need to continue to stay in a solution mode."

Participation as the Permeating Theme

The Permanent Forum strongly believes that indicators and disaggregated data are important not just as a measure of the situation of Indigenous peoples, but as a vital strategy in improving their lives by capturing their aspirations and world views, promoting development with identity, protecting and promoting their cultures and integrity as Indigenous peoples and empowering them to utilize such information to their benefit.

I am confident to state today that, what we heard with the most clarity in the discussions we held is that **unless Indigenous peoples themselves participate fully and effectively in data collection and the establishment of indicators, efforts will likely be incomplete, baseless, or irrelevant, and essentially provide too fragile a foundation for wise policies, including public resource allocations**.

It is ironic and unacceptable that a number of mainstream discourses on poverty and development still continue to exclude and marginalize Indigenous peoples. It is only through the full and effective participation of Indigenous peoples in research, including in data collection and the setting of indicators, that we can go beyond the discourses to action that will improve Indigenous peoples' lives.

In the final analysis, indicators are about listening to Indigenous peoples, they are about a true dialogue between Indigenous peoples and the rest of society, they are about being open to Indigenous world views and respecting them.

The theme of the Second International Decade of the World's Indigenous People adopted by the General Assembly last December is "Partnership for action and dignity." The word "dignity" is linked to fundamental human rights and freedoms. **And we all know, that there is no dignity without participation**.

This is our major challenge. Let us respond to it.

Endnotes

1 Report of the Workshop on Data Collection and Disaggregation for Indigenous Peoples to the Permanent Forum on Indigenous Issues, Third Session, E/C.19/2004/2.

2 Paragraph 15, Report of the UN Permanent Forum on Indigenous Issues on its Fourth Session, E/C.19/2005/9

Part One:
Measuring Well-being

1

Introduction:

Aboriginal Well-being: Canada's Continuing Challenge

Dan Beavon and Jerry White

Introduction

Canada was founded on the principles of peace, order, and good government.[1] It would be fair to say that most Canadians view our society as peaceful, civil, and just. As Canadians, we are often shocked or dismayed when we see civil unrest in other countries, particularly when police or military force are used against civil populations in order to quell popular uprisings or to restore order. When we see such events unfolding in the news, we breathe a collective sigh of relief and count our blessings that we live where we do. However, it may be that our collective memories are quite short, and our knowledge of history quite limited, because police forces and the military have intervened thousands of times against many different segments of civil society in Canada. Some of these interventions have been against protestors (e.g., such as the police action during the 1997 Asia-Pacific Economic Cooperation summit meeting in Vancouver), unruly sports fans (e.g., the 1955 Rocket Richard riot in Montreal), unions (e.g., the 1919 Winnipeg general strike), and sometimes against Aboriginal peoples.

Some of the more recent and notable police and military interventions against Aboriginal peoples include: Oka (1990), Gustafsen Lake (1995), and Ipperwash (1995). The Oka crisis of 1990[2] is particularly noteworthy because it represents the last time in Canadian history that the military was used against a segment of civil society.[3] The Oka crisis resulted in the death of Sûreté du Québec Corporal Marcel Lemay and it led to the Royal Commission on Aboriginal Peoples.[4] The Gustafsen Lake seige represented the largest paramilitary operation in the history of British Columbia[5] and the incident at Ipperwash resulted in the death of Aboriginal protestor Dudley George.

Usually these police and military interventions are the result of Aboriginal occupations and protests. As the Ipperwash inquiry noted (Linden, 2007, p.15):

> Aboriginal occupations and protests can be large or small, short or long, peaceful or violent. They occur in urban areas, rural areas, and in the remote north ... The immediate catalyst for most major occupations and protests is a dispute over a land claim, a burial site, resource development, or harvesting, hunting and fishing rights. The fundamental conflict, however, is usually about land.

Aboriginal occupations and protests are quite common and the vast majority of these events are resolved peacefully, without violence or property damage.[6] Many of these incidents, however, garner considerable media coverage, especially when these events expose major fault lines within Canadian society. For example, the Burnt Church crisis of 1999 and 2000 resulted in angry non-Aboriginal fishermen damaging and destroying a number of Mi'kmaq lobster traps. The local Mi'kmaq retaliated by destroying non-Aboriginal fishing boats and buildings. The Caledonia dispute (2006 and on-going at press time) has been the catalyst for several confrontations between Aboriginal protestors, local non-Aboriginal residents, and the Ontario Provincial Police. While such incidents make for good news stories, they often expose the underlying racist underbelly that still permeates some segments of Canadian society. While many critics may question the economic effectiveness of Aboriginal occupations and protests, they clearly do not understand the intrinsic value that Aboriginal peoples place on their traditional lands and how this attachment is integral to their culture and identity (Burrows, 2005).

While Aboriginal occupations of land will continue in the foreseeable future, Canadians witnessed an entirely new type of Aboriginal protest on June 29, 2007. On this date, the Assembly of First Nations (AFN) organized a National Day of Action. This one day event was part of a broader strategy of the AFN, launched in the fall of 2006 to create awareness of First Nations issues; more specifically, it was a call for action against poverty.[7] This book deals with this same issue, not from an advocacy or political viewpoint, but from an empirical and scientific perspective.

The "Make Poverty History for First Nations" campaign was initiated to highlight the struggles facing First Nations people and communities. The "National Day of Action" was unique for several reasons.

First, the event was one of the largest rallies in Canadian history based on the sheer number of events and locations across the country.

Second, the event was peaceful. There was considerable tension before the event and some in the media and some less sympathetic groups were anticipating confrontations between the Aboriginal peoples and the general public or police. But many of the anticipated tensions were reduced prior to the event through a series of actions. Minister Prentice made a major announcement for an action plan to reform and speed up the specific claims process. The slow pace with which specific claims were resolved has often created tensions between many First Nations and the government. He also defused the threat of blockades at one potential hot spot, by conferring official reserve status to 75 acres of land recently purchased by the Roseau River Fist Nation in Manitoba. AFN Grand Chief Phil Fontaine also did his part to calm the waters. He repeatedly urged Aboriginal people to make the Day of Action a peaceful demonstration aimed at generating public awareness of, and support for, Aboriginal issues. Chief Fontaine also signed a protocol between the AFN and the RCMP that set out ground rules for dealing with any crisis that might occur during the Day of Action. In summary, the event was so peaceful that it was anticlimactic.

Third, the event was not an occupation of a specific piece of land. In fact, protest was not really about land at all. What we witnessed was a shift from a *rights-based agenda* (e.g., specific and comprehensive claims, self-determination, self-government, Indian status, membership, citizenship), which have dominated the Aboriginal political landscape over the last thirty years, to a *needs-based agenda*. While all of these latter rights-based issues are important, there is no direct evidence to suggest that the disproportionate attention that has been paid to them has improved the quality of life of Aboriginal people or their communities. That is not to say we will not see improvements coming from these actions, but only that to date such gains have not been measurable (see Chapter 9).

Aboriginal issues will clearly present Canada with some of its most complex challenges in the twenty-first century. Will this century be the one where we finally address the issues of poverty, lack of educational attainment, poor health, and social problems that beset Aboriginal peoples? Or, will it be one that replicates the past, maintains the status quo, and condemns the next generation of Aboriginal children to a life of mediocrity, suicides, substance abuse, and poverty?

The National Day of Action reminded us that there is a growing understanding and impatience with respect to the relative deprivation that Aboriginal peoples face in Canada. The well-being of the general population far exceeds that of its Aboriginal population. Now instead of turning that inequality into despair and internal violence, it is being channelled outward.

We decided to title this book, "Aboriginal Well-being: Canada's Continuing Challenge." We had considered calling it, "Canada's Shameful Legacy"; however, shame is not what is needed. What is needed is better policies developed from solid research evidence created in partnership with the Aboriginal peoples themselves.

In our 2003 book *Aboriginal Conditions*, we said that "we need to develop better measures of the First Nation communities and tailor our programs and policies to match the reality of the country." In that book we discussed our preliminary attempts to adapt the United Nations Human Development Index (HDI) to the First Nations in Canada (Beavon and Cooke 2003). We also presented a "Community Capacity Index" which aimed to assess the relative capacity of Aboriginal communities to accept and handle their socio-economic development. As we have repeatedly argued, we can not download programs to communities that have not got the capacity to take them on. It serves no one's interests to dump programs as fast as people can fail at managing them (Maxim and White 2003).

We also argued that there are real differences between Aboriginal communities. Some are thriving and relatively self-reliant, while others are facing or have suffered virtual collapse. Within many communities there are vast differences in the resources that families have available. In *Aboriginal Conditions* we also

presented research on the intra-Aboriginal inequalities that plague the populations. We concluded that we needed better ways of understanding capacity and
well-being and that we also needed to develop Canada-wide initiatives that target
the intra-Aboriginal differences.

This book is our next generation of models and tools that are developed to give us
a better understanding of the levels of development and well-being of the Aboriginal peoples of Canada. Some might ask why we are doing this (see Salée, 2006).
We would argue that it is our responsibility, as social scientists, to try and improve
our understanding of the world. That in itself is true. However, we have a selfish
reason as well. Our own well-being is tied to the well-being of the others who
inhabit this great country. In order to keep the high standards of living, level
of prosperity, relative social calm, and exceptional living conditions, we have to
recognize that there is an important, on-going disadvantage that is experienced
by the Aboriginal peoples of Canada. Unless we address this central problem,
Aboriginal relative deprivation will lead to the erosion of the well-being of all
those living in Canada.

What Is at Stake in this Relative Deprivation?

One of the most powerful of human motivators is relative deprivation. Sociolo-
gists, have argued that relative differences in well-being and resources, including
wealth, are often more important than the absolute differences in determining
the perceived quality of life (Gurr, 1970; Griffin, 1988). This means that policies
that increase the societal wealth but leave relative inequalities may not actually
increase the overall well-being of a country.

An understanding of deprivation develops as people compare themselves to
those around them. If the comparison group is reasonable, then people will react
to differences. It is not some absolute level that is used in comparisons. Inequalities that remain even as the absolute levels of prosperity increase still lead to
group resistance. If we think of a village of subsistence farmers that has only
their crops and a small amount of generated income to live on, it may be that they
develop a lifestyle where they are happy despite limited resources. If that village
is moved to the outskirts of a big city or is integrated through digital means to the
wider world, it will begin to assess its relative position. In this case the villagers
will become angry about their circumstances and may begin to protest.

Feeling deprived as an individual differentiates from feeling deprived as a group ...
particularly if there are strong identifiers for that group (see Walker and Smith,
2002). We also know that social identity, social comparison, and understandings
of distributive justice are involved in relative deprivation (ibid). These are collective or social theories, and when we integrate them with relative deprivation we
get what we call integrated relative deprivation theory.

This integrated theory is important because it captures how a group sees itself,
how an individual belongs or identifies their place in the group, whether there

is or could be any explanation for their similar treatment and whether there is a measure of fairness or lack of fairness in their deprivation.

We have argued in other works (White and Beavon, 2003) that understanding the collective identity of Aboriginal peoples is important. The world today is composed of peoples bound together in groups that share some characteristics that create bonds between them. These groups coalesce for a variety of reasons. More often than not, these bonds of cohesion have some relationship to cultural and physical similarities. Social scientists have spent countless research hours studying these ethnic and racial ties. Ties that bind groups together also create differences with others. These differences between collectivities can often involve the development of hierarchies and inequalities. Socio-economic conditions, sometimes measured and sometimes assumed, are used to rank peoples. The roots of some of the most complex social problems are the differential development of ethnic groups and the social ranking that comes with these variations. Public policy in this era of human development is confronted by these social problems and the set of questions that issue from them.

If we look at this racialized and ethnicized understanding of differences in resources and resulting hierarchies and overlay this understanding with an appreciation of the integrated relative deprivation theory we can understand the import of the current situation. Aboriginal people, seeing and experiencing the differences in their lives in comparison with other groups in Canada will inevitably draw conclusions about their relative worth. At an individual level this can result in a lack of respect for themselves, which leads to intragroup violence and self-abuse (drugs, alcohol, suicide, marital violence, etc.). The individual might blame society and strike out individually against that society (through crime or violence). Most assuredly, over time, the ties that create the collective identity will assert themselves in a collective understanding. Those who share history, culture, territory, and common understandings, who become bound together in groups that share some characteristics that create bonds between them, will assess that they are not treated fairly. Collective response to relative deprivation can become a challenge to the fabric of a country that has multiple collectivities such as ethnic or racial groups.

This book is about identifying clearly that there is relative deprivation. It is also about wanting to spur us to move forward in dealing with that deprivation.

It was Francis Bacon who argued for an understanding of the world free from theologically distorted realities. We would concur that there should be a drive to develop the most appropriate and accurate assessments of the well-being and development of different peoples as is possible.

Why Should We Be Developing Well-being Indicators?

There are many reasons why we need to proceed quickly on the development of indicators. If we learn from the United Nations Human Development Index (HDI) and our own work on the Registered Indian Development Index we can see there is an important policy relevance. The HDI has been used to:

- stimulate national political debate—often used for advocacy and to hold governments accountable.
- give priority to human development—an analysis of the three components of the HDI can identify areas requiring policy attention.
- highlight disparities within countries—disaggregation by social group or region can enable local community groups to lobby for more resources.
- open new avenues for analysis—allows comparative studies to be undertaken with respect to the testing of development theories and practices.
- stimulate dialogue on aid policy—HDI has been used by some countries as the basis for aid allocations.

There have been debates internationally on a series of issues related to developing well-being indicators as well. The World Bank and International Monetary Fund have been grappling with several complex issues. There are some who believe that we should send aid and development dollars to those countries that are, by accepted measures, the worst off. Still others think that we should reward the countries that have shown improvement when they have been assisted. The question is, how can we even determine who is who, without measures to assess them? Measures can therefore allow debates on real conditions and let policy be developed. As well, when a policy is put into place, these measures can track the change over time, allowing us to assess success or failure.

We said in 2003 that we were going to develop better measures of the First Nation communities. The reason was that this could assist us to tailor our programs and policies to match the reality of the country. We believe the Canadian public is concerned and ready to address the kinds of problems and difficulties that face Aboriginal people. However, they also seem to want some assurance that the resources are apportioned where most needed and have some success, given clear policy benchmarks and goals. The most cynical may say this is a demand for a "bang for the buck" while the most optimistic may say they want to see more rapid improvement of the Aboriginal condition.

Another reason for developing these measures relates to international prestige. Canada has relied on its positive image around the world in many ways. It helps us play a greater role than our population size should ever permit. It gains us economic advantage, facilitating our negotiations with those that might otherwise be hostile. Finally, it aids us as Canadians in our international dealings and travel

Table 1.1: **Comparing Levels of Development: Registered Indians in Canada and the Canadian Population**

		1981	1991	2001
Life Expectancy at Birth (years)	Registered Indians	65.7	70.6	72.9
	Canadian Population	75.6	77.9	78.7
Proportion Completed High School or Higher[1]	Registered Indians	0.33	0.55	0.57
	Canadian Population	0.60	0.68	0.75
Proportion Completed Grade 9 or Higher[2]	Registered Indians	0.60	0.72	0.83
	Canadian Population	0.80	0.86	0.90
Average Annual Income (2000$)[3]	Registered Indians	$6,840	$8,243	$10,094
	Canadian Population	$16,554	$20,072	$22,489

Notes:

[1] The proportion completed high school or higher is estimated by the population with a secondary school graduation certificate, some post-secondary or trades education, or some university with or without degree, divided by the population aged 19 years and over.

[2] The proportion completed grade 9 or higher is the population aged 15 years and over that has completed grade 9 or higher, divided by the total population aged 15 years and over.

[3] The average annual income is the average income from all sources for the year before the Census enumeration, adjusted by the Statistics Canada Consumer Price Index to year 2000 constant Dollars (Statistics Canada 2005b).

Sources: Statistics Canada Census Data custom tabulations; Statistics Canada 1984, 1990, 1995, 1998, 2005a; Rowe and Norris, 1995; Nault et al. 1993; Norris, Kerr, and Nault, 1996; DIAND, 1998; Verma, Michalowski, and Gauvin, 2003; authors' calculations.

as individuals. The relative deprivation and disadvantage of the Aboriginal people that live in Canada has come under more and more scrutiny and criticism in recent years.[8] It is in our interest to have a clear, acceptable, and valid set of measures so we can accept or reject such commentaries and most importantly make the changes we need to avoid the criticisms in the first place.

When we are asked why we think we should develop the Community Well-being Index (CWB), we note that such an index will allow us to measure well-being at the community level, identify determinants of well-being problems, and assess well-being trends in First Nations and other Canadian communities across time. This is a critical step in making the lives of First Nations, Métis, and Inuit peoples in Canada better.

Before we explore how we have proceeded with the development of these indicators and benchmarks, it is important to give an overview of the relative deprivation that exists in Canada for Aboriginal peoples.

Table 1.2: **Key Labour Market Indicators for Aboriginals and Non-Aboriginals in Canada 2001**

	Non-Aboriginal	Registered Indian
Not in the Labour Force	28%	42%
Unemployed	7.6%	22.4%

Based on the 2001 Census Public Use Microdata File

Figure 1.1: **Comparing the Proportion of Aboriginal Population with Post-secondary Education to All Other Canadians**

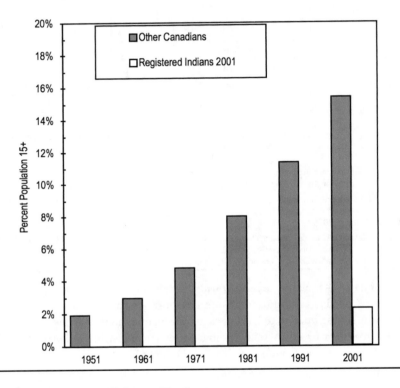

Aboriginal Conditions Today

While many Canadians are aware that the First Nations peoples face certain hardships, they are not aware of the extent of the problems nor how persistent these differences are over time. There was a disturbing indication of this in the results of a poll conducted shortly after The Royal Commission on Aboriginal Peoples Report, which was released in the mid-1990s. In that survey nearly half of the Canadians polled thought that Indian reserves had similar standards of living and well-being as non-Aboriginal communities (Insight Canada 1996). This is a problem for everyone. Unless we understand the real situation we can never confront it and make real improvements.

In **Table 1.1** (page 9), we summarize some trends that we have observed over the 1981 to 2001 period, comparing some basic indicators between Registered Indians and the Canadian population.

Registered Indian life expectancy improved from 65.7 years in 1981 to 72.9 years in 2001, an increase of 7.2 years, compared with an increase of 3.1 years for the Canadian population. This means that there has been a narrowing of the gap; however, the Registered Indian population remains nearly 6 years behind the Canadian population.

We find that educational attainment also lags behind the Canadian population. While we can see overall improvement for Registered Indians between 1981 and 2001, improvement in educational attainment has not been continuous. In the 1981 to 1991 period there was a narrowing of the gap with the Canadian population in terms of the proportion with high school or higher, whereas in the 1991 to 2001 period the gap actually increased.

The average annual income of both the Registered Indian population and the Canadian population increased over the 1981 to 2001 period. In terms of dollars, there was much less improvement in the average annual income of Registered Indians between 1981 and 2001. The income gap between Registered Indians and other Canadians grew over the entire period, from $9,714 in 1981 to $12,395 in 2001. It is interesting to note that over the twenty-year period we see a slight improvement in the relative annual income. As a proportion of the Canadian population's average income, the Registered Indian population narrowed the average income gap over the twenty-year period. Registered Indian 's average income as a proportion of the Canadian population's average income improved from 41.3% in 1981 to 44.9% in 2001. All of the improvement took place between 1991 and 2001.

If we look at labour force participation, we can see the same patterns of disadvantage.

Compared to the non-Aboriginal population, many more Registered Indians have chosen (or been forced) not to seek employment, as reflected in the substantially lower labour force participation rates. As well, of those seeking employment, nearly three times as many Registered Indians are unemployed.

We argued above that there is a relative disadvantage for Aboriginal people compared to the Canadian population, and it would appear to us that the patterns of relative disadvantage extend much further than most people understand. In fact, the disadvantage we note here captures only a portion of the issues. For example, we have seen that there is a serious and on-going problem with potable water (Chapters 8 and 9 in White et al. 2006), higher rates of suicide (Chandler and LaLonde, 2004), and high rates of self-reported health problems (Spence, 2007; Chapter 10).

Educational Attainment: A Detailed Perspective

We generally agree that the development of human capital is very important in the self-actualization of a person. It allows one to choose when and how to integrate

Figure 1.2: Comparing the High School Graduation Rates of Registered Indians in 2001 to All Other Canadians Over Time

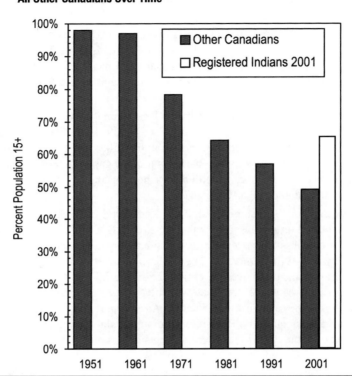

into the economic enterprise of the country, region, or community in which one lives, and it also contributes to the production of citizenship.

There is a long scientific tradition in sociology and economics that has established that educational attainment, that is, the acquisition of human capital, is highly correlated with income, wealth, occupational diversity, and a host of other positive outcomes (see Becker, 1964 and Coleman, 1988). This relationship has been demonstrated to hold for Aboriginal people as well (Spence et al., 2007; Spence, 2007; White, Maxim, and Spence, 2004; and White, Spence, and Maxim, 2005).

If we look closely at the situation for education, we see two trends. We can see in **Figure 1.2** that the Registered Indian population (measured in 2001) has a high school completion rate roughly equal to the rate of non-Aboriginals in 1981; thus, the former are twenty years behind the latter. When we look at post-secondary education, the story is even less positive. **Figure 1.1** (page 10) shows us that the Aboriginal population are at the same levels as the general population was in the 1950s.

When we look at post-secondary education, the story is even less positive. **Figure 1.2** shows us that the Aboriginal population are at the same levels as the general population was in the 1950s. In fact, we have shown in our research that the gap has been increasing in the last decade (see Hull, 2005). If we examine **Figure 1.4** (page 14), we observe this gap in the younger cohorts. In a knowledge-based economy such as Canada's, this means that the chances for economic integration and higher well-being are going to be reduced as the century moves forward.

We wanted to raise one final disturbing issue. In **Figure 1.3** (page 14) we look at how Aboriginals (white bars), aged 18–29, compare in terms of educational attainment, when compared to a range of other ethnic groups in Canada in 2001. We can see that all Aboriginal groups have much lower rates of high school completion than the other ethnic groups. This indicates to us that there is an exceptional problem facing Aboriginal populations.

This is not the only exceptional problem that faces Aboriginal people. In a study of economic development projects by the Strategic Research and Analysis Directorate of Indian and Northern Affairs Canada (INAC), it was found that compared to the average, it takes between three and four times as long to get businesses developed on reserves (Fiscal realities 1999).

Scientists and policy makers have been faced with the ongoing problem of understanding the relative levels of human development and predicting the capacity of a community (or nation or people) to develop given the resources they have at their disposal. Those interested in development have long sought to discover techniques for measuring social and economic progress. Even more challenging is trying to pinpoint the weaknesses in the mix of resources in order to increase the likelihood of success.

Despite the fact that Canadian social policy has, for the last half-century, focused on reducing inequalities through the removal of economic barriers, First Nations and other Aboriginal people face serious issues, as we noted in our brief description of the relative deprivation facing Aboriginal people in Canada.

What Should We Be Learning From this Book?

The advances we have made in well-being and development measures for First Nations can give us a better idea of where we ought to be concentrating our policy energies and resources. We remain convinced that the more articulate, clear, and valid understandings we can develop of the true conditions, as well as the causes of those conditions, the closer we will be to find the solutions. We made this argument in *Aboriginal Conditions: Research as a Foundation for Public Policy* (2003) and in our volumes originating from the Aboriginal Policy Research Conferences from 2002 and 2006 (White et al. 2007a, 2003, 2004a, 2004b, 2002a,

Figure 1.3: Educational Attainment of Youth Proportion With Less Than High School, 2001

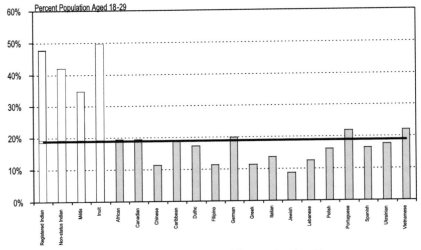

Source: Statistics Canada, 2001 Census of Canada, public use microdata file

Figure 1.4: Proportion of Registered Indians and Other Canadians With a University Degree, 2001

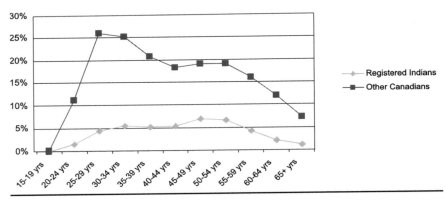

2002b, 2005, 2006, 2007b). This volume on Aboriginal well-being underscores this point as well.

We are calling on Aboriginal and non-Aboriginal leaders, policy makers and researchers to make the tough questions part of our dialogue.

Our book raises some very important and controversial issues. Here are a few of them.

We are not saying "spend more" or "spend less." We have no idea whether $8 billion or $16 billion is what is necessary to solve the problems plaguing Aboriginal conditions. We are saying, "let us figure out what is best." What is the proper

Figure 1.5: The Relationship Between the Community Well-being Index and Government Transfers

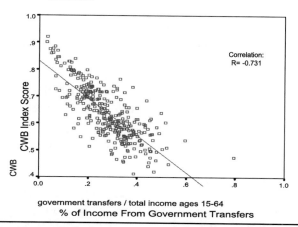

Correlation:
R= -0.731

government transfers / total income ages 15-64
% of Income From Government Transfers

Preliminary analysis of 2001 data reveals that individuals living in First Nations communities with higher well-being are less dependent on government transfers.

way to approach the government transfers and claims settlements to communities? We would say that is not clear right now. Our studies of the CWB in this volume indicate that settlements of specific claims do not impact well-being in the short run. Will they or can they impact development and well-being in the long-run? That is to be determined. For example, **Figure 1.5** shows that when we looked at the relationship between transfers and the CWB scores, there is a strong negative relationship between levels of transfer payments and the well-being of a community. Thus, transfers are not, on the surface, creating equality between communities, which is what they are supposed to do. They are supposed to make up for the shortfalls experienced by communities that are suffering some disadvantage. This raises two very complex and controversial questions. Should we be subsidizing the "worst-off" communities or stratifying our transfers to reward those that are making gains? The second question is even more controversial. Are there some communities that are simply not sustainable? As hard a discussion as this would be, it is certainly not one we can avoid forever. The Kashechewan story most certainly raised the spectre of this issue. Indeed, the suggestion was made to move the community.[9]

The demand for tools to be able to assist all of us, Aboriginal and non-Aboriginal, in making these choices is heartbreakingly obvious. It is not that people are incapable in some individual way; instead, it may be that history has passed some communities by. If we think of non-Aboriginal communities where a natural resource is the driving force behind the local economy, there are cases in which this resource becomes exhausted. The result is that these communities may slowly disappear in the absence of the necessary capacity for long-term sustainability. In the face of climate change, cultural change, and the corresponding change in ways of life in some Aboriginal communities, there may be communities that simply cannot be sustainable, productive, successful places to build families and live one's life.

This whole discussion requires great care. Some Canadians might say, "Why can't Aboriginal people simply move to another town or city if their home community is not working?" We are well aware that this is not the solution. Aboriginal people have a strong attachment to the land, they desire to have proximity to their families and clans, and many hold to the traditions and cultures of their past. Their home communities are part of their identity. This makes simply dispersing as individuals, when troubles increase, a difficult, if not impossible choice. However, our research indicates that nearly half of all reserve band members (recognized citizens of First Nations communities) live off-reserve in non-Aboriginal towns and cities (see Norris et al. 2003).

We do not know which, if any, of the First Nations and Inuit communities might be unsustainable, but we do know that we have to have the tools to supplement our understanding, so that we can discuss the problem. *This is an issue that must be debated by Aboriginal people themselves. Solutions can never work if they are imposed.* There must be a widespread buy-in to whatever course of action is decided. Intra-Aboriginal debate would be paralleled by dialogue between the Aboriginal people and the Canadian government.

The foundation of such a debate must be empirical evidence, otherwise we rest on nothing but ideologies and pre-conceived ideas, including prejudice. We have consistently identified the need to continue developing measures of well-being so that we can assess the impact of policies, examine human development and well-being over time, and ground the many policy debates that we are having or—in the case of the above questions—should be having.

We have not touched all the issues in our introduction. That would take an entire book in and of itself. We can say that the policy implications are manifold. This book represents the best we have achieved thus far. We welcome the responses we will receive—both positive and negative.

Have we stopped our work? Not at all. Even as this book goes to press our research teams in the First Nations Cohesion Project at The University of Western Ontario and in the Strategic Research and Analysis Directorate at INAC are working on ways to enhance the well-being measure. We believe the next step is to determine whether we can capture culture and intra-Aboriginal inequality in the measure. The hard slogging work is being done to test these assertions. We hope that in the next two years we will make even greater headway. We also continue our work trying to make these measures universally applicable so other countries and other Aboriginal people can utilize them for their benefit.

Outline of the Book

This book is divided into three distinct sections. Section One deals with issues related to measuring well-being. It contains this introductory chapter and one by Martin Cooke. Cooke explores some of the major conceptual and methodological issues that underpin our approach to measuring development and well-being.

In his chapter he describes the rationale behind the development of the Registered Indian Human Development Index (HDI) and the Community Well-being Index (CWB) and how they can be used to assess the well-being of Aboriginal people in Canada. The measures developed by our research teams are compared to other composite indicators of well-being. Cooke carefully outlines that these are relatively simple measures, based on the comparable data currently available, and he concludes that we will be enhancing the measures in the future. He notes a very important caveat that "...these measures do not reflect the totality of well-being, and may particularly omit some aspects that are important to Aboriginal peoples." With these limitations in mind, we can still conclude that " ... the dimensions that are captured: overall health, education, and income in the HDI and labour force activity and housing quality in the CWB, are objectively important aspects of quality of life. Improvements in these indicators would reflect unambiguously positive advances in the conditions in which people live, and are worthy goals for policy." Cooke concludes that one of the tremendous advances of this framework is that "these measures do allow comparison between Aboriginal and non-Aboriginal populations and communities and the construction of reasonably reliable time series," and this "allows us to address one of our main questions, which is whether social and economic conditions have been improving for Aboriginal people in Canada. They will also allow us to undertake more analytic research, in order to identify the specific factors that influence well-being, and to identify 'what works'."

In Section Two of the book, we assess and report our work on the Human Development Index (HDI). It begins with a chapter by Martin Cooke and Dan Beavon in which they outline how the United Nations HDI has been applied to First Nations communities. They set out to create a picture of how the health, educational attainment, and income of the Registered Indian population has changed over time using the Registered Indian Human Development Index (HDI). The analysis spans a twenty-year period from 1981 to 2001, comparing Registered Indians to the general population of Canada and documenting differences by on- and off-reserve residence, region and province.

Beavon and Cooke find that the Human Development Index scores for Registered Indians and the general Canadian population improved over the 1981–2001 period; the improvements occurred at a faster rate for the former than the latter, but important gaps still remain. Also, they reveal important differences by province with notable problems in the Prairie region. They conclude, however, that the "general picture painted by these measures is therefore one of inconsistent and uneven progress, both in terms of the temporal trends and regional variation." They caution us that "although the general improvement in these measures of economic, social, and physical well-being is clearly good news, these results also show that future improvement should not be taken for granted." We will have to work hard to be able make headway in the future if we want the gaps to narrow.

Chapter 4, by Martin Cooke and Kate Hano, examines gender equality and well-being. They examine a range of issues related to the HDI and beyond, such as occupational distributions. The chapter provides an examination of First Nation women in comparison to men and other women, as well as tracks changes over time.

They conclude that there is evidence of improving gender equality, but the situation is somewhat mixed. They find that "... women's scores have improved on nearly all of the indicators, including income, education, and representation in management and professional and technical occupations, for both the Registered Indian and reference populations. On several of these measures, this resulted in women narrowing the gap with men, particularly in representation among management occupations." However, they note that the gap between men and women changed with respect to life expectancy. Historically, men experience lower life expectancy than women, but in recent years men have gained ground.

Finally, there are many implications for policy that are outlined. One particular issue raised is the increasing advantage that Registered Indian women have in primary and secondary education, compared to Registered Indian men. This stands out as a growing problem for men that we must explore.

In Chapter 5, Martin Cooke, Francis Mitrou, David Lawrence, Éric Guimond, and Dan Beavon develop an international comparison of the application of the United Nations Human Development Index to Aboriginal people in Australia, Canada, New Zealand, and the United States. Cooke et al. analyze the countries to determine if there have been improvements in terms of the gaps between Aboriginal people and the non-Aboriginal populations during the decade 1990–2000. The team uses the same methodology as in the Canadian studies reported in this book. The countries make good comparators given their origins as mainly British colonies, their shared language, and the presence of sizeable indigenous populations.

The conclusions they draw are complex given the many elements compared across the four countries. Overall well-being, measured using the HDI methodology, improved for all Aboriginal people in these four countries. That said, across the sub indices, such as education, income, life expectancy, and others, there was great variation. For example, life expectancy rose in all countries but Australia.

The researchers write that "despite some improvements, the gaps between Aboriginal and non-Aboriginal people on several of these indicators increased." They find that Aboriginal people in Canada and the United States had higher levels of overall well-being than did Australian Aboriginals or Torres Strait Islanders or the Maori of New Zealand. However, "in Canada, the gap in well-being was particularly large between Registered Indians and other Canadians, although the total Canadian Aboriginal population had higher levels of human development." They note that "New Zealand stands out for the rapid improvement in the well-being of the Maori, particularly on educational and income measures ... characterized as poor but improving ... [T]he US had consistently high levels of human development among the Aboriginal population, and small gaps between Aboriginal and non-Aboriginal people. Gaps between Aboriginal and non-Aboriginal people are generally the largest in Australia, and may be growing wider."

The chapter gives us important insights into patterns that exist across the four countries and also where we might learn from the practices of others. It also demonstrates that our work can be applied in the international scene, allowing interesting comparisons and enabling us to understand the particular situations of indigenous people globally.

Part Three is an exploration of the Community Well-being Index. There are five chapters that look at a wide range of issues and report substantial research findings.

The opening Chapter, "The Community Well-being Index (CWB): Well-being in First Nations Communities, Present, Past, and Future," prepared by Erin O'Sullivan and Mindy McHardy, explains the genesis of the measure, details the methodologies employed, and reports the results of the investigation of First Nation communities. This chapter represents a summary of many teams' research efforts. It is a single source for many studies that went into the development of the CWB and contains results of many applied research projects.

The chapter reports many key findings. A national overview comparing First Nation communities with non-Aboriginal communities across all of the components of the CWB—income, housing, labour force participation, and education—is provided. Regional differences and temporal changes from 1981–2001 are also given strict attention. The detailed presentation of methods and data analysis leads to the following conclusion: while there have been improvements in the well-being of First Nations over the last two decades, there remains a major gap between Aboriginal and non-Aboriginal well-being.

O'Sullivan and McHardy conclude that we cannot assume the gap will gradually disappear. Importantly, they note that this is not the entire story concerning well-being. They point out that while we are confident that this represents an accurate assessment of the conditions, there is much more sophistication to be developed. Indeed, we are getting closer to being able to understand the dynamics at play in the process of well-being development and will continue to improve our capacity.

We note that even as we publish this book, we are already examining whether intra-community inequality might have an effect we can measure, and if it would be wise to integrate an inequality component into the CWB measure.

In Chapter 7, Senécal, O'Sullivan, Guimond, and Uppal use the HDI and the CWB to assess the well-being of the Inuit people of Canada. Inuit communities are compared to all First Nations and all other Canadian communities, regardless of size and location. Senécal et al., illustrate the marked disparity in socio-economic well-being between Inuit communities and Other Canadian communities. Their analysis also highlights the great disparities that exist between different

Inuit communities; that is, some communities experience relatively high levels of well-being while others are facing serious difficulties.

In Chapter 8, White and Maxim utilize their matching communities analysis, which involves matching each reserve (First Nation communities) with its best matched non-Aboriginal community, to develop a pairwise comparison between reserves and the matched non-reserve communities across four zones of remoteness. The CWB reveals a disparity in well-being between First Nations communities and other Canadian communities. This study examines the degree to which that disparity is a function of the small size and remote locations of many First Nations communities, as opposed to the fact that they are reserves.

Overall, they found that only a small portion of the disparity between reserves and other communities can be attributed to either location or population size. Once gross geography is taken into account, they notice that reserve communities closer to urban areas are more similar to their non-reserve matched community than are reserves in more isolated parts of the country. With few notable exceptions, the disparities between reserves and their non-reserve community matches increase with geographic isolation.

Chapter 9 tries to unravel an extremely important complex and difficult problem. Jerry White, Nicholas Spence, and Paul Maxim pose the question, "Does the settlement of specific claims have a direct effect on the well-being of First Nation communities?" Trying to assess this is difficult because change takes place over time and the data are not easily found nor analyzed. They conclude that there is little evidence to support that settling claims leads to improvements in well-being. However, they note that there may be many explanations for this result. First, the settlement of a claim today may not result in the flow of resources for some time. Second, those resources need to be invested, and seeing a return from those investments could take an extended period of time. Also, there is the issue of how the claim is settled. For example, if the claim results in a cash settlement that flows to individuals, it may have only a temporary impact; whereas, if the First Nations community invests in business development, there could be long term employment, which would increase income and the measures would reflect that change.

The lack of a significant positive relationship between specific claims settlement and increases in well-being is troubling, but the researchers state that they will continue to monitor this relationship and develop more sophisticated approaches for future assessments.

The last chapter is by Susan Wingert, who uses the EKOS research firm's First Nation community survey data to assess the well-being of those communities and compare it to the CWB analysis. Working with the First Nations Cohesion Project at Western, Wingert sets out to examine the relationship between objective measures of community well-being and the subjective assessments of residents who live in those First Nations communities. Wingert notes that "we are interested in determining whether there are patterns in residents' responses depending on whether they live in a below-average, average, or above-average CWB community." She addresses three research questions: "1) What do residents of First Nations communities identify as the top priorities for their communities, and do they vary by CWB scores? 2) Is there an association between residents' subjective assessments of their community and its CWB score? 3) Is there a relationship between community well-being, as measured by the CWB, and subjective dimensions of individual well-being?" She was looking for any correspondence between the self-reported health indicators and the CWB. This would give us confidence that the CWB is in part a proxy measure of community well-being. In the case of discrepancies, it calls on us to find explanations, and increase our understanding of the interaction of external conditions and the individual assessments.

She concludes that the CWB captures key issues for community residents. Among many assessments that she makes, Wingert reports that "in general, we find the expected pattern with above average CWB community respondents providing more favorable assessments, with the exception of education. Further investigation is needed to uncover whether the quality of education is relatively poor in high CWB communities or whether there are higher expectations."

One of many interesting findings is that respondents in higher CWB categories report more positive perceptions of themselves and their lives. This gives us an another indication of the validity of the CWB.

Endnotes

1   This phrase is often abbreviated as "POGG." These principles are from the introduction to section 91 of the *Constitution Act*, 1867.

2   The Oka crisis was the result of a land dispute between the Mohawk community of Kanesatake and the town of Oka, in Quebec during the summer of 1990. This crisis was sparked by a Municipality of Oka decision to extend a nine-hole golf course on land that the Mohawks claimed was, and had always been, theirs. The 39 hectares of land in question included a Native cemetery and parts of a pine forest. Several books provide detailed accounts of the Oka crisis (e.g., MacLaine et al., 1991; Alfred, 1995).

3   During the 65-year period following confederation (1867–1933), Canada's military was engaged 132 times in law enforcement activities in order to restore civil order (Pariseau, 1973; Haslip, 2006). However, since 1933, Canada's military has been used only twice to restore civil order: the October crisis of 1970 and the Oka crisis of 1990. It is interesting to note that the Canadian Army mobilized over 2,000 troops to restore order in Oka, yet during that same summer in 1990, Canada sent slightly less than 1,000 soldiers to fight in Iraq. The Oka crisis drew worldwide attention, catapulting native land rights into the spotlight.

4   This royal commission was established in 1991 to address many of the Aboriginal issues that had come to light as a result of the Oka crisis and the failed Meech Lake Accord. The Commission culminated in a final report published in 1996. The final report consisted of five volumes and the 4,000 pages represent the most in-depth study ever undertaken of the historical relations between the Canadian government and Aboriginal peoples.

5   After failed negotiations, 400 tactical assault members of the RCMP, backed by helicopters and armored personnel carriers supplied by the military, were deployed against the Aboriginal occupants and their supporters. In one particularly tense moment, the RCMP fired thousands of rounds during a 45-minute blaze of gunfire (Steele, 1997).

6   Wilkes (2004) analyzed media reports and noted that there were roughly 100 Aboriginal occupations or protests between 1968 and 2000. Using the same methodology, but different criteria, Clairmont and Potts (2006) found 616 incidents between 1951 and 2000. Chapter two of the Ipperwash Inquiry provides an excellent primer on Aboriginal occupations (Linden, 2007).

7   In some respects, this call for action against poverty was probably an off-shoot of the Kelowna Accord. The Kelowna Accord is the common name given to a working paper entitled "Strengthening Relationships and Closing the Gap" which resulted from 18 months of roundtable consultations cumulating at the First Ministers' Meeting in Kelowna in November, 2005. This working paper established targets to improve the education, employment, and living conditions for Aboriginal peoples through additional governmental funding. This accord was never signed, nor were monies ever budgeted for it, before the minority government of Paul Martin fell. The subsequent minority government of Steven Harper identified different priorities with respect to Aboriginal affairs. While the Kelowna Accord is clearly a political hot potato, Wikipedia provided a brief, but balanced discussion of it at press time.

8   See for example: Amnesty International's criticism of Aboriginal womens' treatment in Canada <**www.carleton.ca/jmc/cnews/27012006/n3.shtml**>; the United Nations Human Rights Commission's criticisms of Canada over serious concerns about human rights performance with regards to Aboriginal peoples <**www.prisonjustice.ca/starkravenarticles/UNhuman-rights_1105.html**>; and accusations of self-interest in blocking UN human rights for indigenous peoples. <**www.ctv.ca/servlet/ArticleNews/story/CTVNews/20070606/indigenous_rights_07 0606/20070606?hub=Canada**>. Given our treatment of Aboriginal peoples in Canada some see it to our advantage to mute the UN.

9   This has unsuccessfully been tried in the past. See White (2003) for a discussion of the Davis Inlet and Port Harrison relocations.

References

Alfred, G.R. 1995. Heeding the Voices of Our Ancestors: Kahnawake Mohawk Politics and the Rise of Native Nationalism. New York: Oxford University Press.

Beavon, D. and Cook, M. 2003. "An Application of the United Nations Human Development Index to Registered Indians in Canada, 1996." In White, J.P., Maxim, P., and Beavon, D. (Eds.). *Aboriginal Conditions: Research as a Foundation for Public Policy.*. Vancouver: UBC Press. 201–221.

Becker, G. 1964. *Human Capital.* New York: The National Bureau of Economic Research.

Burrows, J. 2005. "Crown and Aboriginal Occupations of Land: A History & Comparison," background paper prepared for the Ipperwash Inquiry, October, 2005.

Clairmont, D. and Potts, J. 2006. "For the Nonce: Policing and Aboriginal Occupations and Protests," background paper prepared for the Ipperwash Inquiry, May, 2006.

Chandler, M. and Lalonde, C. 2004. "Transforming Whose Knowledge? Exchanging Whose Best Practices? On Knowing about Indigenous Knowledge and Aboriginal Suicide." In White, J.P., Maxim, P., and Beavon, D. *Aboriginal Policy Research: Setting the Agenda for Change, Vol. 2*, edited by Toronto: Thompson Educational Publishing, Inc. 111–124.

Coleman, J. 1988. "Social Capital in the Creation of Human Capital." *American Journal of Sociology.* 94 Supplement.

Department of Indian Affairs and Northern Development. 1998. *Population Projections of Registered Indians, 1996–2021.* Ottawa: DIAND.

Fiscal Realities. 1999. "Expanding Commercial Activity on First Nations Land: Getting First Nation Land Development Regulations Right." Strategic Research and Analysis Directorate. Ottawa: Indian and Northern Affairs Canada.

Griffin, D. (Ed.). 1988. *Spirituality and Society: Postmodern Visions.* New York: State University of New York Press.

Gurr T.R. 1970. *Why Men Rebel.* Princeton: Princeton University Press.

Haslip, S. 2002. "The Bisons Now Hunt the Indians: A Critical Consideration of Contemporary Provisions Providing for the Use of Military Force Against Aboriginal Peoples (in Canada)." LL.M., University of Ottawa, Faculty of Law.

Hull, J. 2005. Post-secondary Education and Labor Market Outcomes: Canada, 2001. Ottawa: Indian and Northern Affairs Canada.

Insight Canada Research Inc. 1996. *Perspectives Canada.* 5(1).

Linden, S.B. 2007. *Report of the Ipperwash Inquiry.* Toronto: Publications Ontario.

MacLaine, C. and Boxendale, M.S. 1991. *This Land Is Our Land: The Mohawk Revolt at Oka.* Montreal: Optimum Publishing International.

Maxim, P. and White, J.P. 2003. "Toward an Index of Community Capacity: Predicting Community Potential for Successful Program Transfer." In White, J.P., Maxim, P., and Beavon, D. (Eds.). *Aboriginal Conditions: Research as a Foundation for Public Policy*, Vancouver: UBC Press. 248–263.

Maxim, P., White, J.P., and Beavon, D. "Dispersion and Polarization of Income among Aboriginal and Non Aboriginal Canadians." In *Aboriginal Conditions: The Research Foundations for Public Policy.* Vancouver: UBC Press. 2003. 222–247

Nault, F., Chen, J., George, M.V., and Norris, M.J. 1993. *Population Projections of Registered Indians, 1991–2016.* Report prepared by the Population Projections Section, Demography Division, Statistics Canada. Ottawa: Indian and Northern Affairs Canada.

Norris , M.J., Cooke, M., and Clatworthy, S. 2003. "Aboriginal Mobility and Migration Patterns and the Policy Implications." In White, J.P., Maxim, P., and Beavon, D. (Eds.). *Aboriginal Conditions: Research as a Foundation for Public Policy*, Vancouver: UBC Press. 108–130.

Norris, M.J., Kerr, D., and Nault, F. 1995. *Projections of the Population with Aboriginal Identity in Canada, 1991–2016.* Report prepared by the Population Projections Section, Demography Division, Statistics Canada, for the Royal Commission on Aboriginal Peoples. Ottawa: Canada Mortgage and Housing Corporation and the Royal Commission on Aboriginal Peoples.

Pariseau, Major J.J.B. 1973. *Disorders, Strikes and Disasters: Military Aid to the Civil Power in Canada, 1867–1933.* Ottawa: Directorate of History.

Report of the Royal Commission on Aboriginal Peoples. Canada Communication Group Publishing, Ottawa, Ontario, 1996.

Rowe, G. and Norris, M.J. 1995. *Mortality Predictions of Registered Indians, 1982 to 1996*. Ottawa: Indian and Northern Affairs Canada.

Sallee, D. 2006. "Quality of Life of Aboriginal People in Canada." *IRPP Choices*. 12(6).

Spence, N. 2007. *New Vistas on the Income Inequality–Health Debate: The Case of Canada's First Nations Reserve Population*. PhD Dissertation. Department of Sociology. London: The University of Western Ontario.

Spence, N., White, J.P., and Maxim, P. 2007. "Modeling Community Determinants of Canada's First Nation's Educational Outcomes." Canadian Ethnic Studies. (Forthcoming).

Statistics Canada. 1984. *Life Tables, Canada and Provinces 1980–82*. Catalogue no. 84-532. Ottawa: Statistics Canada.

Statistics Canada. 1990. *Life Tables, Canada and Provinces, 1985–87*. Health Reports Supplement 13. Ottawa: Statistics Canada.

Statistics Canada. 1995. *Life Tables, Canada and Provinces, 1990–92*. Catalogue no. 84-537. Ottawa: Statistics Canada.

Statistics Canada. 1998. *Life Expectancy Abridged Life Tables, at Birth and Age 65, by Sex, for Canada, Provinces, Territories, and Health Regions*. CANISM Table 102-0016. Ottawa: Statistics Canada.

Statistics Canada. 2000. *The Consumer Price Index*. Catalogue no. 62-010-X1B. Ottawa: Statistics Canada.

Verma, R., Michalowski, M., and Gauvin, R.P. 2003. *Abridged Life Tables for Registered Indians in Canada, 1976–80 to 1996–2000*. Paper presented at the annual meeting of the Population Association of America, May 1–3, Minneapolis.

Statistics Canada Census Data custom tabulations; Statistics Canada 1984, 1990, 1995, 1998, 2005a.

Steele, S. "Gustafsen Lake Standoff: 15 Charged." *Maclean's Magazine*, June 2, 1997.

Walker, I. and Smith, H. (Eds.). 2002. *Relative Deprivation: Development, Specification and Integration*. Cambridge: Cambridge University Press.

White, J.P., Anderson, E., Cornett, W., and Beavon, D. (Eds) 2007a. *Aboriginal Policy Research: Moving Forward, Making a Difference*. Vol. 5. Toronto: Thompson Educational Publishing, Inc.

White, J.P., Beavon, D., and Maxim, P. 2003. *Aboriginal Conditions: The Research Foundations for Public Policy*. Vancouver: UBC Press.

White, J.P., Maxim, P., and Spence, N. 2004a. *Permission to Develop: Aboriginal Treaties, Case Law and Regulations*. Toronto: Thompson Educational Publishing, Inc.

White, J.P., Maxim, P., and Spence, N. 2004b "Educational Attainment of Aboriginal Canadians." In White, J.P., Maxim, P., and Beavon, D. (Eds.). 2004. *Aboriginal Policy Research: Setting the Agenda for Change*. Vol. 1. Toronto: Thompson Educational Publishing, Inc.

White, J.P., Maxim, P., and Beavon, D. (Eds) 2002a. *Aboriginal Policy Research: Setting the Agenda for Change*. Volume I. Toronto: Thompson Educational Publishing, Inc.

White, J.P., Maxim, P., and Beavon, D. (Eds) 2002b. *Aboriginal Policy Research: Setting the Agenda for Change*. Volume 2. Toronto: Thompson Educational Publishing, Inc.

White, J.P., Spence, N., and P. Maxim. 2005. "Social capital and educational attainment among Aboriginal peoples: Canada, Australia and New Zealand." In *Policy Research Initiative Social Capital Project Series, Social Capital in Action: Thematic Studies*. Ottawa: Policy Research Initiative, Government of Canada. 66–81.

White, J.P., Wingert, S., Beavon, D., and Maxim, P. (Eds). 2006. *Aboriginal Policy Research: Moving Forward , Making a Difference*. Volume 3. Toronto: Thompson Educational Publishing, Inc.

White, J.P., Wingert, S., Beavon, D., and Maxim, P. (Eds). 2007b. *Aboriginal Policy Research: Moving Forward , Making a Difference*. Volume 4. Thompson Educational Publishing, Inc.

2

The Registered Indian Human Development Indices: Conceptual and Methodological Issues

Martin Cooke

Introduction

The Registered Indian Human Development Index (HDI) and Community Well-Being Index (CWB) were developed by researchers at Indian and Northern Affairs Canada to provide an ongoing indication of progress made in improving the health and well-being of Aboriginal peoples in Canada. In that sense, they are in the tradition of the social indicators movement that began in the late 1960s, and which has generated a wide variety of composite indicators that attempt to measure various aspects of social, economic, physical, psychological, environmental, and spiritual well-being. As we have been careful to make clear in the papers that form the basis for several chapters in this book, none of these indicators are perfect. Each must balance various methodological and conceptual considerations, and all represent some choices about what constitutes "well-being," "quality of life," "human development," or any of the other descriptions of the preferred conditions in which people live. All make some compromise between conceptual completeness and ease of interpretation and calculation, between ideal measures and available data, and between applicability to the local context and validity for broad national or international comparisons.

Despite the inherent shortcomings of any quantitative social indicator, we obviously feel that the ones we have chosen are appropriate, and have the potential to inform policy debates. Nonetheless, it is important to acknowledge the limitations of our measures, while trying to draw attention to what we believe are their strengths and advantages over alternative approaches. This chapter discusses the conceptual and methodological issues and choices that are involved in our adaptation of some of the UNDP's Human Development Indicators to examine well-being among Aboriginal populations in Canada. I first describe the aims of the HDI and CWB indicators and their general form. I then present a number of other indicators, some that are internationally applied and others that have been applied only to specific contexts, in order to situate the indicators in this book within the broader range of social indicators, and to frame a discussion of the various methodological considerations. I conclude by summarizing the limitations of these measures, as well as their strengths.

The Development of the Registered Indian and Inuit Human Development Index

It comes as no surprise that Aboriginal peoples in Canada have lower average incomes, educations, and employment rates, as well as poorer health than other Canadians, and there has been a lot of economic, social, political, and health research aimed at documenting these disparities and uncovering the mechanisms behind Aboriginal disadvantage. Over the past several decades there have been any number of important changes in the political situation of Aboriginal peoples and in the policies and programmes implemented in and by Aboriginal communities that have attempted, successfully or not, to address these inequalities. These have taken place against a background of far-reaching demographic, social, and economic changes in Canadian society. This complexity makes it rather difficult to answer the simple question, *are things getting better?*

The answer to that question, of course, depends on the indicators chosen and the time period over which they are examined. Our work on this series of indicators began in 1998, with the aim of creating a reliable and valid time series of measurements that address a broad conception of "well-being" or "quality of life," and which would be available to identify progress into the future. These indicators would be used to answer the question of whether the disparities between Aboriginal people and other Canadians had indeed decreased, and by how much. These measures could also serve as potential dependent variables to be used in analyses that would identify the causal factors that have lead to changes in these indicators. As well, we intended that these national and regional-level indicators would form the basis for more local measures that could identify communities that had particularly high levels of well-being, as well as those that faced the most challenges.

We took the United Nations' Human Development Index (HDI) as a starting point for the development of these indicators, for reasons that will be discussed in the remainder of this chapter. Our first published application was an adaptation of the HDI to examine the differences in well-being between Registered Indians and other Canadians in 1996 (Beavon and Cooke, 2003). We called this adaptation the Registered Indian Human Development Index, and we used life expectancy estimates and Census data to compare HDI scores of Registered Indians on- and off-reserve to those of other Canadians, by province and region. We found, again to no surprise, important differences on the index, as well as important differences across regions within Canada. As part of this project, we also compared the HDI scores of Registered Indians living on- and off-reserve in 1996 to countries in the United Nations's *Human Development Report*. Although not particularly important in terms of policy implications, we presented these comparisons in order to empirically address the question of whether First Nations people in Canada did live in "Third World conditions," as was sometimes claimed. We found that indeed there were large gaps, but that conditions were comparable to countries nearer to the middle of those in the *Human Development Report*, with "medium" levels of human development.

These measures were then used to investigate the changes in the relative well-being of Registered Indians over the period from 1981 to 2001 (Cooke, Beavon, and McHardy, 2004). This analysis found that indeed the average educational attainment, income, and life expectancy had increased, both on- and off-reserve. Despite this progress, considerable gaps remained between the Registered Indian population and other Canadians on the index. What was more surprising was that gaps on some indicators increased in some Census periods, as the improvements in the Registered Indian population did not keep up with those made by other Canadians. As part of that report, we looked at the trends in gender differences on the HDI indicators, and found that education and income of Registered Indian women had indeed improved between 1981 and 2001. However, progress in closing gender gaps in income was uneven, despite the fact that Registered Indian women were increasingly surpassing Registered Indian men in terms of education. The patterns that we found are presented in Chapter 4 of this volume, along with some supplemental measures and analysis.

The Community Well-Being Index (CWB) is an adaptation of the general HDI methodology to the community level (O'Sullivan and McHardy, 2005). Using Census data, it measures labour force participation and employment, income, housing, and education within communities. Research using the CWB has included mapping and geographic analyses to help understand the role of remoteness and isolation in producing community outcomes, as well as comparisons between First Nations and other Canadian communities with the CWB indicators, which are presented in Chapter 8 of this volume. The HDI and CWB measures have also been used to examine the well-being of other populations, within Canada and internationally. Senécal et al have applied these measures to Inuit populations and communities, the results of which are in Chapter 7.

The Registered Indian HDI and CWB are part of a tradition of social indicators research that has produced a number of useful indices and scales, as well as some that are less practical. In the following section, I present an array of other indicators for comparison, and the rationale behind their development. This is not nearly a complete list, but includes some of the most cited ones, as well as the one other indicator that has been developed in the context of Aboriginal populations.

Social Indicators and the Social Indicators Movement

Social indicators, including the HDI, were developed in order to balance what was seen as an over-emphasis on economic measures in the determination of progress or "development." Gross Domestic Product (GDP) or employment levels are informative, but, it was argued, address only one dimension of human well-being. In the late 1960s and early 1970s, the time at which the development of many of these social indicators began, purely economic approaches to development had come to be viewed with some suspicion, particularly by those who saw the growth in human economic and industrial activity as at odds with the natural environment, and therefore unsustainable. Concerns about crime and social conflict in developed countries, environmental degradation, as well as the slow progress of development in many parts of the world led to a search for indicators that captured more of the totality of human life. Some of the more ambitious social indicators researchers sought to create a system of measures that would compliment the *national accounts* data collected by most countries. These social accounting frameworks would be used to measure whether "real" progress was being made, or whether economic growth was being pursued at the cost of social and economic conditions (Michalos, 2003: 5).

After the initial interest, work on the development of social indicators waned somewhat, but there was a revival in the early 1990s. Since then, many different composite indices and scales have been developed, incorporating a wide variety of social, economic, and environmental measurements. Some of them are quite complex, while others are fairly simple. Below, twelve of these more recently developed indicators, including the UNDP's Human Development Index and the Registered Indian HDI and CWB, are discussed. These include several specifically Canadian measures, and one that has been developed specifically for use with Indigenous populations in Australia.

The UNDP's Human Development Index (HDI)

The United Nations Development Programme made a major contribution to the development of composite indicators with the publication of the first Human Development Report in 1990. This report contained a new indicator, the Human Development Index (HDI), which captured three dimensions of the development process; income, health, and knowledge, in a single indicator (UNDP, 1990). The HDI was a response to the previous emphasis on GDP growth in studies of international development, and the recognition that high national product does not necessarily translate into high average standards of living, particularly if income is not equitably distributed, or investments are made in military expansion instead of health and social infrastructure (Rao, 1991).

The UNDP conceives "human development" as an expansion of choices, made possible by knowledge, material standard of living, and a long and healthy life (UNDP, 1990). The HDI measures countries' progress toward various maximum values on literacy and education, life expectancy at birth, as well as per capita GDP, and publishes a league table ranking countries based on their HDI score. Canada's high ranking, leading the list of countries with "high human development" for most of the 1990s, became a point of pride for some Canadian politicians, despite the fact that there is very little difference in the HDI scores of the most developed countries.

Figure 2.1: Equations

Equation 1
$$I_{Index} = \frac{X_{actual} - X_{min}}{X_{max} - X_{min}}$$

Equation 2
$$I_{HDI} = \frac{\left[I_{LEB} + \left(\frac{2}{3} I_{LIT} + \frac{1}{3} I_{GER} \right) + I_{GDP} \right]}{3}$$

Equation 3
$$I_{GDP} = \frac{\log y - \log y_{min}}{\log y_{max} - \log y_{min}}$$

The HDI is a composite of three sub-indices; an Income Index, an Education Index, and a Life Expectancy Index, each with equal weight in the overall HDI. The life expectancy index and the income index are calculated from single indicators, life expectancy at birth and per capita national product. The education index is composed of two indicators, adult literacy and gross enrolment rates. The general formula for each indicator is shown in **Equation 1** (**Figure 2.1**).

In this way, the sub-indices describe the distance from the theoretical maximum and minimum values, given for 1999 in **Table 2.1** (page 30), as set by the UNDP. Literacy is given a two-thirds weight within the education index, and enrolment a one-third weight. The HDI is simply the arithmetic mean of the Income, Education, and Life Expectancy indices.

The UNDP methodology uses per capita GDP, expressed in Purchasing Power Parity Dollars (PPP$), as a proxy for income, which itself is taken to be a measure of the people's ability to satisfy their basic material needs. The use of per capita GDP is partly due to the difficulty in gathering average annual income data in many developing countries (UNDP, 1999: 128–9). In the calculation of the Income Index, GDP is heavily discounted in order to reflect the decreasing marginal utility of income, the assumption that a given increase will have a larger impact on the lives of those with less income. The logrithmic discounting formula is shown in **Equation 3** (**Figure 2.1**), in which y is per capita GDP and (ymin) and (ymax) are the minimum and maximum income values, expressed in PPP$.

The simplicity of the HDI is offset to some degree by the inclusion of many other statistics in the annual *Human Development Report*. Since 1990, the UNDP has refined some of these measures in its annual reports, and has developed supplementary measures, such as the Gender Development Index and the Gender Empowerment Measure, in response to criticisms that the HDI was not sensitive to gender differences (UNDP, 1995).

Table 2.1: Components, Minimum, and Maximum Values for the HDI and CWB Indices

Indicator	Minimum Value	Maximum Value
UNDP HDI Indicators		
Life expectancy at birth	25 years	85 years
Adult literacy	0%	100%
Combined enrolment ratio	0%	100%
GDP per capita	PPP$100	PPP$40,000
Registered Indian HDI Indicators		
Life expectancy at birth	25 years	85 years
Proportion 15+ with grade 9 or higher	0.0	1.0
Proportion 20+ with high school or higher	0.0	1.0
Per capita total annual income	CDN$100	CDN$40,000
Community Well-being (CWB) Indicators		
Proportion 15+ with grade 9 or higher	0.0	1.0
Proportion 20+ with high school or higher	0.0	1.0
Labour force participation age 20 and older	0.0	0.8895
Employment as proportion of labour force	0.0	1.0
Per capita total annual income	CDN$2,000	CDN$40,000
Proportion of the population with no more than one person per room	0.0	1.0
Proportion of the population living in residences with no need of major repairs	0.0	1.0

The Registered Indian Human Development Index

Calculating a Human Development Index score for the Registered Indian population requires data that are regularly produced and form a reliable time series, and which allow comparison to other Canadian populations. They also need to distinguish between on- and off- reserve residence and be available by province or region to be useful for the types of analyses we had planned.

These requirements limit the sources of data for education and income characteristics to the Census. Life expectancy estimates for the general Canadian population are generated regularly by Statistics Canada using vital statistics data, and the Indian Register is used to produce estimates for the Registered Indian population, as part of projections for the Registered Indian population.

Whereas the UNDP's HDI uses adult literacy and enrolment rates, these measures are not available from Census data. Instead, we use the proportion of the 15 and older population with grade 9 or higher education as a proxy for adult literacy, the measure of the "stock" of basic education in the population. As a measure of higher education, and which is more sensitive to the "flow" of education in to the population, we use the proportion of the population aged 20 and older, which has completed high school, or some technical or community college, or some university.

Per capita GDP, the income measure in the UNDP indices, is replaced in the Registered Indian HDI by a measure of average annual income from all sources. However, whereas Statistics Canada generally reports this measure as averaged for the population 15 and over and with income, we use the average for the total population with and without income, to account for the higher proportion of children and others without income in the Registered Indian population.

These three components are combined in the Registered Indian HDI index using the same procedure and weighting as in the UNDP's HDI. We also use the same maximum and minimum values as the UNDP's HDI (**Table 2.1**), although average income is adjusted using Statistics Canada's Consumer Price Index (Statistics Canada, 2005a).

The Community Well-being Index (CWB)

The CWB (McHardy and O'Sullivan, 2004) combines elements of the HDI, which is applied at a national and provincial/regional level, and elements of the community-level analyses by Armstrong (2001). The dimensions of well-being included in the CWB are education, labour force participation and employment, income, and housing. These indicators are derived from the Census, which provides information at the Census Subdivision (CSD) level, which allows identification of individual reserves and other Aboriginal communities. These measures combined to form an index score for each community, roughly following the methodology of the HDI, with each individual indicator scaled to reflect the difference between a theoretical minimum and maximum.

The CWB contains the two indicators for education from the Registered Indian HDI. It also includes two measures pertaining to labour force activity and paid work in a community. The first is labour force participation in the week prior to the Census, by those aged 20 and over. However, this variable is re-scaled, so that the upper limit is not the 1.0, or 100% labour force participation, an impossible and perhaps undesirable target. Rather, the authors set 0.8895, two standard deviations above the average Census Subdivision (CSD) labour force participation rate in 2001, as the maximum. The second labour force measure is the proportion of the total labour force that was employed in the week prior to the Census. In order to avoid unduly penalizing communities for school enrolment, the denominator for this measure includes only those aged 20 and older. These labour force participation and employment measures are given equal weight within the labour force activity component of the CWB.

The CWB also includes average income per capita. As in the HDI, $40,000 is used as the theoretical maximum (**Table 2.1**). However, whereas the UNDP uses PPP$100 as the minimum value for per capita GDP, the CWB uses CDN $2,000 as a more realistic minimum average annual income in the Canadian context (McHardy and O'Sullivan, 2004: 7, Chapter 6 in this volume).

In addition to education, labour force activity, and income, the CWB includes two indicators pertaining to housing, a particularly important issue in First Nations

Table 2.2: Key Characteristics of Selected Composite Indicators

	Number of Dimensions	Number of Indicators	Sources of Data			Weighting of Concepts			Income Scaling	
			Census	Administrative	Other	Equally Weighted	Theoretical	Empirical	Income Logged	Income Linear
Registered Indian Human Development Index (HDI)	3	4	•	•		•			•	
Community Well-being Index (CWB)	4	6	•			•			•	
UNDP Human Development Index (HDI)	3	4	•	•		•			•	
Weighted Index of Social Progress	10	40	•	•						•
Quality of Life Index (QOL)	7	7	•	•	•			•		•
Prescott-Allen's Indices of the Well-being of Nations	10	87	•	•	•		•			•
Conference Board of Canada's Quality of Life Scorecard	5	24	•	•	•	•				•
Genuine Progress Indicator *	9	27	•	•	•	•			-	•
Fordham Index of Social Health (ISH)	4	16	•	•	•	•				•
Fraser Institute Index of Living Standards	8	8		•	•	•				•
Ontario Social Development Quality of Life Index	4	12	•	•	•	•			-	•
Index of Relative Indigenous Socioeconomic Disadvantage	4	4	•					•	-	-

1 The Ontario Social Development Quality of Life Index and the Index of Relative Indigenous Socioeconomic Disadvantage include income in the form of a poverty rate.

* The Genuine Progress Indicator uses personal consumption, rather than income, and discounts this by the Gini coefficient.

communities. Housing quantity is measured by the proportion of the population living in dwellings with no more than one person per room. Housing quality is measured by the proportion of the population that reported in the Census that their dwellings were not in need of major repairs. Both of these indicators are given equal weight in the housing component.

Other Socio-economic Indicators of Well-being

As described above, the UNDP's HDI and our own Registered Indian HDI and CWB are two of many different composite social indicators, each with a different conception of well-being or "quality of life." Below, I briefly present some of these alternative measures, in order to situate our own indicators within this field. Some of their key characteristics are summarized in **Table 2.2**.

The Weighted Index of Social Progress (WISP)

The WISP was developed by Richard Estes (1997) of the University of Pennsylvania, as an improvement on his *Index of Social Progress* (Estes, 1984). The new index uses statistically-derived weights and 46 indicators in 10 sub-indices to identify changes in the "adequacy of social provision" in countries throughout the world since 1970. The sub-indices include education, health status, women's status, defence effort, economy, demography, geography, political participation, cultural diversity, and welfare effort.

Quality of Life Index (QOL)

The QOL (Diener, 1995) was developed to include "subjective" or value-based elements of the quality of life, as well as the "objective" measures of physical health and economic activity (Diener and Suh, 1997). The measures chosen represent three "universal requirements of human existence"; biological needs, coordinated social interaction, and the survival and welfare needs of groups. The QOL also uses different indicators for developed and developing countries, in order to account for their substantially different social and economic contexts. Following Schwartz (1994), Diener identifies seven "value regions," each of which is measured by a separate indicator. These regions and their indicators for developed countries are mastery (physicians per capita), affective autonomy (subjective well-being), intellectual autonomy (college/university attendance), egalitarian commitment (income equality), harmony (major environmental treaties), conservatism (monetary savings rate), and hierarchy (per capita income). These components contribute equally to the "total quality of life," which is an average of the scores on these variables.

Prescott-Allen's Indices of The Well-being of Nations

The indices of *The Well-being of Nations* were developed by Robert Prescott-Allen (2001), and focus on sustainable development with the central idea that an index of economic and social well-being must also include the environmental costs of human activity. *The Well-being of Nations* report assesses sustainability in 180 countries using a 36-indicator Human Wellness Index and a 51-indicator Ecosystem Well-being Index. The intersection of the two provides a country's overall well-being index, with the ideal of both high human and ecosystem well-being.

Conference Board of Canada's Quality of Life Scorecard

Since 1986, the Conference Board of Canada has annually compared Canada to other Organisation of Economic Co-operation and Development (OECD) countries based on their performance in six categories: economy, innovation, environment, education and skills, health, and social development with the Quality of Life Scorecard. In the 2002 report these are measured by 24 indicators, including income, crime, the availability of social programmes, the confidence of foreign investors, and air and water quality (Conference board of Canada, 2002).

The Genuine Progress Indicator (GPI)

The Genuine Progress Indicator (GPI) was developed by San Francisco-based research and policy organization Redefining Progress to measure social, environmental, and economic well-being of the US by adjusting per capita GDP to account for other variables. The basic idea of the GPI is that economic expansion is not progress if it comes at a high cost to social life and the environment.

The GPI is built upon consumer expenditures, which are then adjusted for inequality in the distribution of goods and income, the rate of depreciation in durable goods, and expenses due to crime and social problems, as well as costs associated with underemployment and pollution. The estimated value of non-market work, such as child care and volunteer work, is added to GDP. The GPI also considers the long-term cost of dependence on fossil fuels, and the loss of wetlands, forests, and farmland (Cobb, Goodman, and Kliejunas, 2000; Sharpe, 1999).

Fordham Index of Social Health (ISH)

The Index of Social Health (ISH) was developed at Fordham University's Institute for Innovation in Social Policy (Miringoff and Miringoff, 1999) to measure social health trends in the US. There are 16 indicators in this index, dealing with health, mortality, inequality, and access to services. Different indicators are used to monitor social health in different life cycle stages. Infant mortality, child abuse, child poverty, teen suicides, drug abuse, and high school dropout rates are included for children and youth. Unemployment, weekly earnings, and health insurance coverage focus on the well-being of adults. The social health of the elderly is measured by the poverty rate and cost of health care for those 65 and older. Homicide and alcohol-related traffic fatality rates, and access to housing, income inequality, and food stamp coverage apply to all ages. Brink and Zeesman (1997) have produced a modified version for Canada, which uses the rate of social assistance use, rather than food stamp coverage.

Fraser Institute Index of Living Standards

Economist Christopher Sarlo has developed this exploratory index for the Fraser Institute, to follow changes in the quality of life of Canadians over time. This index includes per capita consumption and income, the poverty rate, an index of household facilities, post-secondary education, unemployment, life expectancy, and networth per capita. These are equally weighted and calculated from Census and other data (Sarlo, 1998).

Ontario Social Development Quality of Life Index

The Ontario Social Development Quality of Life Index was developed in 1998 by the Ontario Social Development Council (Shookner, 1998). It was designed as a community development tool which would monitor key indicators of quality of life in Ontario on four dimensions; social, health, economy, and the environment. Social indicators include the number of social assistance recipients and children in the care of Children's Aid societies, as well as public housing waiting lists. Economic indicators include the number of people who are employed and unemployed, and bankruptcies. The 12 indicators are given equal weights, and there is no separate income indicator.

The Index of Relative Indigenous Socioeconomic Disadvantage

Researchers at the Centre for Aboriginal Economic Policy Research at Australian National University have developed the only other composite index to be specifically applied to Aboriginal populations (Gray and Auld, 2000). The Index of Relative Indigenous Socioeconomic Disadvantage includes indicators of income, the proportion of the population below the poverty line, an indicator of housing quality, the proportion of the population with secondary school qualification, and the proportion of the population employed. The authors apply the index to Aboriginal and Torres Strait Islander Commission regions in Australia, using 1991 and 1996 census data.

Comparing Indicators: Methodological Considerations

There has been a lot written about the methodological issues in developing these kinds of measures. Indeed, there are social science journals devoted to them. In the space allotted here, we will review some of the larger conceptual and methodological issues, particularly the ones that have lead to criticisms of our own approach, or which figured prominently in the choices we have made.

Conceptual Issues: Dimensions of Well-being

The first question, and the one that is at the heart of the development of these indicators, is just what dimensions of well-being are important to measure in a given context. To some degree, this is a normative question about what constitutes the "good life," and which we cannot hope to address here. We can see that among the indicators briefly described above, some include a very large number of separate dimensions, addressing economic, physical, environmental, spiritual, subjective, and social well-being. Clearly, all of these dimensions are important to human happiness or quality of life, and most of the criticisms of the relatively smaller indices, such as the HDI, are that they omit important dimensions of well-being (e.g. Veenhoven, 1996). On the other hand, indices have also been criticized for including dimensions with too much conceptual or empirical overlap. McGillivray (1991) has criticised the HDI on the grounds that the HDI and GDP per capita are highly correlated, and that adding the dimensions of education and life expectancy do not significantly improve our ability to identify countries in which conditions are improving, and those in which progress is more elusive. Alternatively, Ogwang and Abdou (2003) find justification from principle component analysis for using only life expectancy at birth to rank nations, and omitting the other HDI measures.

The choice of the dimensions to include is obviously limited by the availability of data. In the case of the Registered Indian HDI and CWB, the data limitations are discussed below, but it is worth mentioning them here, in relation to the choice of dimensions. One of the reasons for the relative simplicity of the UNDP's HDI is its use in the context of developing countries, many with relatively limited national statistics systems. For example, although including environmental degradation is important in the international context, the comparability of these indicators over time may be compromised by changes in the availability of data. Environmental measures are certainly an important aspect of the quality of life, and this may be more so the case for Aboriginal peoples than other Canadians, given historical, spiritual, and economic connections to the physical environment. At the same time, for the Registered Indian HDI, which is mainly about comparing the well-being of populations, rather than geographic regions, measures of environmental health are not applicable. Important aspects of the physical environment, such as air quality, defy identification with a particular location or region. For community-level measures, such as the CWB, it might be possible to include some measures of the environment, such as water quality. Many of those measures are not easily available, however, and would require special data collection. The CWB does include a measure of housing quality and quantity, perhaps one of the most important aspects of the very local physical environment that affects human well-being. However, at this point we have not incorporated the health of the natural environment as a dimension of these measures.

One of the major problems with some of the dimensions included in some of these indices is their subjectivity. Diener's Quality of Life Index, for example, has a specific focus on subjective measures of well-being, and he has elsewhere sought to construct an "index of happiness" (Diener, 2000). Veenhoven (1996) has proposed a happiness-adjusted life expectancy measure. However, we believe including such subjective indicators in these indices is ill-advised, even if data were available. The cultural specificity of something like "happiness" would put any comparisons between Aboriginal peoples and other Canadians on shaky theoretical ground. Other subjective aspects of life such as autonomy (Diener, 1995) are also too difficult to include, and defy definition and measurement. We have therefore chosen to include only the dimensions that are more or less objectively measurable in the HDI and CWB.

We are aware that we have omitted aspects of life that may be particularly important to Aboriginal peoples, including access to traditional lands and activities and retention of Aboriginal languages, and we have been criticized on this point (Salée, 2005; Ten Fingers, 2005). Spirituality and traditional cultural activities are clearly important to many Aboriginal people, as they are to many non-Aboriginal Canadians. There is evidence that retention of culture has beneficial effects for other aspects of well-being, including education and health outcomes (eg. Chandler and Lalonde, 1998). However, measuring cultural retention is difficult, to say the least. We take cultural activities and language retention as factors which very likely improve social, psychological, and physical well-being, rather than as dimensions of this well-being themselves (O'Sullivan, 2003).

We have also not included some objective measures that are included in other indices. Rates of crime and violence, included in the Fordham Index, are not included in the Registered Indian HDI or CWB. We know that Aboriginal peoples are disproportionately victims of crime, as well as disproportionately incarcerated (Brzozowski, Taylor-Butts, and Johnson, 2006). However, these results come from General Social Survey (GSS) data, the only source of data about victimization that also includes questions about Aboriginal identity or Registered Indian Status. Crime report statistics generally do not include this information, and the GSS, like most Statistics Canada Surveys, is not administered in reserve communities. This, and the lack of an ongoing source of time-series data, makes it impractical to incorporate victimization into the Registered Indian HDI. Crime report data do show that crime rates are higher in reserve communities than in other communities (Brzozowski, Taylor-Butts, and Johnson, 2006), raising the possibility that one could include some measures of crime report into a community-level index. However, in small communities we can expect only a few reports of crime in any given year. The effect of this on annual rates is the same as that of community death rates on life expectancy—there will be dramatic fluctuations between years, making any conclusions about trends in community well-being highly suspect.

Some of the indices described in the preceding pages, such as the Conference Board of Canada's Scorecard, include measures of social spending as a positive measure of quality of life. Others, such as the GPI, include measures of military spending, higher values of which are presumed to reflect a lower quality of life.

These measures are untenable for comparing populations within a single state, such as comparing Registered Indians and other Canadians using the HDI, or for community-level measures such as the CWB. However, there are more important reasons for avoiding expenditures as a dimension of well-being in these indicators. Choices about expenditures do indeed have implications for well-being. However, the direction of these effects is often unclear. For example, The Ontario Social Development Quality of Life Index and Brink and Zeesman's (1997) application of the Fordham index include rates of social assistance and health care provided to the elderly as negative indicators of social well-being. However, these are determined to a great extent by availability and eligibility, and the range of services covered. Cuts in benefit eligibility would result in an instant increase in measured well-being (Michalos, 2003: 31). This is a problem with many of the indicators that are included in the larger indices described above.

Within the Canadian context, research and debate about program design, funding levels, and implementation is obviously an important focus for policy research, and part of the rationale behind these indicators is to identify what policies, programmes, and approaches seem to "work" to improve standards of living. In our previous work, we have examined the correlation between HDI scores for Registered Indians on-reserve and the level of spending on DIAND programs (Cooke et al., 2004). However, as with cultural retention and cultural activities, we consider spending levels to be important factors influencing well-being, rather than indicators.

Clearly, our choices about the dimensions to include in the HDI and the CWB are limited by the available data. Nonetheless, we think that there are also some good theoretical reasons behind the UNDP's choice of including just three dimensions; health, income, and education, as well as practical reasons. Health, measured in the HDI by life expectancy at birth, is affected by accidents and homicides that are included as separate measures in some of the other indices. Similarly, income, which is included in the HDI as a measure of material standard of living captures the effects of unemployment, including reliance on social assistance or transfer payments, which are included separately in other indices.

In the end, the Registered Indian HDI and CWB do not include as many dimensions of "well-being" as some of the other indices presented here. However, the ones that are included are also widely represented among the other indices. **Table 2.3** (page 42) shows the degree to which the HDI and CWB dimensions are also captured by the other indices, indicating a general agreement that these dimensions are important, even if other indicators are much more inclusive. However, the question of the conceptual definition of well-being is different from the question of measurement and calculation.

The Calculation of the HDI and CWB Indicators

Any single dimension of "well-being" in a composite index can be measured many ways, using different sources of data. The indicators presented above also use different schemes for combining individual indicators into a composite index and for assigning weights. Below, I discuss some of the issues related to the data sources, the selection of measures, and the combining of measures into the HDI and CWB.

Data Quality and Availability, and Comparability Over Time

Comparability and availability over time are among the major considerations that lead some to prefer indices which have fewer, rather than more, indicators. This has been particularly important in the case of developing countries, where, with even the relatively few indicators included in the *Human Development Report* there are inevitably problems with definitions, and data collection has changed from year to year. **Table 2.2** (page 32) shows the sources of data used in each of the indicators presented here. For many, administrative and national accounts data are used. These include domestic and national product estimates, as well as the mortality rates used to calculate life expectancy. Some, such as the CWB and the Index of Relative Indigenous Socioeconomic Disadvantage, use census data, while others use sample surveys.

One of the goals of the HDI and CWB was to compare Registered Indian populations and other Canadians populations. As described above, although Canada collects a great deal of vital statistics, few of these data contain identifiers of Aboriginality or Registered Indian Status, or on- or off-reserve residence. Most sample surveys with content covering the domains included in the CWB and HDI—such as the Labour Force Survey (Statistics Canada 2005b), which is the usual source of data on the Canadian labour force—do not collect data from reserve communities. The 1991, 2001, and 2006 post-censal Aboriginal Peoples Surveys (APS) would seem promising for the construction of these indicators, but the 2001 APS sample is not considered to be representative of the on-reserve population[1] (Statistics Canada, 2005c). Regardless, the APS surveys collect data *only* for those identifying themselves as Aboriginal, and do not allow comparison to other Canadian populations or communities. There is also no guarantee of the continuation of these surveys, casting doubt on their ability to provide time series data.

Nonetheless, there are problems with the Census as a source of data for the income, education, labour force participation, and housing indicators in the HDI and CWB. There have been some problems and changes to the question used to establish who is a Registered Indian in the Census, as well as to the legal definition of Registered Indian status, that may confound any observed changes in the characteristics of this population between census years. In 1981, Registered Indian status was determined by the Census Ethnic Origin question, which included "Status Indian" and "Non-Status Indian" as possible responses (Statistics Canada, 1982). The 1986 Census included a new question about Aboriginal ethnicity. It asked, "Do you consider yourself an Aboriginal person or a Native Indian of North America, that is, Inuit, North American Indian, or Métis?" (Statistics

Canada, 1987). Possible responses to this question included "Status or Registered Indian" and "non-status Indian," as well as other single and multiple responses. In the 1986 Census, problems were identified with the so-called "identity question," requiring estimates using a cross-classification of the identity and residency questions. Because of this, the 1986 Registered Indian population may not be strictly comparable to the 1981 population (Laroque and Gauvin, 1989). In later Censuses, a question that asked directly if the respondent was registered under the *Indian Act* was used, and was separate from the ethnicity question (Statistics Canada, 1992).

Also, in 1985 Bill C-31, the *Act to Amend the Indian Act*, resulted in the registration of Aboriginal women who had lost their claim to status through out-marriage, and their children, as well as others who may have lost their claim to status through military service, or other stipulations of the Act. This amendment resulted in the reinstatement of over 114,000 people by 1999, increasing the Registered Indian population considerably. These C-31 registrants are predominantly women, many of who continue to live off-reserve, and who may differ from other Registered Indians in terms of education, income, and health status. Their addition to the Registered Indian population will have affected the characteristics of this population to some degree (Clatworthy, 2003).

An additional consideration is that there have been changing patterns of ethnic identification among Canadians, as seen in the Census. Guimond (2003) has found that the "identity" population, the population of Canadians who identify themselves as members of an Aboriginal group, has grown because of an increased tendency of Canadians to identify themselves as such. This has mainly occurred amongst those self-identifying as Métis or non-status First Nations people. However, the census data also rely on self-report of Registration Status, and as such, there may be a similar increased tendency for people to report being Registered Indians.

Finally, in each Census, a number of reserve communities do not participate, with the number fluctuating with each Census, and there is also some amount of undercoverage on- and off-reserve (Guimond, Kerr, and Beaujot, 2004: 65–66). The existing data are re-weighted to account for nonresponse, but it is possible that these changes will also affect the estimated socio-economic composition and health status of that population.

In Canada, vital statistics systems do not record Aboriginal identity when registering births or deaths. As a result, estimating life expectancy for Aboriginal populations for use in the HDI is very difficult. One of the only sources of appropriate data for constructing age-specific mortality rates is the Indian Register, the list of Canadians registered under the *Indian Act* (Rowe and Norris, 1985; Nault, Chen, George, and Norris, 1993; INAC, 2000). However, these data have some limitations as well. Separate estimates for provinces and regions, and by on- and off-reserve residence are not available for all years, and in some cases estimates must be interpolated. The Indian Register data also suffer from late and non-report of births and deaths, as described by Nault and colleagues (1993: 5) likely resulting in overestimates of life expectancy. Lastly, the Indian Register data do not provide any information about the Inuit or other Aboriginal populations. Senécal and colleagues have had to overcome this by using an "ecological" approach in their application of the HDI to the Inuit.

Applicability of the Indicators to Aboriginal Populations

The question of applicability of the HDI and CWB indicators to Aboriginal populations is really a question of their validity. That is, do the various measures capture what they are supposed to measure? Although they may be appropriate for measuring the education and material well-being of non-Aboriginal Canadians, differences in Aboriginal populations may make these measures less applicable.

Average annual income, intended to measure material quality of life, considers only money income and does not capture the numerous other kinds of income that may be important. Residents of Aboriginal communities may benefit significantly from traditional activities, including trapping, hunting, and fishing, and the proceeds of these activities might be spread widely among family and friends. This and any other material that is exchanged outside of the money economy will not be measured. Furthermore, instrumental help such as help with child care and other caring activities can contribute significantly to one's quality of life, and are not captured in these measures. The labour force participation measures in the CWB also capture only participation in the paid labour force, providing no information on productive activity outside of the formal economy. The education measures capture only education within the formal education system, missing the important learning that takes place informally, through spending time with elders and other older community members, and participating in traditional activities. The proxy for adult literacy, the proportion aged 15 and older with grade 9 or higher, is really only a proxy for literacy in one of Canada's official languages and does not address knowledge of Aboriginal languages.

To the degree that informal work and education outside of the school system are more important in First Nations or other Aboriginal communities, these measures will under-estimate material well-being. Life expectancy at birth and the housing quality indicator in the CWB index are less problematic in this regard, and are probably equally valid in Aboriginal or non-Aboriginal contexts. Some well-being measures, such as the GPI, do include measures of non-market work, although these are not available from the Census. Although we recognize that there are aspects of education and income that are not captured in these measures, we nonetheless believe that these aspects of formal educational and labour force participation are important to measure, and do contribute to the quality of life for people and communities.

Sensitivity to Change: Stock and Flow Measures of Well-being

One of the considerations in choosing a measure is whether it is able to capture change resulting from policy interventions or external causes. Hagerty and

Table 2.3: Inclusion of the HDI and CWB Dimensions in Other Quality of Life Indices

	Income	Education	Labour Force Activity	Housing	Health Status
Human Development Index (HDI)	•	•			•
Community Well-being Index (CWB)	•	•	•	•	
Weighted Index of Social Progress (WISP)	•	•			•
Quality of Life Index (QOL)	•	•			•
Prescott-Allen's Indices of Well-being of Nations	•	•	•		•
Conference Board of Canada's Quality of Life Scorecard	•	•	•		•
Genuine Progress Indicator (GPI)	•			•	
Fordham Index of Social Health (ISH)	•	•	•	•	•
Fraser Institute Index of Living Standards	•	•	•	•	•
Ontario Social Development Quality of Life Index	•		•	•	•
Index of Relative Indigenous Socioeconomic Disadvantage	•	•	•	•	

colleagues (2001) refer to this as the "sensitivity" of an indicator. Some measures, such as per capita GDP as a proxy for average annual income, or average income measured using Census data, are inherently sensitive to year-to-year changes. On the other hand, measures of education, such as the proportion of the population with a high school education, reflect the "stock" of knowledge in a population, but are unlikely to change much between years, because those most likely to gain a high school education in a given year are those in a relatively limited age range. As a result, even programmes that dramatically reduce high school dropout rates are unlikely to be reflected in such a measure. The UNDP recognized this problem in the 1995 Human Development Report, in which the education component of the HDI was changed to include the adult literacy rate, reflecting the "stock" of education in a population, and the combined primary, secondary, and tertiary school enrolment ratios, reflecting the "flow" of education into a population.

Capturing both "stock" and "flow" is more important for some dimensions of well-being than others. It is similar to the importance of reporting both incidence and prevalence in order to understand the amount of disease in a population, but also the contribution made by new cases. Sensitivity is a weakness in many of the indicators reviewed here, particularly in the domains of education and environmental impact. In the case of the CWB, the income, labour force, and housing measures are sensitive to changes between years. Although the education measures taken in the Registered Indian HDI and CWB are valid measures of the stock of knowledge and functional literacy in a population, they are not sensitive to annual changes. One way that the measure of the proportion with high school or higher education might be changed to reflect the flow of education into a community may be to limit the proportion to young adults, who are more likely to be involved in education or training. However, the overall proportion of a population with post-secondary qualifications remains an important indicator of the stock of human capital and knowledge in a community. Ultimately, sensitivity is only one consideration in the choice of indicators, and given that the income, labour force, and housing measures are inherently sensitive to changes between Census periods, including educational attainment as a "stock" variable represents a compromise.

Weighting and Scaling of the Components and Indicators

One of the most interesting questions is how each component of such an index should be weighted. **Table 2.2** (page 32) indicates which of three general approaches to weighting are taken in each of the indices. Some indices, such as the Quality of Life Index, and the Community Well-being Index weight each component of well-being equally. Prescott-Allen's Indices for the Well-being of Nations gives indicators different weights, according to their theoretical importance to the concept being measured. The HDI and the CWB give equal weight to each dimension of the index, but weight each of the two education indicators differently. Following the UNDP, primary education is weighted most heavily, reflecting the theoretical importance of literacy as a fundamental prerequisite for social participation. Other indicators use statistical techniques, such as principal components analysis, to empirically determine weights for each indicator (Slottje, 1991). The components in the Index of Indigenous Socioeconomic Disadvantage and the WISP are weighted using this method.

Statistical methods for determining weights raise some questions. For example, if the aim is to compare the change of indicators over time, and the weights are re-calculated for each year, as in the Index of Relative Indigenous Socioeconomic Disadvantage, some of the change in index scores will be due to the different weighting, and some will be due to the changes in the indicator scores. With few indicators, the goal of examining change over time, and in the absence of a compelling theoretical reason to give some indicators more weight than others, the equal-weighting approach taken by most of these indices may be the best (Hopkins, 1991: 1471).

Another consideration is whether the indicators in an index will be re-scaled or transformed, or left in their original metrics. This is particularly important in the case of income, which is often considered to have decreasing marginal utility. At higher levels of income, the effects of each additional dollar on overall well-being are less, and this is reflected in indices such as the HDI, which has used a logarithmic transformation of income since 1999 (UNDP, 1999). However, most of the indices that include income or its proxy, per capitaGDP, leave the measure untransformed (**Table 2.2** – page 32). Emes and Hahn (2001) argue that the HDI's log formula is arbitrary, and results in an under-valuation of the impact of income on human development, and particularly too low a score for the US.

Ultimately, such arguments for not discounting income are not more convincing than the decreasing marginal utility argument for the log formula, or other transformations. Indeed, the decision of the weighting of individual indicators and the ways in which these indicators might be transformed, are often value judgments, as are the components to be included in an index. For example, the discounting of GDP in the HDI has meant that Canada generally scores higher than the US on this index, whereas this would not be the case without the transformation. The important point is to be aware of the effects of these transformations and weights in interpretation. In the CWB index applied to First Nations and other Canadian communities, it will be the higher income non-First Nations communities whose income scores are most reduced by this formula and the differences between First Nations and other communities on the income indicator will therefore be affected more than the differences among First Nations.

There is no single answer to the methodological or conceptual problems encountered in creating a composite index of well-being. We believe that the decisions we have made in taking the UNDP HDI as a model have been reasonable, but accept that others will suggest alternatives. This is the case with the UNDP's measures as well, and they have nonetheless proved themselves to be useful in international and national policy discussions and research.

Conclusions: Measuring Well-being

This chapter has described the intentions behind the development of the HDI and CWB and their use in measuring the well-being of Aboriginal peoples in Canada, and places these measures within the context of other composite indicators of well-being. These are relatively simple measures, and capture relatively few of the many possible dimensions of well-being, due partly to the limited availability of data. However, these measures do allow comparison between Aboriginal and non-Aboriginal populations and communities and the construction reasonably reliable time series. This allows us to address one of our main questions, which is whether social and economic conditions have been improving for Aboriginal peoples in Canada. They will also allow us to undertake more analytical research, in order to identify the specific factors that influence well-being, and to identify "what works."

As we have tried to emphasize here and in the other papers using these indices, it is recognized that these measures do not reflect the totality of well-being, and may particularly omit some aspects that are important to Aboriginal peoples. However, we feel that the dimensions that are captured; overall health, education, and income in the HDI and labour force activity and housing quality in the CWB, are objectively important aspects of quality of life. Improvements in these indicators would reflect unambiguously positive advances in the conditions in which people live, and are worthy goals for policy.

Nonetheless, these are only partial measures of well-being. They provide a set of basic indicators of social and economic conditions and how they have changed over time. As with any set of qualitative social or economic measures, they need to be augmented and elaborated with other measures and observations in order to give a complete picture of the social and economic conditions of Aboriginal peoples in Canada. We do, however, believe these indicators give us important information about the changing social and economic conditions of Aboriginal peoples in Canada.

Endnotes

1 One can extract those persons living on-reserve and complete an analysis, but this raises other methodological issues that complicate comparability and representivity.

References

Armstrong, R.P. 2001. "The geographical patterns of socio-economic well-being of First Nations communities in Canada," in Agriculture and Rural Working Paper Series—Working Paper No. 46. Ottawa: Statistics Canada.

Beavon, D. and Cooke, M. 2003. "An Application of the United Nations Human Development Index to Registered Indians in Canada." in White, J.P., Maxim, P. and Beavon, D. eds. *Aboriginal Conditions*. Vancouver: UBC Press.

Brzozowski, J-A., Taylor-Butts, A. and Johnson, S. 2006. "Victimization and Offending Among the Aboriginal Population in Canada," *Juristat*, 26(3): Ottawa: Canadian Centre for Justice Statistics, Statistics Canada.

Brink, S., and Zeesman, A. 1997. *Measuring Social Well-being: An Index of Social Health for Canada*. Research Paper R-97-9E. Ottawa: HRDC.

Canada Mortgage and Housing Corporation. 1996. *The Housing Conditions of Aboriginal People in Canada*, 1991. Ottawa: CMHC.

Chandler, M.J. and Lalonde, C.E. 1998. "Cultural Continuity as a hedge against suicide in Canada's First Nations." *Transcultural Psychiatry*, 35(2), 193–211.

Cobb, C., Goodman, G.S., and Kliejunas, J.C.M. 2000. *Blazing Sun Overhead and Clouds on the Horizon: The Genuine Progress Report for 1999*. Oakland, CA: Redefining Progress.

Conference Board of Canada. 2002. Performance and Potential, 2002-03—Canada 2010: Challenges and Choices at Home and Abroad (Ottawa) (retrieved January 5, 2005 from <**www.conferenceboard.ca**>

Cooke, M., Beavon, D., and McHardy, M. 2004. "Measuring the Well-Being of Aboriginal People: An Application of the United Nations Human Development Index to Registered Indians in Canada, 1981–2001." Report for the Strategic Analysis Directorate, Policy and Strategic Direction Branch. Ottawa: INAC.

Diener, E. 1995. "A value based index for measuring national quality of life." *Social Indicators Research*. 36:107–127.

Diener, E. and Suh, E. 1997. "Measuring Quality of Life: Economic, Social, and Subjective Indicators." *Social Indicators Research*. 40:189–216.

Emes, J. and Hahn, E. 2001. "Measuring Development: An Index of Human Progress." Fraser Institute Occasional Paper Number 36. Vancouver: The Fraser Institute.

Estes, R.J. 1997. "Social Development Trends in Europe, 1970–1994: Development Prospects for the New Europe," *Social Indicators Research*. 42:1–19.

_____. 1984. *The Social Progress of Nations*. New York: Praeger.

Frenette, M. and Picot, G. 2003. "Life After Welfare: The Economic Well Being of Welfare Leavers in Canada During the 1990s." Statstics Canada Analytical Studies—Research Paper Series No 192. Ottawa: Statistics Canada.

Gray, M.C. and Auld, A.J. 2000. "Towards an Index of Relative Indigenous Socioeconomic Disadvantage." Discussion Paper 196. Centre for Aboriginal Economic Policy Research. Canberra: ANU.

Hagel, A. and Tudge, J. 1998. "Illiterate Adults in Literate Societies: Interaction with a Social World." in de Oliveira, Marta Kohl and Jaan Valsiner, eds. *Literacy in Human Development*. London: Ablex. pp. 163–182.

Hagerty, M.R. et al. 2001. "Quality of Life Indexes for National Policy: Review and Agenda for Research." *Social Indicators Research*. 55: 1–96.

Hopkins, Michael. 1991. "Human Development Revisited: A New UNDP Report." *World Development*. 19(10):1469–1473.

Land, K. 2000. "Social Indicators" in Edgar F. Borgatta and Rhonda V. Montgomery (eds). *Encyclopedia of Sociology*, revised ed. New York: Macmillan.

Maxim, P. 1999. *Quantitative Research Methods in the Social Sciences*. New York: OUP.

McGillivray, M. 1991. "The Human Development Index: Yet Another Redundant Composite Development Indicator?" *World Development*. 19(10):1461–1468.

McHardy, M. and O'Sullivan, E.. 2004. "Nations Community Well-being in Canada: The Community Well-being Index (CWB), 2001." Strategic Research and Analysis Directorate, Indian and Northern Affairs Canada. Ottawa: INAC.

Michalos, A.C. 2003. *Essays on the Quality of Life*. Dordrecht: Kluwer Academic Publishers.

Miringoff, M. and Miringoff, M.L. 1999. *The Social Health of the Nation: How America is Really Doing*. New York: OUP.

O'Sullivan, E. (2003) "Aboriginal Language Retention and Socio-Economic Development: Theory and Practice." in White, Maxim, and Beavon (Eds.) *Aboriginal Conditions: Research as Foundation for Public Policy*. Vancouver: UBC Press, 136–163.

Ogwang, T. and Abdou, A. 2003. "The Choice of Principle Variables for Computing some Measures of Well-being." *Social Indicators Research*. 64: 139–152.

Prescott-Allen. R. 2001. *The Well-being of Nations: A Country-by-Country Index of Quality of Life and the Environment*. London: UNEP/Island Press.

Rao, V.V.B. 1991. "Human Development Report 1990: Review and Assessment." *World Development*. 19(10): 1451–1460.

Sarlo, C. 1998. "Canadian Living Standards: 1998 Report." Fraser Institute Critical Issues Bulletin. Vancouver: The Fraser Institute.

Salée, Daniel. 2006. "Quality of Life of Aboriginal People in Canada: An Analysis of Current Research." *IRPP Choices*. 12(6).

Schwartz, S. H. 1994. "Beyond Individualism and Collectivism: New Cultural Dimensions of Values" in U. Kim et al. (eds.) *Individualism and Collectivism Theory, Method, and Applications*. Thousand Oaks: Sage.

Sharpe, A. 1999. "A Survey of Indicators of Economic and Social Well-being." Paper Prepared for Canadian Policy Research Networks.

Shookner, M. 1998. "A Quality of Life Index for Ontario." Paper presented at the Centre for the Study of Living Standards conference on the State of Living Standards and the Quality of Life in Canada. October 30–31, Ottawa.

Slottje, D. J. 1991. "Measuring the Quality of Life Across Countries." *The Review of Economics and Statistics*. 72(4): 684–693.

Statistics Canada (2005a). Consumer Price Index, Historical Summary. Ottawa: Statistics Canada. Retrieved September 1, 2005 from: <**www40.statcan.ca/l01/cst01/econ46.htm**>

Statistics Canada (2005b) Labour Force Survey. Retrieved February 22, 2005 from: <**http://stcwww.statcan.ca/english/sdds/3701.htm**>

Statistics Canada (2005c) Aboriginal Peoples Survey. Retrieved February 22, 2005 from: <**http://stcwww.statcan.ca/english/sdds/3250.htm**>

Statistics Canada. 2003. Geographic Units: Census Subdivision (CSD). Retrieved January 24, 2005 from <**www12.statcan.ca/english/census01/Products/Reference/dict/geo012.htm**>

Ten Fingers, Keely. 2005. "Rejecting, Revitilizing, and Reclaiming: First Nations Work to Set the Direction of Research and Policy Development." *Canadian Journal of Public Health*. 96: S60–S63.

United Nations Development Programme. 1990. *Human Development Report 1990*. New York: Oxford University Press.

_____. 1995. *Human Development Report 1995*. New York: Oxford University Press.

_____. 1999. *Human Development Report 1999*. New York: Oxford University Press.

Veenhoven, R. 1996. "Happy Life-Expectancy: A comprehensive measure of quality-of-life in nations." *Social Indicators Research*. 39: 1–58.

Part Two:
The Human Development Index (HDI)

3

The Registered Indian Human Development Index, 1981–2001

Martin Cooke and Dan Beavon

Introduction

One of the most important applications of quantitative social indicators is to create a picture of how overall well-being has changed over time. Most observers of Canadian politics and public life will be able to identify a number of important events relating to the social, economic, and political situations of Aboriginal peoples in Canada in the past several decades. The Oka crisis in 1990, the report of the Royal Commission on Aboriginal Peoples, the *Delgamuuku* and *Marshall* decisions, the creation of Nunavut, and the signing of the Nis'gaa Agreement are only the most obvious. Largely in the shadow of these large events are any number of local programs and policy changes by Aboriginal, local, provincial, and federal governments; legal challenges and litigation; and private, non-governmental initiatives that can potentially affect the lives of Aboriginal peoples. As well, these must be considered against the backdrop of other social and economic changes in Canada. In this rapidly changing context it is important to have an understanding of how the overall social, economic, and health status of populations are changing, and to have some consistent indicators that can complement other information about changing conditions.

As described in Chapter 2, the Registered Indian Human Development Index (HDI) has been developed in order to measure the degree to which the health, educational attainment, and income of the Registered Indian population has changed. The Registered Indian HDI is calculated using population averages at the national and the provincial levels. As such, it provides a broad picture of how attainment on these basic indicators has changed, while leaving local conditions, programs, and situations to other measures, such as the CWB, and to other research strategies. This chapter presents the results of our use of the HDI to answer three basic questions; how has the overall level of well-being of Registered Indians changed in recent decades, how does this compare to the patterns seen in the general Canadian population, and what are the regional differences in these indicators?

Methodology: The Registered Indian Human Development Index

As described more completely in Chapter 2, the HDI consists of three sub-indices; life expectancy at birth, educational attainment, and income. Each of the individual indicators reflects the population's distance from theoretical minimum and maximum scores, so that an indicator score of 1.0 reflects the theoretical maximum. These are combined with equal weights to form a single composite measure between 0 and 1.0 (UNDP, 2003: 340).

To construct an index for the Canadian context, we use Census education and income measures, rather than the literacy and enrolment rates and national product used by the United Nations Development Programme (UNDP) to compare countries. The two Census education measures are the proportion of the population aged 15 and older with grade 9 or higher, and the proportion of the population aged 20 and older with high school, some technical school or post-secondary educational attainment. These are given a two-thirds and a one-third weight, respectively, within an Educational Attainment Index. The Census income measure is the annual total income, averaged over the entire population with and without income. This is discounted according to the log formula in Chapter 2 (see page 29). These measures are combined with life expectancy estimates from Canadian vital statistics (Statistics Canada 1984, 1990, 1995, 1998, 2005a) and the Indian Register (Nault et al. 1993; Norris, Kerr, and Nault; Rowe and Norris 1995;1996; Verma, Michalowski, and Gauvin 2003) to form the Registered Indian HDI.[1]

In the following sections, we will present the changes in the indicator values for Registered Indians living on- and off-reserve and other Canadians, between 1981 and 2001, as well as provincial and regional scores. It should be noted that one of the important dimensions upon which all of these indicators can be expected to differ is gender, with women and men having different incomes, educational attainment, and life expectancy. However, gender differences in these scores are discussed in Chapter 4 in this volume, and so in this chapter we present only figures for men and women combined. Although our main purpose is to understand the trends in the Canadian context, in the final section we also place the HDI scores for the Canadian populations in international context, by comparing them to the countries in the UNDP's *Human Development Report 2003* (UNDP, 2003).

Human Development Index Scores, 1981–2001

Overall, the Human Development Index scores for Registered Indians improved over the 1981–2001 period, and did so at a faster rate than did the general Canadian population. **Table 3.1** presents the scores on the HDI and components for Registered Indians and the reference population, defined as the Canadian population that is not registered under the *Indian Act*. The HDI score for Registered Indians improved from 0.626 in 1981 to 0.765 in 2001. Although the HDI scores for the reference population also improved, the gap between reference population and Registered Indian HDI scores fell from 0.18 in 1981 to 0.12 by 2001.

Despite this overall improvement, when we examine the indicators separately we see that not all have contributed equally to this overall improvement in well-being. Life expectancy at birth increased relatively steadily for both

Table 3.1: **HDI and Component Measure Scores, Registered Indian and Reference Population, 1981–2001**

Indicator	Population	1981	1986	1991	1996	2001
Life Expectancy at Birth (years)	Registered Indians	65.7	67.5	70.6	72.2	72.9
	reference population	75.6	76.2	77.9	78.5	78.7
Life Expectancy Index	Registered Indians	0.678	0.708	0.760	0.786	0.799
	reference population	0.843	0.853	0.881	0.891	0.896
Proportion completed High School or higher[1]	Registered Indians	0.330	0.341	0.456	0.514	0.567
	reference population	0.597	0.618	0.680	0.717	0.754
Proportion completed Grade 9 or higher[2]	Registered Indians	0.597	0.628	0.721	0.781	0.825
	reference population	0.802	0.829	0.863	0.881	0.903
Educational Attainment Index	Registered Indians	0.508	0.533	0.633	0.692	0.739
	reference population	0.733	0.759	0.802	0.826	0.853
Average Annual Income (2000$)[3]	Registered Indians	6,840	6,795	8,243	8,887	10,094
	reference population	16,554	18,132	20,072	19,979	22,489
Income Index	Registered Indians	0.694	0.693	0.725	0.737	0.759
	reference population	0.841	0.856	0.873	0.873	0.892
HDI Score	Registered Indians	0.626	0.644	0.706	0.739	0.765
	reference population	0.806	0.823	0.852	0.863	0.880

Notes:

1 The proportion completed high school or higher is estimated by the ratio of the population with a secondary school graduation certificate, some post-secondary or trades education, or some university with or without degree, to the population aged 19 years and over.

2 The proportion completed grade nine is the population aged 15 years and over completed grade 9 or higher, divided by the total population aged 15 years and over.

3 The average annual income is the average income from all sources, for the total population with or without income, for the year before the Census enumeration, adjusted by the Statistics Canada Consumer Price Index to year 2000 constant Dollars (Statistics Canada, 2005b).

Sources: Statistics Canada, custom tabulation, unpublished data (Statistics Canada), 1984, 1990, 1995, 1998, 2005a; Rowe and Norris 1995; Nault et al. 1993; Norris, Kerr, and Nault 1996; DIAND, 1998; Verma, Michalowski, and Gauvin, 2003; authors' calculations.

populations between 1981 and 2001, and resulted in a narrowing of the life expectancy gap. Registered Indian life expectancy improved from 65.7 years in 1981 to 72.9 years in 2001, an increase of 7.2 years, compared with an increase of 3.1 years for the Reference Population, as shown in **Table 3.1**. However, improvement in educational attainment was not as consistent. Despite an overall improvement in the total Educational Attainment Index score, from 0.508 in 1981 to 0.739 in 2001, reducing the gap between Registered Indians and other Canadians from 0.23 to 0.11, there was little improvement in this gap during the first five years of the period (**Table 3.1**).

There was much less improvement in the average annual incomes of Registered Indians between 1981 and 2001. Although the average income for Registered Indians improved, from $6,840 to $10,094 over the period, incomes fell slightly between the 1981 and 1986 censuses. Overall, the income gap between Registered Indians and other Canadians grew over the entire period, from $9,714 in 1981 to $12,395 in 2001. This difference did decline somewhat between 1991

Figure 3.1: Contribution of the HDI Components to Registered Indian HDI, 1981-2001

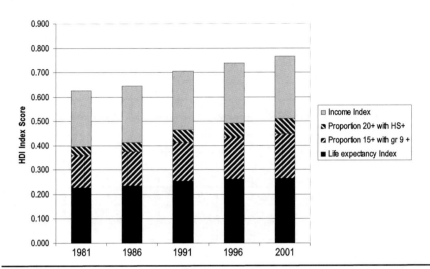

and 1996, but this was due to the falling average income for the reference population rather than to increases among Registered Indians (**Table 3.1**— page 53).

These results indicate that, despite the overall improvement in HDI scores, the differences between the Registered Indian population and other Canadians in the measures of overall health and educational attainment fell while the differences in income grew. However, the calculation of the index, with the different weights assigned to each of the education indicators and a discounting formula for income, mean that changes on the raw scores of these indicators do not equally contribute to the overall HDI. **Figure 3.1** shows the total HDI scores for the Registered Indian population, decomposed into each of the components. This figure makes clear that most of the growth in the Registered Indian HDI scores over the period has been due to improvements in the educational attainment index, especially after 1986. Within this index the adult literacy proxy, the proportion of individuals 15 years and over with grade 9 or higher, receives two-thirds weight, meaning that the increase in this indicator from 0.618 to 0.754 between 1986 and 2001 contributed heavily to the overall HDI improvement. Although the proportion individuals aged 20 and older with high school or higher contributes less to the overall index, its improvement also contributed to the increased HDI score. Overall, increases in educational attainment accounted for 55% of the observed improvement in the HDI, compared to 29% due to the steady increase in life expectancy, and 16% to improvements in average annual income.

Differences by On- and Off-reserve Residence (1981–2001)

In general, improvements in the HDI scores of the Registered Indian population reflect improvements in average levels of well-being among those living in

Figure 3.2: HDI Index Scores, Registered Indian On- and Off-reserve and Reference Population, 1991–2001

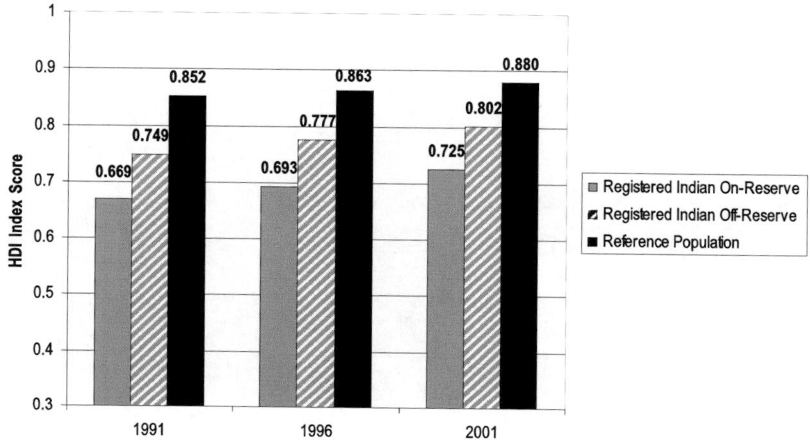

reserve or First Nations communities, as well as those living in other areas, urban and rural. However, those living on-reserve continued to have lower scores on the HDI and its components in 2001. **Figure 3.2** presents the HDI scores for the on- and off-reserve Registered Indian populations and the reference population for 1991–2001.[2] Over the 1991–2001 period, the gap between the on- and off-reserve population fell from 0.080 to 0.077, although it widened slightly between 1991 and 1996. Note that the relative contributions of improvements in well-being of on- and off-reserve populations to the overall HDI are effectively weighted by their share of the total Registered Indian population. As the proportion of Registered Indians living off-reserve has grown over the period, conditions off-reserve have had a greater impact on the overall Registered Indian HDI.

Figure 3.3 (page 56) shows the change in the educational attainment index scores for the on and off-reserve Registered Indian populations and the reference populations, between 1981 and 2001. Although those living on-reserve had lower average educational attainment over the whole period, this difference declined between 1991 and 2001, while they had remained basically constant from 1981 to 1991. By the end of the period, off-reserve educational attainment index score was 0.802, compared to 0.853 for the reference population and 0.668 for the on-reserve population.

As was the case with the overall HDI scores, much of the improvement in the educational attainment index was due to increases in the proportion of the population with elementary-level education. Only 53% of the Registered Indian population living on-reserve had grade 9 or higher in 1981 and this had risen to 76% by 2001 (**Figure 3.4**). Among those living off-reserve, values on this indicator improved from 69% to 89%, approaching the reference population value of 90% in 2001. The difference in elementary educational attainment between the on- and

Figure 3.3: Educational Attainment Index Score, Registered Indians On- and Off-reserve and Reference Population, 1981–2001

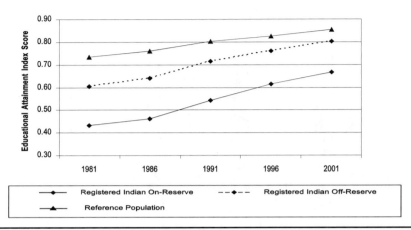

Figure 3.4: Proportion Aged 15 and Older With Grade 9+, Registered Indians On- and Off-reserve and Reference Population, 1981–2001

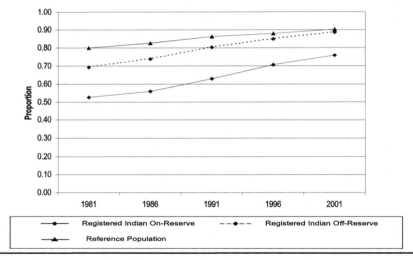

off-reserve populations also declined after 1991, although they widened between 1981 and 1991. Much of this may be due to the addition of Bill C-31 registrations to the off-reserve population[3] (Clatworthy, 2003).

The improvement in secondary and post-secondary educational attainment has been much stronger since 1986, as shown in **Figure 3.5**. The fact that this is observed in the reference population as well as the Registered Indian population suggests that this is not mainly due to Bill C-31 registrations. The proportion of those aged 20 or older with high school or higher educational attainment increased from 0.25 of those living on-reserve and 0.43 of those living off-reserve in 1981,

Figure 3.5: Proportion Aged 20 and Older With High School+, Registered Indians On- and Off-reserve and Reference Population, 1981–2001

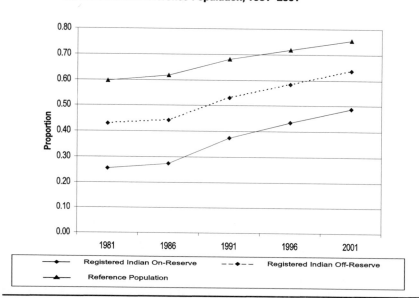

to 0.49 and 0.64 in 2001 (**Figure 3.6** – page 58). However, unlike our measure of elementary educational attainment, the gap between the on- and off-reserve Registered Indian populations declined in the beginning of the period, from 1981 to 1991, but increased slightly between 1996 and 2001. Although the difference between the off-reserve population and other Canadians declined between 1996 and 2001, on-reserve scores improved more slowly and diverged slightly from the other two populations.

Average annual income scores are shown in **Figure 3.6**, which illustrates the continuing large gaps between Registered Indians and other Canadians on this measure. Average incomes of both on- and off-reserve populations increased over the 1981–2001 period. However, while incomes on-reserve grew at a fairly steady pace, off-reserve incomes were less consistent, likely reflecting the increased importance of market income and greater vulnerability to the effects of economic downturns. Among Registered Indians living off-reserve, average income fell between 1981 and 1996, from $8,168 to $7,607, rising again to $11,729 by 2001. The 1981–1986 decline in off-reserve incomes meant that the gap between those living on- and off-reserve narrowed during that period. However, over the whole 1981–2001 period, the gap in average annual income between those living on- and off-reserve increased, from $2,285 to $3,327.

Provincial and Regional Differences (2001)

The Census and life expectancy data allow HDI and component index scores to be calculated separately for provinces or regions in 2001. As shown in **Figure 3.7**,

Figure 3.6: Average Annual Income, Registered Indians On- and Off-reserve and Reference Population, 1981–2001 (Year 2000 $)

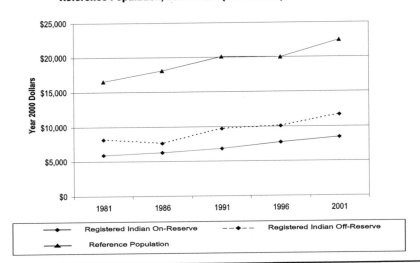

there was considerable regional variation in HDI scores. Registered Indian HDI scores were highest in Ontario, at 0.847 for the off-reserve population and 0.757 for the on-reserve population. The lowest HDI scores were for the Registered Indian population in Manitoba and Saskatchewan, where off-reserve scores were 0.758 and 0.757 and on-reserve HDI scores were 0.674 and 0.687 (**Figure 3.4 –** page 56). Despite having relatively low reference population HDI scores as well, the gaps between Registered Indians and other Canadian were also the largest in the Prairie provinces. The smallest differences between the reference and Registered Indian populations were found in the Atlantic and the North, followed by Quebec and Ontario.

Provinces also varied with respect to the gaps between the on- and off-reserve Registered Indian populations. The largest gap in HDI scores between those living on- and off-reserve was found in Quebec and Alberta, while the smallest gaps between on- and off-reserve were in the Atlantic region, British Columbia, and the North (**Figure 3.7**).

The regional differences on the individual components of the HDI are more striking. **Figure 3.8** presents the 2001 Educational Attainment Index scores for on- and off-reserve Registered Indian populations and the reference population. Among Registered Indians living in reserve communities, the lowest average levels of educational attainment were found in Quebec, Manitoba, Saskatchewan, and the North, while the highest levels were in the Atlantic Region, British Columbia, and Ontario (**Figure 3.8**). Quebec and the North also had the largest gaps between Registered Indians living on- and off-reserve. Educational attainment index scores for those on-reserve were 0.574 and 0.633 for Quebec and the North, respectively, compared to off-reserve scores of 0.756 and 0.834. The gap

Figure 3.7: Human Development Index Scores, Registered Indians On- and Off-reserve and Reference Population, Canada, Provinces and Regions, 2001

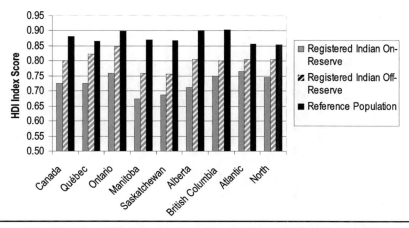

Figure 3.8: Educational Attainment Index Scores, Registered Indians On- and Off-reserve and Reference Population, Canada, Provinces and Regions, 2001

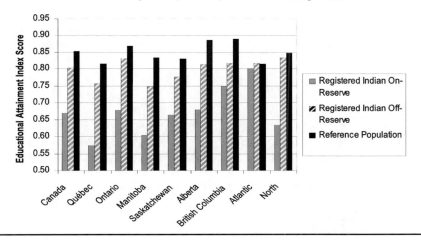

between the Registered Indian and reference population was the lowest in the Atlantic Region, where Registered Indians off-reserve had a slight advantage in educational attainment over the reference population.

Regional and provincial estimates of life expectancy at birth in 2001 are presented in **Figure 3.9**. As with the Educational Attainment Index, Registered Indians in Manitoba and Saskatchewan had the lowest scores on this indicator, with total life expectancy at birth of 70.3 and 70.1 years, respectively. These provinces also had large differences between the Registered Indian population and other Canadians, at 9.4 and 9.0 years. The difference in British Columbia was also large, at 9.2 years, whereas the total Canadian difference in life expectancy between Registered Indians and other Canadians was 5.8 years. Manitoba

Figure 3.9: Life Expectancy at Birth Both Sexes Combined, Registered Indians On- and Off-reserve and Reference Population, Canada, Provinces and Regions, 2001.

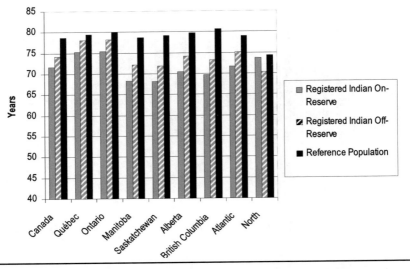

Figure 3.10: Average Annual Income, Registered Indians On- and Off-reserve and Reference Population, Canada, Provinces, and Regions, 2001 (Year 2000 $)

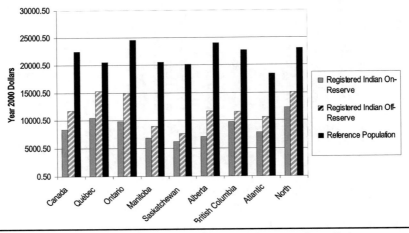

and Saskatchewan also had the largest difference between those living on-reserve and those living off-reserve in 2001, at 3.9 years in Manitoba and 3.7 years in Saskatchewan (**Figure 3.9**).

Life expectancy among Registered Indians was highest in Quebec and Ontario in 2001, where life expectancy was nearly 77 years and the difference between the on- and off-reserve populations was less than 3 years. However, the difference in life expectancy between Registered Indians and other Canadians was the lowest in the North, where Registered Indians on-reserve had a higher life expectancy than both the off-reserve Registered Indian population and the reference population (**Figure 3.9**).

The large differences in average annual income that were found at the national level can also be seen at the provincial and regional levels, and average annual incomes for the on- and off-reserve and reference populations are presented in **Figure 3.10**. Again, the provinces with the lowest levels of Registered Indian income were Manitoba and Saskatchewan. These low levels also meant that there was the smallest difference between those living on- and off-reserve in 2001. Registered Indians living on-reserve in these provinces had an average income of $6,900 and $6,173, respectively, compared to the Canadian on-reserve average of $8,402. Those living off-reserve had an average income of $8,973 in Manitoba and $7,668 in Saskatchewan, compared to a national off-reserve average of $11,729. Although the average reference population income in these provinces was also below the national average, there were nonetheless large gaps between Registered Indians and other residents. The difference in average income between Registered Indians and other Manitobans was $12,691, and the difference in Saskatchewan was $13,144. The only province with a larger income gap in 2001 was Alberta, where average reference population incomes were $14,333 higher than the Registered Indian average.

Average incomes were highest for Registered Indians living off-reserve in Quebec and Ontario, with averages of $15,318 and $14,986, respectively. Quebec, the Atlantic, and the North regions had the smallest differences in income between Registered Indians and other Canadians (**Figure 3.10**).

International Comparisons (2001)

Lastly, the Registered Indian HDI scores can be used to place these Canadian populations in international context. It should be stressed that it is really the changes in the Registered Indian scores in Canada that are important, rather than any international comparison. However, Canada's high ranking in the HDI had become part of political debates about the relative well-being of Aboriginal peoples, leading us to rank Registered Indians among the countries in the Human Development Report as part of our 1996 HDI calculations (Beavon and Cooke, 2003). These are updated in **Table 3.2** (pages 66–68), using the 2001 data to place the on- and off-reserve Registered Indian populations among the countries in the 2003 *Human Development Report*, which uses 2001 data (UNDP, 2003).

The differences between the indicators in the Registered Indian HDI and those used by the UNDP mean that the two are not strictly comparable. However, we approximate the UNDP measures by adjusting the Canadian index components to be equal to the Canadian figures presented by the UNDP. Each of the education, life expectancy, and income indicators are adjusted by the ratio of the UNDP's published value for Canada to the national values for the indicators used in the Registered Indian HDI. Assuming that the ratio of the adult literacy rate to the proportion of individuals 15 and older with grade 9 or higher, for example, holds for the Registered Indian and reference populations to the same degree as for Canada generally, this provides a means by which we can roughly compare the populations described above to the countries in the *Human Development Report*.

Table 3.2 presents the ranking of the total Registered Indian population, the on- and off-reserve Registered Indian populations, and the reference population among the countries included in *Human Development Report 2003* (UNDP, 2003). It should be noted that Canada's rank on the HDI fell from 1 to 7 between 1996 and 2001. However, there is relatively little difference among the countries at the top of the international ranking, and this change in Canada's status has been due mainly to changes in the reporting of enrolment ratios.

As **Table 3.2** shows, the reference population had an HDI score that was slightly higher than the total Canadian population, indicating that Canada would rank about fourth in the world in 2001 if the HDI scores for the Registered Indian population were the same as for other Canadians. The off-reserve Registered Indian population would rank approximately 32nd, alongside Czech Republic and Malta, with an HDI score of .856. The total Registered Indian population would rank approximately 48th, below Croatia and above the United Arab Emirates, with an HDI score of .817.

Of course, changes in these international rankings are due both to the changing situation in other countries as well as to the improvement in the Registered Indian HDI scores. Note that in 1996 the Registered Indian population would have held the same position in the international HDI Rankings, although the HDI score increased between 1996 and 2001 (Beavon and Cooke, 2003: 208). In 1996, the Registered Indian population ranked among the countries considered to have "medium human development" by the UNDP, with an HDI score of .793. In the 2001 ranking, the Registered Indian population HDI of .819 was high enough to place among countries with "high human development." Despite this overall improvement, however, the on-reserve Registered Indian population continued to rank among countries with "medium" levels of human development. The HDI score for the on-reserve population was .772 in 2001, indicating a level of human development similar to Romania and Saudi Arabia. However, this represents an improvement in international ranking, from 79th to 73rd, reflecting an improvement in HDI score from .739 in 1996.

Conclusions

This chapter has presented the changes in the Registered Indian Human Development Index Scores between 1981 and 2001. By the end of this period the overall well-being of Registered Indian populations, as measured by these indicators, had improved, and the differences between Registered Indians and other Canadians in terms of life expectancy, educational attainment, and average income were reduced. The improvement in Registered Indian HDI scores was reflected in international ranking, achieving levels comparable to countries with "high human development."

Despite these overall improvements, we find that important gaps remain, and that similar gains have not been made on all indicators. Although higher educational attainment contributed strongly to the higher HDI scores for Registered Indians, this does not seem to be reflected in a closing of the income gap. In the last decade of this period, the difference in average income between Registered Indians and other Canadians widened, reflecting especially slow growth in income on-reserve.

The continuing difference between Registered Indians living on- and off-reserve was also seen in educational attainment, particularly secondary and post-secondary education. However, these differences varied considerably with province and region. At the end of the period, Registered Indians living on-reserve in Manitoba and Saskatchewan had the lowest scores on all of the HDI indicators. Scores for those off-reserve in these provinces were also low, and the differences in well-being between Registered Indians and other residents was wide in these provinces, which have large Aboriginal populations.

The general picture painted by these measures is therefore one of inconsistent and uneven progress, both in terms of the temporal trends and regional variation. Although the general improvement in these measures of economic, social, and physical well-being is clearly good news, these results also show that future improvement should not be taken for granted. It remains to be seen whether some of the gaps between Registered Indians and other Canadians, some of which have recently been widening, can be narrowed in the near future.

Endnotes

1   The calculations, minimum and maximum values, and data issues involved in these indices are discussed in detail in Chapter 2.

2   Whereas the income and educational attainment indicators from the Census are available for the on- and off-reserve populations separately, life expectancy at birth is not available for the earlier years by on- and off-reserve residence. Although we have previously published HDI scores by on- and off-reserve residence in 1981 and 1986 (Cooke, Beavon, and McHardy, 2004), those figures rely on extrapolation of life expectancy trends from 1991–1996 backwards to 1981–1986, and we do not present them here.

3   In 1985 the federal government passed Bill C-31. Bill C-31 was intended to bring the *Indian Act* into conformity with gender equality rights provided under section 15 of the Canadian Charter of Rights and Freedoms and section 35(4) of the Constitution Act, 1982. It changed the rules for Indian registration under the *Indian Act* and substantially increased the number of individuals eligible for registration. It also allowed First Nations to have limited control over their memberships, but only after certain individuals who had lost Indian status under the *Indian Act* prior to 1985 were granted reinstatement upon application to both Indian status and First Nation membership. This legislation gave women who had lost status when they out-married to regain that status. It has meant that many who had lived and been educated off-reserve would now be counted in educational attainment data.

References

Beavon, D. & Cooke, M. 2003. "An Application of the United Nations Human Development Index to Registered Indians in Canada." In White, J.P., Maxim, P, and Beavon, D. (Eds.) *Aboriginal Conditions*. Vancouver: UBC Press. pp. 201–221.

Cooke, M., Beavon, D. & McHardy, M. 2004. "Measuring the Well-being of Aboriginal People: An Application of the United Nations Human Development Index to Registered Indians in Canada, 1981–2001." Report for the Strategic Analysis Directorate, Policy and Strategic Direction Branch. Ottawa: INAC.

Clatworthy, S.J., 2003. "Impacts of the 1985 Amendments to the *Indian Act* in First Nations Populations." In White, J.P., Maxim, P.S., and Beavon, D. (Eds.) *Aboriginal Conditions*.Vancouver: UBC Press. pp. 63–90.

Nault, F., Chen, J., George, M.V., and Norris, M.J. 1993. "Population Projections of Registered Indians, 1991–2016." Report prepared by the Population Projections Section, Demography Division, Statistics Canada for Indian and Northern Affairs Canada. Ottawa: INAC.

Norris, M.J., Kerr, D., and Nault, F. 1995. "Projections of the Population with Aboriginal Identity in Canada, 1991–2016." Report prepared by the Population Projections Section, Demography Division, Statistics Canada, for the Royal Commission on Aboriginal Peoples. Ottawa: Canada Mortgage and Housing Corporation and the Royal Commission on Aboriginal Peoples.

Rowe, G., and Norris, M.J. 1985. "Mortality Projections of Registered Indians, 1982 to 1996." Ottawa: Indian and Northern Affairs Canada.

Statistics Canada. 1984. "Life Tables, Canada and Provinces 1980–82." Cat. no. 84-532. Ottawa: Statistics Canada.

Statistics Canada. 1990. "Life Tables, Canada and Provinces 1985–87." *Health Reports Supplement* 13. Ottawa: Statistics Canada.

Statistics Canada. 1995. "Life Tables, Canada and Provinces, 1990–92." Cat. no. 84-537. Ottawa: Statistics Canada.

Statistics Canada. 1998. "Life Expectancy Abridged Life Tables, at Birth and Age 65, by Sex, for Canada, Provinces, Territories, and Health Regions." CANSIM Table 102-0016. Ottawa: Statistics Canada.

Statistics Canada. 2005a. Table 102-0511—Life expectancy: abridged life table, at birth and at age 65, by sex, Canada, provinces and territories, annual (Years). 360 series. Ottawa: Statistics Canada. Retrieved 1. Sept. 2005. <**www.statcan.ca/english/freepub/84F0211XIE/2002/tables.htm**>.

Statistics Canada. 2005b. "Consumer Price Index, Historical Summary." Ottawa: Statistics Canada. Retrieved September 1, 2005 from: <**www40.statcan.ca/101/cst01/econ46.htm**>.

United Nations Development Programme. 2003. *Human Development Report 2003*. New York: OUP.

Verma, R., Michalowski, M., and Gauvin, R.P. 2003. "Abridged Life Tables for Registered Indians in Canada, 1976–1980 to 1996–2000." Paper presented at the annual meeting of the Population Association of America, May 1–3, Minneapolis.

Table 3.2: Ranking of Selected Countries and Registered Indian and Reference Populations by Human Development Index, 2001

HDI Rank	Country	HDI Score
Countries with High Human Development		
1	Norway	.944
2	Iceland	.942
3	Sweden	.941
4	Australia	.939
	Reference Population	*.939*
5	Netherlands	.938
6	Belgium	.937
7	United States	.937
8	*Canada*	*.937*
9	Japan	.932
10	Switzerland	.932
13	United Kingdom	.930
16	Austria	.929
17	France	.925
19	Spain	.925
20	New Zealand	.917
23	Portugal	.896
30	Republic of Korea	.879
31	Brunei Darussalam	.872
32	Czech Republic	.861
	Registered Indian off-Reserve	*.856*
33	Malta	.856
34	Argentina	.849
35	Poland	.841
36	Seychelles	.840
37	Bahrain	.839
38	Hungary	.837
39	Slovakia	.836
40	Uruguay	.834
41	Estonia	.833
42	Costa Rica	.832
43	Chile	.831
44	Qatar	.826
45	Lithuania	.824
46	Kuwait	.820
47	Croatia	.818

Table 3.2 Continued

HDI Rank	Country	HDI Score
	Registered Indian Population	*.817*
48	United Arab Emirates	.816
49	Bahamas	.812
50	Latvia	.811
51	St. Kitts and Nevis	.808
52	Cuba	.806
53	Belarus	.804
54	Trinidad and Tobago	.802
55	Mexico	.800
Countries with Medium Human Development		
56	Antigua and Barbuda	.798
57	Bulgaria	.795
58	Malaysia	.790
59	Panama	.788
60	Macedonia, TFYR	.784
61	Libyan Arab Jamahirya	.783
62	Mauritius	.779
63	Russian Federation	.779
64	Colombia	.779
65	Brazil	.777
66	Bosnia and Herzegovina	.777
67	Belize	.776
68	Dominica	.776
69	Venezuela	.775
70	Samoa (Western)	.775
71	Saint Lucia	.775
72	Romania	.773
	Registered Indian On-Reserve	*.772*
73	Saudi Arabia	.769
74	Thailand	.768
75	Ukraine	.766
76	Kazakhstan	.765
77	Suriname	.762
78	Jamaica	.757
79	Oman	.755
80	St. Vincent and the Grenadines	.755
81	Fiji	.754
82	Peru	.752

Table 3.2 Continued

HDI Rank	Country	HDI Score
83	Lebanon	.752
84	Paraguay	.751
85	Philippines	.751
...85–102 deleted		
103	Cape Verde	.727
104	China	.721
105	El Salvador	.719
...106–135 deleted		
135	Lao People's Democratic Republic	.525
136	Bhutan	.511
137	Lesotho	.510
138	Sudan	.503
139	Bangladesh	.502
140	Congo	.502
141	Togo	.501
Countries with Low Human Development		
142	Cameroon	.499
143	Nepal	.499
144	Pakistan	.499
145	Zimbabwe	.496
146	Kenya	.489
147	Uganda	.489
148	Yemen	.470
149	Madagascar	.469
...150–175 deleted		

Source: Data from HDI table, p. 237-240 from "Human Development Report 2003" by UNDP (2003) by permission of Oxford University Press; Remaining data: Authors' Calculations

4

Using the UNDP Indices to Examine Gender Equality and Well-being

Martin Cooke (with the assistance of Kate Hano)

Introduction: Gender Equality and Well-being

As we have explained in Chapter 2, the Human Development Index (HDI), as developed by the United Nations Development Program (UNDP), compares countries' average scores on what the UNDP has identified as three main dimensions of well-being; education, income, and health. Of course, considering only the national average scores is limited, and our application of the HDI methodology to Aboriginal populations in Canada has been premised on the understanding that national-level measures hide important differences in the social conditions experienced by different groups in Canadian society.

One dimension which the UNDP does specifically examine in its annual Human Development Report (1990; 1995; 2004) is gender. Gender inequality is important in the context of international development, but it also remains a key dimension of income, employment, and health inequality in Canada, despite dramatic changes in recent decades. This chapter uses the HDI indicators as a means to examine the changes in gendered inequality between 1981 and 2001, and to measure the gender differences in the Registered Indian population and among other Canadians. We also introduce adaptations of two UNDP measures of gender inequality, the Gender-Related Development Index (GDI) and the Gender Empowerment Measure (GEM), and evaluate their use in examining changing patterns of gender equality in the Registered Indian population and among other Canadians.

Background: Gender Equality in Canada

It is worth pointing out the dramatic changes that gender relations in the general Canadian society have undergone in the past several decades. By 2001, women's labour force participation rate had closed to within ten percentage points of that of men (Statistics Canada, 2006), and women have surpassed men in terms of university enrolment and graduation (Statistics Canada, 2003; Christofides, Hoy, and Yang, 2006). Women's representation in business and political organizations has improved considerably over the past few decades, and leadership roles are now much more likely to be occupied by women than was the case in the past. But despite these changes, gender remains an important dimension of de facto inequality in Canadian society on a number of measures, generally to the disadvantage of women. Women's labour force participation does remain lower than men's, partly due to absences from the paid labour force to care for children and others. Women earn less than men on average, even among full-time, full-year employees (Drolet, 2001). Canadian women have been under-represented among high-status, high-paying jobs and professions, and over-represented in short-term service work providing low wages and few benefits (Armstrong, 1994). Women, including employed women with spouses, remain responsible for the bulk of unpaid household work, (Beaujot, 2000: 194). These factors, as well as discrimination in the labour market, leave Canadian women at increased risk of living in poverty, particularly as lone parents (Christopher et al., 2002).

In development studies, gender equality has long been identified as an important factor in social and economic development. In the context of industrializing countries, for which the UNDP created the HDI measures, women's education and health have been found to have important and beneficial effects on infant and child mortality (e.g.Caldwell, 1979). Women's roles in families and communities mean that their education and physical and economic well-being has crucial implications for the health and well-being of others, and this has been found in Canada as well as in developing countries (e.g. Chen and Millar, 1999).

Of course, gender equality is an important goal for its own sake, in addition to its implications for the well-being of others. To that end, the UNDP has identified gender equality as a critical dimension of an expanded conception of human development (UNDP, 1995). In the Canadian context, less is known about the relative equality of men and women in Aboriginal populations, and how this has changed in recent decades. There are reasons to believe that gender may be observed differently in Aboriginal and non-Aboriginal populations. Some authors have pointed to the important leadership roles traditionally held by women in some Aboriginal cultures, forming a different basis of gender relations than that in European cultures (Fiske, 1991). Aboriginal women have also had different experiences with the Canadian state than have other Canadian women, particularly in relationship to Registered Indian status and the *Indian Act*. Prior to 1985, the *Act* discriminated against Registered Indian women, who lost registration status when they married non-Registered men, whereas the reverse did not occur (Fiske, 1995). In many cases this loss of status meant loss of band membership and claims on band resources such as housing. This was partly addressed by Bill C-31, although Registered Indian women may still be subject to a somewhat different gender regime than are other Canadian women. In particular, the division of matrimonial real property among Registered Indians on-reserve is not governed by provincial or territorial laws, leaving women less able to claim property after the dissolution of a marriage (Abbott, 2003).[1]

Aboriginal women also tend to live in different family forms than other Canadian women, with implications for their economic and physical well-being. Higher fertility rates and earlier childbearing in Aboriginal populations means that Aboriginal women on average spend more time living with young children, resulting in lower labour force participation rates (Peters and Rosenberg, 1995: 88). Aboriginal women are also much more likely to be the heads of single parent families than are other Canadian women, affecting employment opportunities as well as income (Hull, 2001b). However, the effects of having children at home on women's employment and education may also be less for Registered Indian women than for other women, possibly reflecting greater support available in Aboriginal communities or the success of targeted transfer programs (Hull, 2001b, White et al., 2003).

There has been some empirical research about the changing social and economic situation of Aboriginal women relative to Aboriginal men and non-Aboriginal women. Census data from 1996 and 2001 show that Aboriginal women had lower labour force participation and incomes than Aboriginal men, at all educational levels. Nonetheless, Aboriginal women tended to have higher educational attainment than men, at least in recent years (Hull, 2001a, 2005). However, it is somewhat unclear how gender inequality has changed in recent decades, and whether Aboriginal populations have seen the same kinds of changes that have occurred in the general Canadian population. In order to study these changes, we examined the gender differences on the HDI indicators presented in Chapter 3, as well as the results of two of the measures of gender inequality found in the Human Development Report.

Gender and the Human Development Indicators

In the remainder of this chapter, we use our adaptation of the UNDP's HDI to examine the different levels of attainment for men and for women in the Registered Indian population and amongst other Canadians. As well, we present the results from two indices of gender equality. In its 1995 *Human Development Report*, the UNDP presented new indicators to incorporate gender equality into its measurement of human development. In its "engendered development model," the UNDP asserted that countries' scores on measures of "human development" should be discounted to reflect the extent to which men and women have not shared equally in that development. To that end, the UNDP introduced the Gender-Related Human Development Index (GDI), which discounts a country's HDI scores by the degree to which men and women's scores on the individual indicators differ. The calculation of the GDI involves calculating separate male and female scores for each of the education, life expectancy, and income measures, and combining them into a new measure, discounted by the amount of inequality on each of the indicators.[2]

The Gender Empowerment Measure (GEM) was also introduced in the 1995 Human Development Report. Whereas the HDI/GDI methodology focuses on the relative level of attainment of men and women in education, health, and income, the GEM attempts to measure the participation of men and women in political and economic decision-making. Within the GEM, "empowerment" is measured

Figure 4.1: Life Expectancy at Birth, Registered Indian and Reference Population Males and Females, 1981–2001

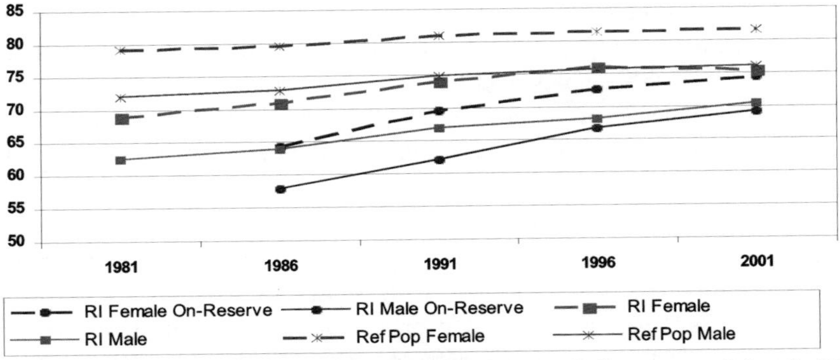

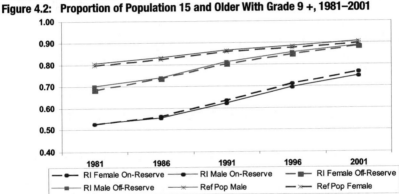

Note: Separate life expectancy estimates are not available for on- and off-reserve populations for 1981.
Source: Statistics Canada, 1984, 1990, 1995, 1998, 2005; Rowe and Norris, 1995; Nault et al., 1993; Norris, Kerr, and Nault, 1996; DIAND, 1998; Verma, Michalowski, and Gauvin, 2003; authors' calculations.

Figure 4.2: Proportion of Population 15 and Older With Grade 9 +, 1981–2001

Source: Statistics Canada, Census of Canada, 1981-2001.; author's calculations.

by men's and women's representation in parliamentary bodies, within professions and technical occupations (UNDP, 1995). While the HDI includes average total income, the GEM includes men's and women's shares of average income from employment, as a measure of economic empowerment.[3]

In the following sections, we present the trends in the HDI indicators for men and women in the Registered Indian and reference populations, for 1981–2001, and use the GDI methodology to discount the HDI scores for gender inequality. We then use the adapted GEM to examine the trends in men's and women's participation in economic and organizational decision-making. We conclude by pointing out the important trends in gender inequality in the Registered Indian population, and some of the limitations of these measures.

Gender Differences in the HDI/GDI 1981–2001

As described in previous chapters, the HDI incorporates three dimensions of well-being. These are health, measured by life expectancy at birth; education, measured by the proportions with grade 9 or higher and high school or higher; and material standard of living, measured by total average income. In this section we present the trends in gender inequality using these indicators for the Registered Indian on- and off-reserve and the reference population from 1981 to 2001. We will also demonstrate the effect of applying the GDI methodology for discounting these measures to account for gender inequality.

Life Expectancy at Birth

One area in which women have consistently out-scored men in industrialized countries is in life expectancy at birth, and in Canada this is true for the Registered Indian population as it is for other Canadians. **Figure 4.1** shows the life expectancy estimates for Registered Indians living on- and off-reserve and for other Canadians, from 1981 to 2001. As described in previous chapters, life expectancy has improved for each of these populations, and the gap between Registered Indians and other Canadians declined over the 1981–2001 period. In terms of gender differences in life expectancy, the female advantage has also declined. In 1981, life expectancy for male and female Registered Indians was estimated at 57.8 and 64.2 respectively, a seven-year difference. This difference declined to five years in 2001, when life expectancy was 70.3 for males and 75.4 for females. This five-year gap was similar for the reference population, despite longer life expectancy of 75.9 years for men and 81.5 years for women. A similar gender difference is observed in the on-reserve Registered Indian population, for whom life expectancy was 69.2 years for men and 74.3 years for women, in 2001.

Education

As described above and in previous chapters, the first education measure on the HDI, the proportion of the population 15 and older with grade 9 or higher, serves as a proxy for adult literacy, or the minimal standard of education required for participation in society. **Figure 4.2** shows the scores on this measure for 1981–2001. In the Registered Indian population, the general pattern is towards equal scores and a slight, but increasing, advantage among women on-reserve. About 53% of both men and women living on-reserve had grade 9 or higher in 1981, compared to 70% of men and 68% of women living off-reserve. However, by the end of the period, women on-reserve had slightly higher attainment on this indicator (77%), compared to men (75%). In the off-reserve population, male advantage disappeared over the period, and 89% of both men and women had grade 9 or higher in 2001. In the reference population, the male advantage on this indicator remained fairly constant, at less than one percent.

These gender differences on this indicator are of a small magnitude, and one should not make too much of the trend toward higher scores for women. However,

Figure 4.3: Proportion of those 19 and Older With High School +, 1981–2001

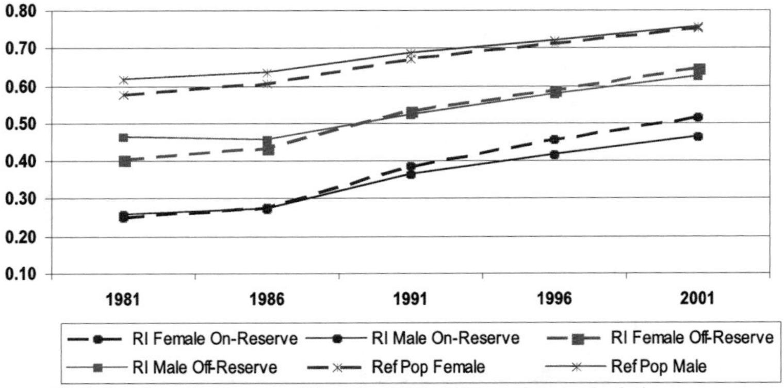

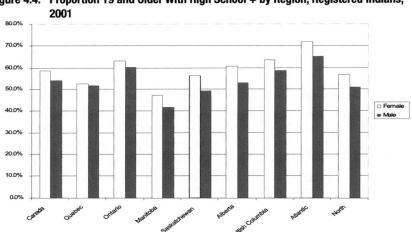

Source: Statistics Canada, Census of Canada, 1981–2001; authors' calculations.

Figure 4.4: Proportion 19 and Older With High School + by Region, Registered Indians, 2001

Source: Statistics Canada, Census of Canada, 1981–2001; authors' calculations.

women's outstripping of male educational attainment among Registered Indians is more clearly shown in the other measure of educational attainment, the proportion of the population aged 19 and older with high school or higher education. The 1981–2001 scores on this indicator are shown in **Figure 4.3**. As with the other indicator, men began the period with higher average scores than did women, both among Registered Indians and the reference population. However, while women in the reference population had caught up to men in 2001, among Registered Indians, women's scores had passed men's by 1991. By 2001, 51% of Registered Indian women living on-reserve had high school, or some technical, college, or university education, compared to 46% of men. Among off-reserve Registered Indians the gender gap was smaller but the trend was similar, and by 2001, 65% of women living off-reserve had high school or higher education, compared to 62% of men. In the rest of the Canadian population, male advantage on this educational

Table 4.1: Education Index Scores, Men and Women 1981–2001

		Educational Attainment Index (HDI)			
		Male	Female	Total	Discounted Education Index (GDI)
On-reserve	1981	0.436	0.433	0.434	0.434
	1986	0.460	0.467	0.463	0.463
	1991	0.535	0.552	0.543	0.543
	1996	0.603	0.626	0.614	0.614
	2001	0.653	0.683	0.668	0.667
Off-reserve	1981	0.590	0.622	0.604	0.604
	1986	0.635	0.646	0.639	0.639
	1991	0.713	0.715	0.714	0.714
	1996	0.760	0.764	0.762	0.762
	2001	0.805	0.799	0.802	0.802
Reference Population	1981	0.743	0.724	0.733	0.733
	1986	0.765	0.751	0.759	0.758
	1991	0.807	0.798	0.802	0.802
	1996	0.830	0.823	0.826	0.826
	2001	0.856	0.850	0.853	0.853

Source: Statistics Canada, 1981–2001 Census of Canada, author's Calculations

attainment indicator also decreased over the period, with men and women very nearly equal by 2001.

This pattern of higher female educational attainment among the Registered Indian population is generally found in all provinces and territories, although to different degrees. As **Figure 4.4** illustrates, the gender gaps were largest in Saskatchewan and Alberta, where there was more than 7% difference, and lowest in Quebec, where registered Indian women had an advantage of only 0.6%. As well, the general pattern of higher female advantage among those on-reserve, compared to off-reserve, held in most regions, although those data are not presented here.

As in the previous chapters, scores on these two measures are combined to form the Educational Attainment Index. **Table 4.1** presents the education index scores for men and women, as well as the discounted education index, according the GDI methodology. The two-thirds weight given to the proportion with grade 9 or higher reduces the difference between men's and women's HDI scores, but the general pattern of higher scores for Registered Indian women is evident. By 2001, the combined HDI score for the on-reserve population (0.668) masked a relatively large difference between women's and men's separate index scores. However, when combined according to the GDI methodology, they do not result in observable discounting of the HDI scores, at least to three decimal places.

Table 4.2: **Average Annual Income and Income Index Scores, 1980–2000 (Year 2000 $)**

		Average Annual Total Income				
		Male Income	**Female Income**	**Male-Female**	**Income Index (HDI)**	**Discounted Income Index (GDI)**
On- reserve	1980	7,857	4,441	3,416	0.669	0.668
	1985	7,846	4,587	3,259	0.679	0.671
	1990	7,980	5,482	2,498	0.692	0.688
	1995	8,445	6,781	1,574	0.713	0.712
	2000	8,651	8,145	506	0.728	0.728
Off-reserve	1980	11,300	5,572	5,728	0.723	0.604
	1985	9,335	6,159	3,176	0.693	0.532
	1990	11,236	8,431	2,805	0.752	0.744
	1995	11,280	9,015	2,265	0.758	0.756
	2000	13,215	10,487	2,728	0.784	0.782
Reference Population	1980	23,380	9,822	13,558	0.834	0.820
	1985	24,557	11,850	12,707	0.856	0.841
	1990	26,018	14,259	11,759	0.873	0.865
	1995	25,228	14,905	10,323	0.873	0.865
	2000	27,931	17,225	10,706	0.892	0.886

Source: Statistics Canada, 1981–2001 Census of Canada, author's Calculations

Average Total Income

Although women generally surpassed men in terms of educational attainment by the end of the 1981–2001 period, quite a different pattern is evident when we examine trends in income. As described in earlier chapters, our adaptation of the HDI methodology uses total annual income averaged over the entire population as a measure of material standard of living, or access to goods and services in the market. In the HDI methodology this income is discounted using a log formula to account for the decreasing marginal utility of income. For simplicity, **Table 4.2** presents the untransformed average incomes for males and females, among the on- and off-reserve Registered Indian population and the reference population, in year 2000 dollars.

For each of these populations, men had an advantage in average total income over the entire period. This is much more clearly the case in the reference population than in the Registered Indian population. In 1980, the average income of reference population men was $23,380 or 2.4 times that of reference population women (**Table 4.2**). Women's average incomes improved fairly steadily over the entire period, while male incomes declined between 1990 and 1995, due to the economic recession. The end result was that the male-female gap closed to $10,300 by 1995, but widened again between 1995 and 2001, as male incomes recovered.

Table 4.3: **Human Development and Gender-related Development Index Scores, 1981–2001**

		HDI Scores				GDI Score
		Male	Female	Total	Male-Female	Total
On-reserve	1981	-	-	-	-	-
	1986	-	-	-	-	-
	1991	0.643	0.663	0.669	-0.02	0.621
	1996	0.676	0.710	0.693	-0.03	0.669
	2001	0.707	0.742	0.725	-0.04	0.700
Off-reserve	1981	-	-	-	-	-
	1986	-	-	-	-	-
	1991	0.764	0.774	0.749	-0.01	0.746
	1996	0.785	0.790	0.777	-0.01	0.760
	2001	0.793	0.810	0.802	-0.02	0.782
Registered Indian Total	1981	0.625	0.622	0.626	0.00	0.606
	1986	0.637	0.656	0.644	-0.02	0.625
	1991	0.688	0.720	0.706	-0.03	0.686
	1996	0.718	0.757	0.739	-0.04	0.718
	2001	0.750	0.780	0.762	-0.03	0.746
Reference Population	1981	0.808	0.793	0.806	0.02	0.779
	1986	0.825	0.817	0.823	0.01	0.799
	1991	0.850	0.849	0.852	0.00	0.828
	1996	0.861	0.861	0.863	0.00	0.840
	2001	0.887	0.883	0.880	0.00	0.863

Source: Statistics Canada, 1984, 1990, 1995, 1998, 2005; Statistics Canada 1981–2001 Census of Canada data; Rowe and Norris, 1995; Nault et al., 1993; Norris, Kerr, and Nault, 1996; Verma, Michalowski, and Gauvin, 2003, authors' calculations.

Registered Indian women living on-reserve also saw their average annual incomes increase over the period, from an average of about $4,400 in 1980 to about $8,150 in 2000. However, the incomes of on-reserve men were basically flat between 1980 and 1990, and rose only slightly thereafter. As a result, the gender gap in incomes on-reserve closed to about $500 by 2000 (**Table 4.2**). Among those living off-reserve, the gender gap in average annual income also closed between 1980 and 2000. In 1980, off-reserve women had an average income of $5,600, compared to $11,300 for men. Because male incomes were about the same in 1995 as in 1980, the increase in female incomes over this period closed the gap. By 2000, the average income for off-reserve males was only $2,730, or 26%, higher than that of off-reserve women.

Table 4.2 (page 76) also presents the income index discounted for gender inequality, according to the GDI methodology. Unlike the discounted education index, gender differences in total average income do result in lower

Table 4.4: Gender Empowerment Measure Scores and Components, Registered Indian and Reference Population, 1991–2001.

		Women's Population Proportion	Female Proportion of Public Sector Managers & Legislators	Female Proportion of Private Sector Managers	Female Proportion of Professional and Technical Employment	Female Share of Employment Income	Gender Empowerment Measure Score
Registered Indian	1991	0.54	0.31(-.23)	0.49(-.05)	0.55(+.01)	0.48(-.06)	0.751
	1996	0.54	0.31(-.23)	0.51(-.03)	0.57(+.03)	0.48(-.06)	0.756
	2001	0.54	0.39(-.15)	0.49(-.05)	0.58(+.04)	0.47(-.07)	0.801
On-reserve	1991	0.50	0.27(-.23)	0.40(-.10)	0.50(0.0)	0.44(-.06)	0.707
	1996	0.49	0.28(-.21)	0.43(-.06)	0.52(+.04)	0.46(-.03)	0.728
	2001	0.50	0.35(-.15)	0.46(-.04)	0.55(+.05)	0.47(-.03)	0.773
Off-reserve	1991	0.60	0.43(-.17)	0.53(-.07)	0.59(+.01)	0.50(-.10)	0.804
	1996	0.58	0.41(-.17)	0.56(-.02)	0.61(+.03)	0.51(-.07)	0.807
	2001	0.57	0.47(-.10)	0.50(-.07)	0.60(+.07)	0.48(-.09)	0.834
Reference Population	1991	0.51	0.26(-.25)	0.31(-.20)	0.45(-.06)	0.41(-.10)	0.773
	1996	0.51	0.28(-.23)	0.32(-.19)	0.46(-.05)	0.40(-.11)	0.801
	2001	0.51	0.35(-.16)	0.36(-.15)	0.46(-.05)	0.40(-.11)	0.865

Source: Statistics Canada, 1991–2001 Census of Canada, Author's Calculations. Income data are for 1990, 1995, 2000. The difference between female population share and indicator share is shown in parentheses.

discounted index scores. This effect was greatest in the reference population, but is also seen in the Registered Indian scores, especially off-reserve. However, the declining gender gap in total income among the Registered Indian population meant that by 2000 the discounting formula had very little effect, reducing off-reserve scores by only 0.002 (**Table 4.2**).

Human Development Index Scores

As we described in Chapter 2 , the HDI methodology combines life expectancy, education, and income indicators into Human Development Index scores for each of these populations. The combined HDI, as well as separate scores for men and women are shown for 1981 to 2001, in **Table 4.3** (page 77). As well as the HDI scores, we have presented the Gender-Related Development Index Scores (GDI) which represent the HDI scores discounted for the disparity between men and women on each of the indicators.

In both the Registered Indian and reference populations, women's HDI scores improved, relative to those of men. Among Registered Indians, women's scores were higher than men's in 1981, and this difference increased between 1981 and 2001, while in the reference population the gap between men's and women's scores declined. By 2001, Registered Indian women on-reserve had an HDI score of 0.742, compared to 0.707 for men (**Table 4.3**). For those living off-reserve, women's scores were 0.810, compared to 0.793 for men.

When combined into discounted GDI scores, the gender differences in life expectancy, education, and income resulted in considerably reduced index scores. As shown in **Table 4.3**, among Registered Indians on-reserve, the discounted score was 0.700, compared to an HDI of 0.725 in 2001. Among those living off-reserve, the discounting effect was even stronger, from 0.802 to 0.700 in 2001. However, it should be noted that the GDI methodology results in a lower score regardless of whether it is men or women who have an advantage on any particular indicator. Some of the implications of this are presented in the conclusion to this chapter.

The Gender Empowerment Measure (GEM)

Whereas the HDI/GDI indicators measure the average level of well-being of men and women, the Gender Empowerment Measure (GEM) attempts to capture the relative empowerment of men and women in terms of political and economic decision-making. As described above, the UNDP captures these dimensions of equality by examining male and female shares of parliamentary seats, representation among professionals, managers, and technical occupations, and male and female shares of earned income. In our adaptation to the Canadian case, we use Census data on occupation and industries, and income from employment. Below, we present the results of these indicators for the 1991–2001 period, for the Registered Indian and reference populations.

Table 4.4 shows the main components of the Gender Empowerment Measure for the Registered Indian and reference populations from 1991 to 2001. Because of a change to Statistics Canada's classifications of occupations and industries, we have not calculated GEM scores for 1981 or 1985. The GEM methodology compares men's and women's representation in public administration and private sector management, and shares of employment income to their representation in the population. For example, perfect equality would require that women's share of professional and technical occupations would be exactly the same as women's representation in the population. Note that women make up slightly more than half of the reference population, and 54% of the Registered Indian population. This is due to several factors including men's lower life expectancy and the effects of Bill C-31 re-registration (Clatworthy, 2003). Registered Indian women are over-represented among Registered Indians living off-reserve because of the registration of off-reserve women under Bill C-31, as well as higher migration rates among women (Norris et al., 2004).

Women's under-representation among legislators and managers in public administration was greater in the reference population than in the Registered Indian population in the 1991–2001 period.[4] In 2001, women accounted for only 35% of reference population managers, and 39% of the Registered Indian public administration managers. Women's representation among public sector managers was highest in the off-reserve Registered Indian population, in which women occupied 47% of these jobs in 2001. This was still 10% lower than women's share of the total off-reserve population, however. Nonetheless, women's share of public administration management jobs increased between 1991 and 2001, in each of the study populations (**Table 4.4** – page 78).

Women were much better-represented among Registered Indians in private sector management positions. Although reference population women's representation increased from 31% to 36% over the decade, women accounted for roughly half of all Registered Indians in private sector management occupations over the period. Unlike public-sector management, women's representation in these occupations was higher among on-reserve Registered Indians than among those living off-reserve by 2001. Although women were 50% of off-reserve Registered Indians in these occupations in 2001, the high proportion of women among the off-reserve population meant that representation was better on-reserve. Moreover, while women's relative representation in management positions on-reserve improved over the period, off-reserve it was the same in 1991 and 2001, after improving in 1996 (**Table 4.4**).

The proportion of women in professional or technical employment shows a much different pattern for the Registered Indian and reference populations. Although reference population women are somewhat under-represented in this category, it is men who were under-represented in the Registered Indian population to an increasing degree over the 1991–2001 period. It is important to note that this is a very broad category, and includes highly paid professions such as doctors and lawyers, as well as less well-paid professionals such as teachers and nurses. The technical occupations in the category included, for example, dental hygienists and computer operators. The over-representation of Registered Indians in these occupations is due at least partly to employment in the technical occupations in this category.

Lastly, the GEM incorporates men's and women's relative shares of employment income, as a measure of economic power in the market. **Table 4.4** presents

Figure 4.5: Average Annual Employment Income by Gender, Registered Indians and Reference Population, 1980–2000 (Year 2000 $)

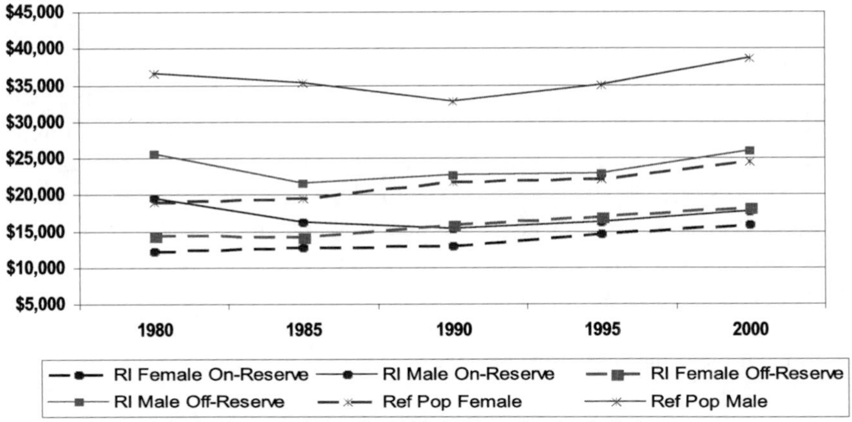

Legend:
— ● — RI Female On-Reserve — ● — RI Male On-Reserve — ■ — RI Female Off-Reserve
— ■ — RI Male Off-Reserve — × — Ref Pop Female — × — Ref Pop Male

Source: Statistics Canada, Census of Canada, 1981–2001; authors' calculations.

the female share of total employment income, from Census data, for each of the study populations. In no case do women receive a greater proportion of employment income than do men. However, the difference between men and women is least among Registered Indians on-reserve, where relative equality was nearly achieved in 2001, while it is greatest among the reference population.

As described in the 1995 *Human Development Report* (UNDP, 1995), the income measure in the GEM captures both the shares of employment income received by men and women, and the absolute level of income, in its calculation. **Table 4.4** presents men's and women's shares of average employment incomes and **Figure 4.5** shows the trends in average income between 1980 and 2000. The figure shows improvement in the gap between men and women in these populations, although some of the improvement has been due to declines in men's incomes, rather than higher employment incomes for women. In the on-reserve Registered Indian population, men received an average of $19,400 in employment income in 1980, $7,200 more than the average for women. By 2000, this gap had decreased to $1,800. However, most of the decline was due to the drop in men's employment income between 1985 and 1990. Although female income rose steadily over the 1980–2000 period, the gap between male and female income widened between 1995 and 2000, as male incomes recovered somewhat.

A similar pattern is observed in the off-reserve Registered Indian and the reference populations. Among Registered Indians living off-reserve, male average employment incomes fell from $25,500 to $21,100 between 1980 and 1985 (**Figure 4.5** – page 81). Male incomes had recovered to $25,800 by 2000, while female incomes increased fairly steadily, from $14,300 to $18,100 between 1980 and 2000. The result was that the gender gap in average annual employment income fell for most of the period, but rose slightly between 1995 and 2000. This pattern is also evident in the reference population, in which male employment incomes fell between 1980 and 1990, and then recovered, resulting in a widening of the gender gap between 1995 and 2000. In both of these populations, these results are observed in a slightly decreasing female share of employment income between 1995 and 2000 (**Table 4.4** – page 78).

These measures are combined in the Gender Empowerment Measure presented in **Table 4.4** The higher level of average employment income results in a higher GEM score for the reference population, despite higher degrees of gender inequality on most indicators. However, the trend for the GEM indicators was to increase between 1991 and 2001, for all of the study populations. This suggests that the relative equality of men and women, at least in terms of the "empowerment" measured by these indicators is increasing. As discussed below, this obscures the different patterns on each of these indicators and the fact that the gender disparity on some of these measures has increased.

Conclusions

What can we conclude from the use of these indicators to examine gender differences in the Canadian context, both in terms of the patterns of gender inequality in the Registered Indian population, and the utility of these measures? In general, the evidence of improving gender equality is mixed. Women's scores have improved on nearly all of the indicators, including income, education, and representation in management and professional and technical occupations, for both the Registered Indian and reference populations. On several of these measures, this resulted in women narrowing the gap with men, particularly in representation among management occupations. The gender gap in life expectancy, the indicator on which women tend to score higher, also decreased among Registered Indians and other Canadians as improvements were made in men's mortality (Manuel and Hockin, 2000; DesMeules, Manuel, and Cho, 2004).

Registered Indian women's incomes improved over the period, both in terms of average employment income and average total income, resulting in a narrowing of the total income gap with men. However, some of these gender gaps widened, as was the case with employment income between 1995 and 2000. Moreover, at least some of the improvement that was seen before 1995 was due to stagnation or decline in men's incomes, as women's incomes continued to improve. This would seem to indicate that further progress in closing this gap is uncertain. It may be that as Registered Indian employment incomes rise, especially off-reserve, the gender gap in income will approach that seen in the rest of the Canadian population.

However, the trends are not all the same in the Registered Indian and reference populations. The increasing advantage of Registered Indian women in primary and secondary education is unmatched among other Canadians, although previous research has found that women have indeed outstripped men in terms of attainment of university degrees and higher education for some time (Christofides, Hoy, and Yang, 2006). It may be that the processes that lead to female advantage in higher levels of education among the total Canadian population is evident at lower levels in the Registered Indian population, again because of the lower average level of attainment.

Regardless of potential similarities in process, and any hypotheses about whether the gender differences in the two populations may converge in the future, current trends in gender equality in the Registered Indian population may have important implications for research and policy. It is clearly important to understand why it appears that Registered Indian men are falling behind in terms of educational attainment, especially on-reserve. At the same time, it is important to ask why the improvements in women's educational attainment and representation in management, professional, and technical occupations, have not resulted in dramatic improvements in employment income, relative to that of men.

The Gender-Related Development Index (GDI) and the Gender Empowerment Measure (GEM) were developed by the UNDP in the context of international development studies, in which the concern is generally improving women's health, well-being, and empowerment, and to close the gap with men. As we have seen, in the case of the Registered Indian population, several of the GDI/HDI and GEM indicators favour women over men. In general, judging by the individual HDI scores shown above, Registered Indian women had a higher level of overall well-being than did men, because of higher life expectancy and education, and relatively small gaps in income. These differences are lost when only the total HDI is examined. As well, the different trends in gender difference on the life expectancy, education, and income indicators led to inconsistent results when the GDI methodology was used. Women's decreasing advantage in life expectancy was offset by their increasing advantage in education and inconsistent changes in income, making the interpretation of the GDI unclear. As with the GEM, the GDI composite index is probably not as useful to examine gender inequality as is the examination of the individual index components.

Endnotes

1   Those interested in exploring the issue of identity in relation to Bill C-31, including the legislation's roots and consequences, should refer to the fifth volume in our series on Aboriginal public policy research, a compilation of articles from the 2006 APRC Conference: White, J.P., et al. (Eds.). 2007. *Aboriginal Policy Research: Moving Forward, Making a Difference*, vol. 5, Toronto: Thompson Educational Publishing, Inc.

2   In the GDI, each of the life expectancy, education, and income indicators in the HDI are discounted according to the formula:

EDI = [female population share (female index$^{1-\varepsilon}$)] + [male population share (male index$^{1-\varepsilon}$)], where ε is the aversion to inequality parameter, and set to $\varepsilon=2$.

The GDI methodology also sets higher minimum and maximum life expectancy values for women, to account for a natural advantage (UNDP, 2004: 261).

3   For each of the indicators on the GEM, an Equally Distributed Equivalent Percentage is calculated, which is the harmonic mean of the male and female indicators, weighted by the male and female shares in the population (UNDP, 2004: 261).

4   Public administration includes occupations in municipal, provincial, federal, and Aboriginal governments.

References

Abbott, K. 2003. Urban Aboriginal Women in British Columbia and the Impacts of the Matrimonial Real Property Regime. Ottawa: Indian and Northern Affairs Canada. Retrieved 10 Dec. 2006. <**www.ainc-inac.gc.ca/wige/ura/index_e.html**>.

Armstrong, H. 1994). *The Double Ghetto: Canadian Women and Their Segregated Work.* Third Edition. Toronto: McClelland & Stewart.

Beavon, D. and Cooke, M. 2003. "An Application of the United Nations Human Development Index to Registered Indians in Canada." In White, J.P., Maxim, P., & Beavon, D. (Eds.). *Aboriginal Conditions.* Vancouver: UBC Press. 201–221.

Beaujot, R. 2000. *Earning and Caring in Canadian Families.* Peterborough. Broadview.

Chen, J. and Millar, W.J. 1999. "Birth outcome, the social environment, and child health." *Health Reports.* 10 (4): 57–67.

Caldwell, J.C. 1979. "Education as a Factor in Mortality Decline: An Examination of Nigerian Data." *Population Studies.* 33: 395–413.

Christofides, L.N., Hoy, M., and Yang, L. 2006. "The Gender Imbalance in Participation in Canadian Universities (1977–2003)." Department of Economics, University of Guelph working paper. April.

Clatworthy, S.J. 2003. "Impacts of the 1985 Amendments to the *Indian Act* in First Nations Populations." In White, J.P., Maxim, P., and Beavon, D. (Eds.). *Aboriginal Conditions.* Vancouver: UBC Press. 63–90.

Cooke, M., Beavon, D., and McHardy, M. 2004. "Measuring the Well-being of Aboriginal People: An Application of the United Nations Human Development Index to Registered Indians in Canada, 1981–2001." Report for the Strategic Analysis Directorate, Policy and Strategic Direction Branch. Ottawa: Indian and Northern Affairs Canada. Retrieved 5 Jan. 2005. <**www.ainc-inac.gc.ca/pr/ra/index_e.html**>.

DesMeules, M., Manuel, D., and Cho, R. 2004. "Mortality: Life and Health Expectancy of Canadian Women." *BMC Women's Health 4*, (Supp 11): S9. Retrieved 1 Feb. 2006. <**www.biomedcentral.com/1472-6874/4/S1/S9**>.

Drolet, M. 2001. "The Persistent Wage Gap: New Evidence on the Canadian Gender Wage Gap." Analytical Studies Branch Research Paper Series No. 157. Ottawa: Statistics Canada.

Fiske, J. 1991. "Colonization and the Decline of Women's Status: The Tsimshian Case." *Feminist Studies.* 17(3): 509–535.

_____. 1995. "Political Status of Native Indian Women: Contradictory Implications of Canadian State Policy." *American Indian Culture and Research Journal.* 19(2): 1–30.

Hull, J. 2001a. "Aboriginal Post-Secondary Education and Labour Market Outcomes in Canada, 1996." Research and Analysis Directorate. Ottawa: Indian and Northern Affairs Canada.

Hull, J. 2001b. "Aboriginal Single Mothers in Canada, 1996 A Statistical Profile." Research and Analysis Directorate. Ottawa: Indian and Northern Affairs Canada.

Hull, J. 2005. "Post-Secondary Education and Labour Market Outcomes Canada, 2001." Strategic Research and Analysis Directorate. Ottawa: Indian and Northern Affairs Canada.

Indian and Northern Affairs Canada. (2001). "Aboriginal Women: A Profile from the 1996 Census." First Nations and Northern Statistics, Cooperate Information Management Directorate, Information Management Branch. Ottawa: Indian and Northern Affairs Canada.

Indian and Northern Affairs Canada. 2000. "Registered Indian Population Projections for Canada and Regions 2000–2021." Ottawa: Indian and Northern Affairs Canada. Retrieved 1 Sept.2005. <**www.ainc-inac.gc.ca/pr/sts/ipp_e.pdf**>.

Indian and Northern Affairs Canada. 2003. Basic Departmental Data. Ottawa: Indian and Northern Affairs Canada. Retrieved 1 Sept. 2005. <**http://dsp-psd.pwgsc.gc.ca/Collection/R12-7-2003E.pdf**>.

Larouque, G. and Gauvin, R.P. 1989. "Census Highlights on Registered Indians—Annotated Tables." Ottawa: Statistics Canada.

Manuel, D. and Hockin J. (2000) "Recent trends in provincial life expectancy." *Canadian Journal of Public Health.* 91(2):118–19.

Nault, F., Chen, J., George, M.V., and Norris, M.J. 1993. "Population Projections of Registered Indians, 1991–2015." Ottawa: Indian and Northern Affairs Canada. Norris, M. J., Cooke, M., Beavon, D., and Guimond, E. 2004. "Registered Indian Mobility and Migration: Patterns and Implications." In *Population Mobility and Indigenous Peoples in Australasia and North America.* J. Taylor and M. Bell (Eds.). London: Routledge.

Peters, E. and Rosenberg, M. 1995. "Labour Force Attachment and Regional Development for Native Peoples: Theoretical and Methodological Issues." *Canadian Journal of Regional Science.* 18(1): 77–105.

Rowe, G. and Norris, M. J. 1985. "Mortality Projections of Registered Indians, 1982 to 1996." Ottawa: Indian and Northern Affairs Canada.

Statistics Canada. 2006. Labour force and participation rates by sex and age group. Ottawa: Statistics Canada. Retrieved 10 Dec. 2006. <**www40.statcan.ca/l01/cst01/labor05.htm**>.

Statistics Canada. 2003. University Enrolment by Field of Study, The Daily, Monday March 31. Ottawa: Statistics Canada. Retrieved 1 Sept.2005. <**www.statcan.ca/Daily/English/030331/d030331b.htm**>.

Statistics Canada. (2003b). 2001 Census Dictionary, Catalogue no. 92-378-XIE. Ottawa: Statistics Canada. Retrieved 5 Sept. 2005: <**www12.statcan.ca/english/census01/products/reference/dict/appendices/92-378-XIE02002.pdf**>.

Statistics Canada. 2005a. Table 102-0511—Life expectancy—abridged life table, at birth and at age 65, by sex, Canada, provinces and territories, annual (Years).360 series. Ottawa: Statistics Canada. Retrieved 1 Sept. 2005. <**www.statcan.ca/english/freepub/84F0211XIE/2002/tables.htm**>.

Statistics Canada. 2005b. Consumer Price Index, Historical Summary. Ottawa: Statistics Canada. Retrieved 1 Sep. 2005. <**/www40.statcan.ca/l01/cst01/econ46.htm**>.

Statistics Canada. 1984. "Life Tables, Canada and Provinces 1980–82." Cat no. 84-532. Ottawa: Statistics Canada.

Status of Women of Canada. 2000. "Aboriginal Women's Roundtable on Gender Equality." Ottawa: Status of Women of Canada.

Townshend, I., MacLachlan, I., and O'Donohue, D. (2004). "Integrated Dis-Integration: Employment Structure of First Nations Communities on the Prairies Relative to their Local Regions." *Canadian Journal of Native Studies.* 24(1): 91–127.

United Nations Development Program. 1990. *Human Development Report 1990.* New York: Oxford University Press.

United Nations Development Program. 1995. *Human Development Report 1995.* New York: Oxford University Press.

United Nations Development Program. 2004. *Human Development Report 2004.* New York: Oxford University Press.

White, J.P., Anderson, E., Cornet, V., and Beavon, D. (2007). *Aboriginal Policy Research: Moving Forward, Making a Difference.* vol. 5. Toronto: Thompson Educational Publishing, Inc.

White, J.P., Maxim, P., and Gyimah, S.O. 2003. "Labour Force Activity of Women in Canada: A Comparative Analysis of Aboriginal and Non-Aboriginal Women." *Canadian Review of Sociology and Anthropology.* 40(4): 391–415.

White J.P., Maxim, P., and Spence, N. 2004. "An Examination of Educational Success" In White, J.P., Maxim, P., and Beavon, D. (Eds.) *Aboriginal Policy Research: Setting the Agenda for Change.* vol. 1. Toronto: Thompson Educational Publishing, Inc. 129–148.

5

Aboriginal Well-being in Four Countries: An Application of the UNDP's Human Development Index to Aboriginal People in Australia, Canada, New Zealand, and the United States

Martin Cooke, Francis Mitrou, David Lawrence, Éric Guimond, and Dan Beavon

Introduction

In this chapter we develop a comparative analysis of Australia, Canada, New Zealand, and the United States. It is unclear just how the socio-economic and health status of Aboriginal people in these countries has changed in recent decades, and it remains generally unknown whether the overall conditions of Aboriginal people are improving and whether the gaps between Aboriginal people and other citizens have indeed narrowed. Utilizing the same approach as was developed in Chapter 2 we have analyzed our comparator countries to determine if there have been improvements or increasing problems in terms of the gaps between Aboriginalpeople and the non-Aboriginal populations during the decade 1990 to 2000.

It is well known that, on average, Aboriginal people in North America and Australasian countries have not shared the same high quality of life enjoyed by other citizens. The colonial histories of these countries are reflected in higher mortality, lower incomes and educational achievement, and higher rates of crime and victimization of Aboriginal people. However, important changes in the relationships between Aboriginal people and state structures have taken place in each of these countries in recent decades. In Canada, Australia, and New Zealand, there have been incremental moves toward more self-determination by Aboriginal peoples, including Aboriginal control over education and health service delivery. In the United States, Aboriginal affairs has occupied a less central place in national politics, but there have nonetheless been changes that have given Aboriginal peoples more control over program delivery in their own communities (Maaka and Fleras, 2005; Fleras and Elliott, 1992: 159; Cornell, 2004).

Nonetheless, it remains an open question as to whether the economic, social, and physical well-being of Aboriginal people has improved, and whether the gaps between Aboriginal people and other citizens have been reduced. In the Canadian context, research using an adaptation of the UNDP's Human Development Index (HDI) has found that disparities between Registered Indians and other Canadians declined over the 1981–2001 period. However, progress was uneven and the gaps on some indicators widened (Cooke, Beavon, and McHardy, 2004). This paper extends that research to use the HDI methodology to investigate the well-being of Aboriginal people in Canada, Australia, New Zealand, and the US and to compare Aboriginal and non-Aboriginal people in terms of income, health, and educational attainment indicators between 1991 and 2001.

Background: Similarities and Differences

These four countries are often thought of as natural comparators due to their origins as mainly British colonies, their shared language, and the presence of sizeable indigenous populations (Lavoie, 2004). This is reflected in comparative studies of the politics of Aboriginal rights and the history of Aboriginal–state relations (Maaka and Fleras, 2005; Fleras and Elliot, 1992; Armitage, 1995), and of the health status of Aboriginal people (Kunitz, 1990; Trovato, 2001; Bramley, Hebert, Jackson, and Chassin, 2004). According to the UNDP's annual *Human Development Report*, these four countries are all among the world's most "highly developed" nations and differences among them in terms of average educational attainment, income, and general health are very slight (UNDP, 2003). They have similar colonial origins and broadly similar systems of state provision, characterized by minimal decommodification and an emphasis on market provision (Esping-Andersen, 1999).

All of these countries currently have minority Aboriginal populations as well as laws and institutions that apply only to Aboriginal people. At the time of arrival of Europeans, a similar approach was taken toward the people of these territories, including attempts to eradicate traditional ways of life and assimilate Aboriginal people into the settler culture, as well as paternalistic policies that were under-taken in order to "protect" them. Although the specific policies and circumstances of colonial rule differed, Aboriginal peoples in North America and Australasia were subject to military domination and were treated as both wards of the state or the Crown, and as a "problem" to be solved by assimilation into the European culture (Armitage, 1995: 9). Nonetheless, there were important differences in the conditions under which colonization occurred, and it is argued that these histori-cal legacies continue to affect Aboriginal–state relations today (Armitage, 1995).

In North America, Europeans found a world in which there were many distinct cultures, spread across a vast continent, and connected by well-developed trade networks and political relationships (Kunitz, 1990). In Canada, Aboriginal people were economically important to settlers engaged in the fur trade. Military and economic relationships between some Aboriginal peoples and the Crown, and the drive to settle the West, resulted in a complex situation in which treaties were signed with some groups, but not others. The result of these historical dynamics in Canada has been a fragmentation of the legal status of Aboriginal peoples and communities. Some Aboriginal people live on reserves—Crown lands held by Aboriginal communities and which have a special legal status. However, not all communities share this special status, and in some provinces there were no treaties signed between Aboriginal peoples and the Crown (Ponting and Gibbins, 1980: 23). First Nations people registered under the *Indian Act* ("Registered Indians") have a unique relationship to the Canadian state, which has a responsibility to provide services, particularly in reserve communities. This responsibility has been extended by the Supreme Court of Canada to include the Inuit. For other Aboriginal people, including the Métis, non-Status First Nations people, and others, health and social services are provincial responsibilities (Dow and Gardiner-Garten, 1998).[1]

In the US, the relationship between Aboriginal peoples and settlers was characterized by somewhat more conflict than in Canada. The *Treaty of Paris*, concluding the American Revolution, allowed the settlement of the West and marked the beginning of an eighty-year period of treaty-making between the government and various tribes. A reservation system has remained in the US, and treaty-based rights are an important basis for negotiation with the federal government. Tribes have been described as "domestic dependent nations," having at least formal sovereignty (Maaka and Fleras, 2005: 60). This government-to-government relationship for recognized tribes may facilitate greater Aboriginal control over services. Although the US is the only country of the four that does not have a universal public health system, the federal Indian Health Service (IHS) does provide primary health services in reservation communities, contributing to lower mortality among Aboriginal Americans (Kunitz 1990).

Australian Aboriginal people were also distributed across a continent, but social organization was generally at the tribal level, in hundreds of small groups with many different languages. Australia stands out as the only one of the four countries in which there were no treaties signed between the colonizers and Aboriginal peoples (Bienvenue, 1983). Kunitz (1990) argues that this has eliminated a legal basis for claims of compensation and services. The creation of the Commonwealth of Australia through the merger of separate colonies resulted in a Constitution that placed responsibility for social and health programmes for Aboriginal people at the state level until a 1967 referendum made Aboriginal affairs an area of Commonwealth jurisdiction (Lavoie, 2004).

When Europeans arrived in New Zealand, the Maori were a large population speaking related dialects and occupying a small total area relative to the other countries. It is argued that this put the Maori in a position from which colonization could be better resisted, and led to the signing of a single treaty, the *Treaty of Waitaingi*, between the Crown and all Maori *iwi* in 1840. This provided a different basis for relations between the Maori and the state than in the other countries (Armitage, 1995; Bienvenue, 1983; Kunitz, 1990). Andrew Armitage (1995) points out that colonization also occurred later in New Zealand than the other

Table 5.1: Aboriginal Population and Urbanization

	Population 2001	% of total Population	% living in urban areas
Australian Aboriginal and Torres Strait Islander	410,000	2.2	72.6%[1]
New Zealand Maori	526,281	14.1	83.0%[1]
Canadian Aboriginal Identity	976,305	3.3	49.1%
US American Indian or Alaska Native[2]	4,119,300	1.5	60.8%

Sources: ABS, 1998; Statistics Canada, 2003; Statistics New Zealand, 2001; US Census Bureau, 2000.
Notes: 1 Urbanization figures from 1996 census data; urban areas are defined as areas with populations of 1,000 or more in Canada, Australia, and New Zealand, and 2,500 or more in the US.
2 US figures are from 2000 census, others from 2001.

countries, and that a middle-class social reform movement had by then taken hold in England, shaping the organization of colonial affairs. As well, New Zealand is a unitary state in which services are provided to all citizens by the national government, rather than by provinces or states. This may have prevented the sorts of jurisdictional issues which have made political action more difficult for Aboriginal groups in Canada and Australia (Kunitz, 1990: 653).

The Changing Situation of Aboriginal People

There have been important demographic and political changes in the situation of Aboriginal people in recent decades. Although fertility and mortality remain higher than in non-Aboriginal populations, Aboriginal populations have largely undergone a demographic transition (Kunitz, 1990). There has also been an epidemiologic transition (Omram, 1971), in which immunization, improved sanitation, medical services, and transportation in remote communities have reduced infant mortality. However, diabetes, suicide, alcoholism, and violence now contribute significantly to the difference in mortality between Aboriginal and non-Aboriginal populations (Trovato, 2001).

Table 5.1 shows the sizes of the Aboriginal populations in these countries in 2001. Although they number over four million people, American Indians and Alaska Natives make up only about 1.5% of the American population. In relative terms, the Maori population is the largest, accounting for 14% of all New Zealanders. Just over 2% of Australians and 4.6% of Canadians identified themselves as Aboriginal people in 2001. About two percent of Canadians were registered under the *Indian Act*, roughly half of whom live in reserve communities.

Another important transition that has taken place in the social demography of Aboriginal people has been increased urbanization. As shown in **Table 5.1**, Australian Aboriginal people and the Maori are more urbanized than North American populations. In the last two decades, however, there has been more migration to Aboriginal communities from the city than in the other direction in Canada and Australia (Norris, Cooke, and Clatworthy, 2003; Taylor and

Bell, 1996). Taylor and Bell (1996) suggest this may be related to changing political and legal situations of Aboriginal people and communities. Broadly speaking, this includes greater political representation and self-determination and increased Aboriginal control over services in communities.

Aboriginal political movements in the late 1960s and 1970s contributed to important changes in the relationship between Aboriginal people and the state in the 1980s and 1990s. In Canada, Aboriginal rights were included in the *Constitution Act* of 1982, and the Royal Commission on Aboriginal Peoples reported on the poor socio-economic and health status of Aboriginal people, prompting an official apology from the Canadian government (Dow and Gardiner-Garten, 1998). The creation of the territory of Nunavut, the Nis'gaa treaty, and the Marshall decision regarding Aboriginal hunting and fishing rights, have been important in entrenching Aboriginal rights and improving the political representation of Aboriginal people in Canada. In the US, there have been fewer recent changes to the constitutional and legal status of Aboriginal peoples. However, in 1982, reservation communities were given taxation rights similar to those held by states, providing tribes with greater resources and contributing to increased control over local affairs (Maaka and Fleras, 2005: 61; Fleras and Elliott, 1992: 161).

In Australia, much of the impetus for future progress in equality for Aboriginal people began in the 1960s, with eligibility to vote in Commonwealth elections coming in 1962, and an equal pay ruling in 1965. A 1967 referendum gave the Federal Government specific power to make laws regarding Aboriginal people and resulted in the newly created Department of Aboriginal Affairs, giving Aboriginal issues representation at the national level (Bennett, 2004). In 1990 the Aboriginal and Torres Strait Islander Commission (ATSIC) was established to advise the government on Aboriginal affairs, and had some executive power with regard to decision making and spending on Aboriginal programs. ATSIC comprised elected regional Aboriginal representatives and government-appointed administration staff (Pratt and Bennett, 2004). The 1992 Mabo decision recognized the native title rights of Aboriginal Australians and overturned the premise that Australia was *terra nullius* (land owned by no one) when settled by Europeans (High Court of Australia, 1992). The subsequent *Native Title Act* paved the way for claims to land by Aboriginal groups. However, a major setback for the government representation of Aboriginal people occurred in March 2005 when ATSIC was formally abolished and many of its functions were transferred to mainstream agencies.

The *Treaty of Waitangi Act* is recognized as the founding document of New Zealand, and was amended in 1985 to strengthen the mandate of the Waitangi Claims Tribunal to hear claims of breaches of treaty. In 1993, the *Te Ture Whenua Maori*, or the *Maori Land Law Act* strengthened Maori land claims (Gilling, 1993). New Zealand is the only one of the four countries in which there are dedicated parliamentary seats for Aboriginal people, and the number of these seats was increased in 1995, a year in which there was also a number of large Maori land claims settled (Dow and Gardiner-Garten, 1998).

Scholars have suggested that the unique histories of these countries have resulted in different relations between Aboriginal people and the state, with implications for the health and well-being of Aboriginal people and their ability to mobilize state resources through political action. The Maori may fare relatively better partly because the *Treaty of Waitaingi* provides a basis for Aboriginal rights that apply to all Maori. The lack of treaties in Australia, it has been argued, weakens the political position of Aboriginal people in that country (Armitage, 1995; Bienvenue, 1983; Fleras and Elliott, 1992). Geographic and legal fragmentation of the Canadian Aboriginal population may contribute to heterogeneity in terms of health and socio-economic well-being, while recognition of US tribes as dependent but self-governing internal nations facilitates direct negotiation with the federal government (Maaka and Fleras, 2005: 60).

Empirically, some of these populations have been compared in terms of specific mortality measures. Australian Aboriginal people and Maori have been found to fare worse than North American Aboriginal populations in terms of life expectancy and cause-specific mortality (Kunitz, 1990; Trovato, 2001; Bramley et al, 2004). However, these populations have not been compared in terms of overall quality of life, including other dimensions of social and economic well-being. As well, despite the changing political and legal situations of Aboriginal people in these countries, it is unclear how the gaps between Aboriginal and non-Aboriginal people have changed in the past decade. Research using the HDI to measure the well-being of Canadian Registered Indians found that overall health, income, and education measures improved between 1981 and 2001 (Cooke et al., 2004). Disparities between Registered Indians and other Canadians remained, however, and progress in reducing them was uneven. It is unclear how the changes seen in Canada compare with those in similar countries and how North American and Australasian Aboriginal people compare in terms of overall quality of life. This paper explores these questions, applying the HDI methodology to compare the education, income, and overall health of these populations.

Methodology: The Human Development Index[2]

The HDI was developed to include dimensions other than national product in measurements of development (Hopkins, 1991; ul Haq, 2003). However, in the context of developing countries it is necessary for an index of well-being to balance theoretical completeness with the constraints of data availability. Therefore, *human development* was defined by the UNDP to include three broad and interrelated dimensions; an income sufficient for a minimal material standard of living, knowledge, which is necessary for full participation in society, and health, identified as a fundamental prerequisite to well-being (UNDP, 1990). Life expectancy, education, and income indicators are each placed on a scale between a theoretical minimum and maximum, and combined with equal weighting, to give an overall HDI score between zero and one, as shown in **Table 5.2** (page 94).

The Aboriginal populations examined in this paper include Australian Aboriginal and Torres Strait Islanders, New Zealand Maori, and American Indian and Alaska Native people. Two Canadian Aboriginal populations are included—those identifying themselves as having Aboriginal origins, and those registered under the *Indian Act of Canada*. These populations are compared to the non-Aboriginal populations in these countries, defined as the total national population, minus the Aboriginal population.

As with the previous applications of the HDI to sub-national populations, some changes had to be made to the HDI methodology in light of the available data. The education and income measures in this paper were taken from custom tabulations of 1991, 1996, and 2001 census data for Australia, Canada, and New Zealand, and from 1990 and 2000 census five % public use sample files for the US. Because of a lack of data on adult literacy or school enrolment in the censuses, we use the proportion that completed the equivalent of grade 9 or higher in the North American systems as a proxy for adult literacy (**Table 5.3** – page 94). Whereas our previous research used the population 20 and over with high school or higher education as a proxy for the gross enrolment ratios used in the UNDP publications (Beavon and Cooke, 2003; Cooke et al., 2004), this paper uses the proportion of the population aged 18 to 25 with secondary school or higher as a measure of the *flow* of knowledge into the population (**Table 5.3**). The UNDP's HDI methodology for comparing countries uses per capita GDP as a proxy for average individual income, and discounts GDP using the log formula in **Table 5.2**. We use median annual individual total income from census data. Following the UNDP, point estimates only are presented, as the census data are tabulated from very large samples. We are interested in the very general trends at the national level, rather than hypothesis tests of small differences.

Data Sources and Quality

Although censuses are the best source of time series data on these populations, there are some problems with the comparability between countries and between years. In the Canadian and Australian censuses, the Aboriginal population refers to people who identify themselves as having Aboriginal ethnicity. The Canadian Registered Indian population is identified by a separate question in the Census, and it is known that this population does not perfectly correspond to the Indian Register. The Canadian Census questions regarding ethnic origin and Aboriginal identity have changed somewhat between years, and the data may also be affected by the continued effects of a major 1985 legislative change to the *Indian Act* (Clatworthy, 2003; Guimond, Kerr, and Beaujot, 2004). The Maori population is defined in response to an ethnicity question that was changed in 1996, possibly affecting the comparability between years (Statistics New Zealand, 2005). The US Aboriginal population is defined using the "race" question, which also changed between 1990 and 2000, to allow multiple write-in responses (US Census Bureau,

Table 5.2: HDI Index Calculation

		Measure	Min.	Max.	Index Formula
Education Index	**Adult Literacy (1/3)**	Proportion 15 and older with grade 9 or higher education	0	100	$I_{Literacy} = \dfrac{X_{actual} - X_{min}}{X_{max} - X_{min}}$
	Education (2/3)	Proportion 18–25 with high school or some post-secondary education	0	100	$I_{Education} = \dfrac{X_{actual} - X_{min}}{X_{max} - X_{min}}$
Income Index		Median total income for those 15 and older	PPP $100	PPP $40,000	$I_{Income} = \dfrac{\log(X) - \log(X_{min})}{\log(X_{max}) - \log(X_{min})}$
Life Expectancy Index		Life expectancy at birth	85 years	25 years	$I_{LEB} = \dfrac{X_{actual} - X_{min}}{X_{max} - X_{min}}$
HDI					$I_{HDI} = \dfrac{\left[I_{LEB} + \left(\dfrac{1}{3} I_{Literacy} + \dfrac{2}{3} I_{Education} \right) + I_{Income} \right]}{3}$

Table 5.3: Educational Attainment Proxy Measures

	Adult Literacy Proxy	Gross Enrolment Proxy
Australia	1991, 1996: Proportion 15 or older that left school aged 15 years or older. 2001: Proportion 15 or older with highest education qualification year 9 or higher.	1991, 1996: Proportion 18–24 still in school or left school aged 18 or older. 2001: Proportion 18–24 still in school, or with highest educational qualification year 12 or equivalent
Canada	Proportion 15+ with grade 9 or higher educational attainment.	Proportion 18–24 with secondary school certificate, some college, trades or technical, or university.
New Zealand	Proportion 15+ with no school qualification	Proportion 18–24 with sixth form or higher qualification.
United States	Proportion 15+ with 9th grade or higher educational attainment	Proportion 18–24 with high school graduation, GED, or higher educational attainment.

2000b). Because we use self-reported ethnicity or race, these data are susceptible to the effects of changing patterns of ethnic identification observed in the US, Australia, and Canada (Guimond, 2003; Esbach, 1993; Taylor, 1998).

Other problems include a change in the Australian census education questions. Whereas the 1991 and 1996 data include the age at which the respondent left school, the 2001 data indicate the highest level of schooling completed (**Table 5.2**). Although this educational attainment measure is more comparable to the census measures in the other countries, it is not comparable with the previous

Australian measures of the age at school leaving. This may especially be the case for Aboriginal people, who have been found to complete school later, at least in Canada (Hull, 2005). In order to describe the 1991–2001 changes, we use the 1991 and 1996 age at school-leaving measures, extrapolating 2001 values and assuming that the non-Aboriginal Australian measures improved linearly between 1991 and 2001 and that the gap between Aboriginal and non-Aboriginal people remained constant between 1996 and 2001. We use the educational attainment measure to compare Australia to other countries in 2001.

Median annual income for those aged 15 and older with income was also taken from the census data. Whereas the other countries reported point estimates of income, the Australian and New Zealand census data provided fourteen income categories, requiring the calculation of a median from grouped data. Fortunately, the categories were of relatively small width, providing confidence in these median incomes. Income measures were converted to Purchasing Power Parity dollars (OECD, 2005). However, these adjustments for price and currency do not take into account higher prices in remote communities and census income measures do not incorporate traditional activities or those reporting no income.

The life expectancy estimates used are the best estimates that are available from official sources. Where the years for which these estimates were available do not correspond to census years, estimates were interpolated. In Canada, Statistics Canada estimates are only available for the Registered Indian population and are used for the total Aboriginal population (Rowe and Norris, 1985; Nault, Chen, George, and Norris, 1993; INAC, 2000). These are calculated from Indian Register data, and are subject to problems of under-reporting of deaths. Life expectancy for American Indians and Alaska Natives, adjusted for under-reporting of Indian race, were taken from Indian Health Service publications (IHS, 1994; 1997; 1998; 1999). New Zealand estimates were taken from official life tables (Statistics New Zealand, 1999; 2004). Estimates for Australia are from adjusted life tables published by the Australian Bureau of Statistics (1997, 2001).

Estimating Aboriginal life expectancy is difficult, and the accuracy of life tables can be influenced by the quality of recording of Aboriginal status within death registers and the total population counts. Resulting numerator–denominator bias can impact on life expectancy estimates, and changes in bias over time can impact gaps over time (Alwaji et al., 2003; Blakely et al., 2005). Aboriginal life tables calculated from vital statistics data and published by official sources have been used for all four countries, and where the estimate years did not correspond with the census years, they were linearly interpolated. Life expectancy estimates used for the Canadian Aboriginal population were for Registered Indians, the only population for which national estimates are available, and which represent about 57% of the Canadian Aboriginal population in the 2001 Census. For New Zealand, a change in the census ethnicity question affected the comparability of 1991 and later life tables. For this reason, we have not used the 1991 Aboriginal life tables for New Zealand, but have backcast the 1996 and 2001 data using linear extrapo-

Table 5.4: Life Expectancy at Birth, Years (Life Expectancy Index Score)

	Australia Non-Aboriginal	Aboriginal and Torres Strait Islander	Aboriginal–Non-Aboriginal Gap
1990/1	80.2 (.920)	59.6 (.577)	20.6 (.343)
1995/6	81.4 (.939)	59.4 (.573)	22.0 (.366)
2000/1	82.8 (.964)	59.6 (.576)	23.2 (.388)
	Canada Non-Aboriginal[1]	Canadian Registered Indian	Gap
1990/1	77.9 (.882)	70.6 (.760)	7.3 (.122)
1995/6	78.5 (.892)	72.2 (.787)	6.3 (.105)
2000/1	78.7 (.895)	72.9 (.798)	5.8 (.097)
	New Zealand Non-Aboriginal	Maori	Gap
1990/1[2]	76.4 (.856)	67.7 (.712)	8.7 (.144)
1995/6	78.0 (.883)	69.4 (.741)	8.6 (.142)
2000/1	79.6 (.910)	71.1 (.769)	8.5 (.141)
	United States Non-Aboriginal	American Indian and Alaska Native	Gap
1990/1	75.4 (.841)	70.2 (.753)	5.2 (0.88)
1995/6	76.2 (.854)	71.1 (.768)	5.1 (.086)
2000/1	76.6 (.859)	70.6 (.760)	6.0 (.099)

Notes

(1) Reliable life expectancy estimates for Canadian Aboriginal populations for these years are only available for the Registered Indian population. The non-Aboriginal population value for this indicator is therefore the total Canadian population, minus the Registered Indian population.

(2) 1990/1 life expectancy estimates for New Zealand are backcast from the later estimates, using linear extrapolation.

lation. The resulting 1991 estimates are similar to those published by Blakely et al. (2003), who identify some overestimation of Maori life expectancy within these tables. They report that although Maori life expectancy increased over the 1980s and 1990s, the gap with non-Maori, non–Pacific Islanders in New Zealand widened over the period, to nearly 10 years. As well, Hill et al.(2007) suggest the gap in life expectancy is around 13 years for Aboriginal Australians, compared with the gap of over 20 years estimated using official life tables. Note that using these revised estimates would not change the ranking of the countries presented below, nor seriously change the overall picture of changes in Aboriginal well-being in these countries. We therefore choose to use the original New Zealand life tables, which are centred on the census years and show a slightly narrowing life expectancy gap, and the original Australian figures, which provide a series of estimates over the period in which we are interested.

Results

In this section, the four countries are compared in terms of the gaps between Aboriginal and non-Aboriginal people in life expectancy, education, and income indices over the 1990/1–2000/1 period. The gaps in the overall Aboriginal HDI scores are then compared. Lastly, we present adjusted Aboriginal HDI scores for these populations in 2000/1, and compare them to some countries in the *Human Development Report 2003* (UNDP, 2003).

Life Expectancy at Birth, 1991–2001

Table 5.4 shows the life expectancy in years for four Aboriginal populations, the total national populations, and the gap between Aboriginal and non-Aboriginal people. As expected from previous research, Australia stands out as having the widest gap in life expectancy with more than 20 years difference between Aboriginal and Torres Strait Islander people and other Australians, who had the highest life expectancies among the four countries. Estimated life expectancy at birth for Aboriginal Australians was the same at the beginning and the end of the period, at about 59 years, resulting in a growing gap in life expectancy.

The gap between Registered Indians and other Canadians declined to 5.8 years by 2001, the smallest gap among these four countries (**Table 5.4**). Maori life expectancy was 8.5 years less than other New Zealanders in 2001. This gap improved between 1996 and 2001, but note that the linear improvement over the entire period is an artefact of our extrapolation of the 1996–2001 trend back to 1991–1996. The gap between American Indians and Alaska Natives and other Americans remained roughly the same over the decade, at between 5.2 and 6.0 years.

Educational Attainment, 1991–2001

Table 5.5 (page 98) presents the scores on the two educational attainment measures. As described above, because of the incompatibility of 2001 Australian educational attainment with previous measures, we extrapolated the 1991–1996 measures forward, assuming that the Aboriginal–non-Aboriginal gap remained constant. This assumption was made because of the *increase* in the observed gap on both age at school-leaving indicators between 1991 and 1996, and is therefore somewhat conservative. The 2001* row presents the Australian educational attainment indicators that are comparable to those of the other countries.

All four countries had high values on the adult literacy proxy measures, and the gaps between Aboriginal and non-Aboriginal populations improved between 1991 and 2001. The Maori population had the lowest proportion with some basic school qualification, at about 57 percent in 2001, and the largest gaps between Aboriginal and non-Aboriginal people. However, these gaps declined considerably between 1991 and 2001, from 30 to 20 percentage points (**Table 5.5**). There was also a wide gap between the Canadian Registered Indian population and other Canadians, but as with the Maori, this population saw considerable improvement. In 2001, the Canadian Registered Indian and Australian Aboriginal populations had similar scores on this indicator, with 83% of the 15 and older population having attained primary school or higher. The total Canadian Aboriginal

Table 5.5: Educational Attainment Measures, 1990/1–2000/1

	Adult Literacy Proxy (2/3 weight)			Gross Enrolment Proxy (1/3 weight)			Educational Attainment Index		
	Non-Aboriginal	Aboriginal	Gap	Non-Aboriginal	Aboriginal	Gap	Non-Aboriginal	Aboriginal	Gap
Australia (Aboriginal and Torres Strait Islanders)									
1991	0.85	0.84	0.02	0.28	0.13	0.15	.659	.598	.061
1996	0.86	0.84	0.02	0.33	0.17	0.16	.686	.618	.068
2001	0.88	0.86	0.02	0.38	0.22	0.16	.713	.644	.069
2001*	0.91	0.83	0.07	0.69	0.31	0.38	.832	.659	.176
Canada (Registered Indians)									
1991	0.86	0.72	0.14	0.74	0.38	0.36	.826	.610	.216
1996	0.88	0.78	0.10	0.77	0.42	0.35	.843	.659	.184
2001	0.90	0.83	0.08	0.79	0.44	0.35	.866	.697	.169
Canada (Aboriginal Identity Population)									
1991	0.86	0.82	0.05	0.74	0.53	0.21	.826	.713	.113
1996	0.88	0.85	0.03	0.77	0.53	0.24	.843	.738	.105
2001	0.90	0.88	0.02	0.79	0.56	0.23	.866	.773	.093
New Zealand (Maori Identity)									
1991	0.65	0.35	0.29	0.54	0.27	0.28	.611	.325	.286
1996	0.70	0.45	0.25	0.63	0.37	0.27	.674	.421	.253
2001									
United States (American Indian and Alaska Native Race)									
1990	0.90	0.88	0.03	0.77	0.63	0.13	.857	.795	.062
2000	0.92	0.91	0.02	0.75	0.67	0.08	.83	.827	.036

Note: Australian 1991–2001 figures are calculated using age at school-leaving; 2001* figures calculated using educational attainment.

population scored somewhat higher, and the American Indian and Alaska Native population had the highest adult literacy proxy scores, at 91% in 2001.

Table 5.5 also presents the proportion of the population aged 18–25 with high school or higher education, our measure of the flow of education. On this indicator, the attainment of all of the Aboriginal populations improved considerably over the decade. However, this improvement did not keep pace with the increasing educational attainment among the non-Aboriginal populations, so nearly all of the countries saw these gaps widen.

By the end of the period, 31 percent of Aboriginal and Torres Strait Islander people aged 18–25 had the equivalent of high school or higher qualifications. This was somewhat lower than the Canadian Registered Indian population, which saw improvement between 1991 and 1996, but not between 1996 and 2001. However, because of the lower scores for the non-Aboriginal Australian population compared to non-Aboriginal Canadians, the gap was only slightly wider in Australia. Although young Aboriginal people in Australia and Canada were increasingly attaining secondary and higher education, they did not keep up with the increases among the non-Aboriginal populations. The gap between Maori and non-Maori was also large, but fairly stable over the period. In the US, where the Aboriginal population had the highest scores on this indicator, the gap narrowed, but this was due partly to a decline in the educational attainment of the non-Aboriginal population (**Table 5.5**).

Combining the two education measures using their respective weights results in an Educational Attainment Index score. Because of the falling gaps on the first indicator, and the two-thirds weight given it in the UNDP's methodology, most of the countries saw the gaps between Aboriginal and non-Aboriginal populations on the Educational Attainment Index fall over the decade. Australia may be an exception, and even with the conservative assumptions about the 1996–2001 gaps described above, the gap in this country increased slightly from 0.061 to about 0.069 (**Table 5.5**). Again, the gap between American Indians and Alaska Natives and other US citizens fell because of a decline in the index score for the non-Aboriginal population, combined with an improvement among the Aboriginal population.

Among Aboriginal populations, American Indian and Alaska Native people had the highest Educational Attainment Index scores in 2001, and the US had the smallest gaps between Aboriginal and non-Aboriginal people, while New Zealand had the largest gaps. The Canadian Registered Indian and Australia Aboriginal populations had fairly similar scores in 2001, and the total Canadian Aboriginal population had somewhat higher educational attainment.

Average Annual Income, 1990–2000

Although the educational attainment of Aboriginal people increased over the decade, real incomes tended to fall over the 1990–2000 period. Median annual incomes for those aged 15 and over with income are presented in **Table 5.6**. Note

Table 5.6: Median Annual Income, 2000 PPP$ (Income Index Score)

	Australia Non-Aboriginal	Aboriginal and Torres Strait Islander	Gap
1990/1	25,795 (.927)	16,283 (.850)	9,512 (.077)
1995/6	25,579 (.925)	15,337 (840)	10,242 (.085)
2000/1	21,767 (.898)	12,268 (.803)	9,499 (.095)
	Canada Non-Aboriginal	Canadian Registered Indian	Gap
1990/1	31,084 (.958)	15,226 (.839)	15,858 (.119)
1995/6	26,441 (.931)	14,035 (.825)	12,406 (.106)
2000/1	27,617 (.938)	14,824 (.834)	12,793 (.104)
	Canada Non-Aboriginal	Canadian Total-Aboriginal	Gap
1990/1	31,084 (.958)	19,970 (.884)	11 114 (.074)
1995/6	26,441 (.931)	16,931 (.857)	9,410 (.074)
2000/1	27,617 (.938)	18,713 (.873)	8,904 (.065)
	New Zealand Non-Aboriginal	Maori	Gap
1990/1	30,973 (.957)	23,936 (.914)	7,037 (.043)
1995/6	29,020 (.946)	22,838 (.906)	6,182 (.040)
2000/1	29,756 (.951)	23,024 (.908)	6,732 (.043)
	United States Non-Aboriginal	American Indian and Alaska Native	Gap
1990/1	19,372 (.879)	12,648 (.808)	6,724 (.071)
2000/1	21,050 (.893)	16,000 (.847)	5,050 (.046)

that for Australia, Canada, and New Zealand, real median incomes fell for the non-Aboriginal populations between 1990 and 2000. In Canada and New Zealand, incomes fell between 1990 and 1995, rising somewhat thereafter, whereas Australian median incomes declined even more steeply between 1995 and 2001.

The absolute gap between Aboriginal people and other Australians was nearly the same in 1990 and 2000, at about PPP$9,500. The real median annual incomes for Aboriginal and Torres Strait Islanders experienced roughly the same decline experienced by other Australians. Because of the logarithmic formula used to calculate the income index, the gap between Aboriginal and non-Aboriginal Australians in Income Index Scores grew, from 0.077 to 0.095.

The greatest absolute gap between Aboriginal and non-Aboriginal incomes was seen between Canadian Registered Indians and non-Aboriginal Canadians. However, this gap decreased from nearly PPP$16,000 to roughly PPP$13,000 between 1990 and 2000 (**Table 5.6**). Median annual incomes for the total Canadian Aboriginal population were considerably higher.

The Maori population had the highest annual median income of all of the Aboriginal populations in this study, at nearly PPP$24,000 in 1990. The gap between

Table 5.7: 1991–2001 Aboriginal Human Development Index Scores

	Australia Non-Aboriginal	Aboriginal and Torres Strait Islander	Aboriginal–Non-Aboriginal Gap
1990/1	.835	.675	.160
1995/6	.850	.677	.173
2000/1	.858	.674	.184
	Canada Non-Aboriginal	Canadian Registered Indian	Gap
1990/1	.886	.736	.152
1995/6	.889	.757	.132
2000/1	.900	.776	.124
	Canada Non-Aboriginal	Canadian Aboriginal	Gap
1990/1	.886	.786	.103
1995/6	.889	.794	.095
2000/1	.900	.815	.085
	New Zealand Non-Aboriginal	Maori	Gap
1990/1	.808	.650	.158
1995/6	.835	.689	.146
2000/1	.867	.728	.139
	United States Non-Aboriginal	American Indian and Alaska Native	Gap
1990/1	.859	.785	.074
2000/1	.872	.811	.061

Maori and other New Zealanders shrank slightly, to PPP$6,700 (**Table 5.6**). Because of the high absolute values, the gap in Income Index Scores was lowest in New Zealand, at about 0.043 in both 1990 and 2000. At the other extreme, the American Indian and Alaska Native population had the lowest annual income among the Aboriginal populations at PPP$12,600 in 1990. The income of the non-Aboriginal US population was also the lowest, at PPP$19,400. However, the incomes of American Aboriginal people improved much more that the rest of the American population, resulting in a decreasing gap in Income Index scores.

Human Development Index Scores, 1991–2001

As described in **Table 5.2** (page 94), the life expectancy, educational attainment, and income indices were calculated and combined into an overall Aboriginal HDI score. **Table 5.7** (page 101) presents overall HDI scores for each of the populations for 1981–2001. The Australian scores presented are calculated using the 1991–1996 age at school-leaving data, extrapolated to 2001. Overall, the HDI scores for Aboriginal people and Torres Strait Islanders fell slightly between 1991

Table 5.8: Selected International and Aboriginal HDI Scores, 2001

HDI Rank	Country	HDI Score
Countries with High Human Development		
1	Norway	.944
2	Iceland	.942
3	Sweden	.941
4	*Australia*	*.939*
5	Netherlands	.938
6	Belgium	.937
7	*United States*	*.937*
8	*Canada*	*.937*
9	Japan	.932
10	Switzerland	.932
13	United Kingdom	.930
16	Austria	.929
17	France	.925
19	Spain	.925
20	*New Zealand*	*.917*
23	Portugal	.896
30	Republic of Korea	.879
	U.S. American Indian and Alaska Native	*.877*
32	Czech Republic	.861
	Canadian Aboriginal Population	*.851*
34	Argentina	.849
42	Costa Rica	.831
43	Chile	.831
52	Cuba	.806
53	Belarus	.804
	Canadian Registered Indian	*.802*
54	Trinidad and Tobago	.802
55	Mexico	.800
Countries with Medium Human Development		
73	Saudi Arabia	.769
	New Zealand Maori	*.767*
75	Ukraine	.766
85	Philippines	.751
94	Dominican Republic	.737
103	Cape Verde	.727
	Australian Aboriginal and Torres Strait Islanders	*.724*
104	China	.721
105	El Salvador	.719
120	Egypt	.648

Source: Data from HDI table, p. 237-240 from "Human Development Report 2003" by UNDP (2003) by permission of Oxford University Press; Remaining data: Authors' Calculations

and 2001, despite some improvement between 1991 and 1996. As a result of the improvements in the HDI scores of the non-Aboriginal Australian population, the Aboriginal–non-Aboriginal gap in HDI scores increased fairly constantly, from 0.160 to 0.184 (**Table 5.7**).

Both the Canadian Registered Indian population and the total Canadian Aboriginal population saw improvements in overall HDI scores in absolute terms and relative to other Canadians. Canadian Registered Indians had lower HDI scores than other Canadian Aboriginal people, but saw considerable improvement. The gap between Registered Indians and other Canadians fell from 0.152 to 0.124. The gap between the total Aboriginal population and other Canadians was much lower, falling from 0.103 to 0.085.

The greatest improvement in overall well-being was observed in the Maori population. Maori HDI scores increased from 0.650 to 0.729 over the decade, and the gap between Maori and non-Maori decreased from 0.158 to 0.139. However, some of the 1991–1996 increase is due to our assumptions about 1991 life expectancy. The US stands out for having the lowest overall gap between Aboriginal people and other citizens. The 1990 gap of 0.704 fell to 0.061 by 2000. As described above, however, some of this reduction is due to the lower attainment of non-Aboriginal Americans.

International Comparison, 2001

The discussion above used our proxies for the UNDP's measures in the calculation of Aboriginal HDI scores. However, some of those measures for the different populations are not strictly identical, as is the case with the educational measures for Australia. In this section, we present Aboriginal HDI scores for 2000–01. The Australian scores have been calculated using educational attainment. The index measures presented in **Table 5.8** are also adjusted by the ratio of the total national measures to those published in the UNDP's *Human Development Report*, to facilitate international comparison.

Table 5.8 presents these adjusted HDI scores of each of the study populations, along with those for selected countries from the 2003 *Human Development Report*. This table clearly shows the high rankings of the four countries among the countries with "high human development." The Canadian Aboriginal population and the American Indian and Alaska Native population would also rank within the top 50 countries of the world in terms of human development. The population of Canadian Registered Indians would rank somewhat lower, along with Trinidad and Tobago and Belarus and slightly higher than the Maori population, which would rank about 74th among countries in the *Human Development Report*. Australian Aboriginal and Torres Strait Islander people, however, would rank about 103rd, also among the countries classified by the UNDP as having "medium" levels of human development.

Discussion and Conclusions

Overall well-being, measured using our adaptation of the HDI methodology, improved among Aboriginal people in these four countries over 1991–2001. Life expectancy rose, except possibly amongst Australian Aboriginal people. Improvements in median income were less consistent, although a decline in income between 1991 and 1996 was experienced by non-Aboriginal as well as Aboriginal populations. Despite some improvements, the *gaps* between Aboriginal and non-Aboriginal people on several of these indicators increased. This is especially true for our measure of the flow of education, on which only the US did not experience a widening gap between Aboriginal and non-Aboriginal population, due partly to a decline in educational attainment among non-Aboriginal people in that country.

Aboriginal people in Canada and the US had higher levels of overall well-being than did Australian Aboriginal or Torres Strait Islanders or the Maori of New Zealand. In Canada, the gap in well-being was particularly large between Registered Indians and other Canadians, although the total Canadian Aboriginal population had higher levels of human development. New Zealand stands out for the rapid improvement in the well-being of the Maori, particularly on educational and income measures. While the situation in New Zealand might be characterized as poor but improving, the US had consistently high levels of human development among the Aboriginal population, and small gaps between Aboriginal and non-Aboriginal people. Gaps between Aboriginal and non-Aboriginal people are generally the largest in Australia, and may be growing wider.

Despite the changing political situation of Aboriginal people in these countries, there has not been uniform progress in reducing the disparities between Aboriginal and non-Aboriginal populations. The declining disparity in New Zealand may be related to the strong political representation of the Maori, as previous research suggests. Likewise, the low levels of well-being among Australian Aboriginal people and the increasing disparity may be related to the lack of treaties as a basis for Aboriginal–state relations. However, the relative education, health, and income levels attained by the Aboriginal people in these countries are affected by many complex policies and programs, as well as geographic, political, and economic factors that are impossible to fully explore here. This research only compares national averages, concealing a great degree of heterogeneity within Aboriginal populations. To understand the processes that have resulted in improvements in well-being among Aboriginal populations, future research needs to move toward examination of community and local-level contexts and the specific policies, programs, and economic circumstances that have led to these improvements.

Limitations of this study include some problems with data quality, as discussed above. The HDI has not been free from criticism (Castles, 1999; Henderson, 2000; Jolly, 2000). Of course, "well-being" or "quality of life" is much more complicated than can be captured in the index and its components. There are many other aspects of overall well-being that are important, including the health of the environment and communities, and social and political freedoms. (Sen, 2003; Fukuda-Parr, 2003). These measures also do not consider linguistic survival and access to traditional activities and ways of life. However, the HDI's three broad dimensions do tell us something about the conditions in which people live, and are useful for monitoring the progress made in overcoming disparity.

Endnotes

1 For a discussion of the treaties, agreements and regulations that impact Aboriginal peoples in Canada see White, J.P. et al. 2004. *Permission to Develop: Treaties, Case Law and Regulations,* Toronto: Thompson Educational Publishing, Inc.

2 To facilitate international comparison, the Canadian measures used in this paper differ from those reported in previous versions of the Aboriginal HDI published by Indian and Northern Affairs Canada (Cooke et al., 2004).

References

Ajwani S., Blakely T., Robson B., Bonne M., and Tobias M. 2003. *Decades of Disparity: Ethnic mortality trends in New Zealand 1980–1999.* Wellington: New Zealand Ministry of Health.

Alwaji S., Blakely T., Robson B., Atkinson J., and Kiro C. 2003. *Unlocking the numerator–denominator bias III: Adjustment ratios by ethnicity for 1981–1999 mortality data.* The New Zealand Census–Mortality Study. *The New Zealand Medical Journal* 116(1175): 6.

Armitage, A. 1995. *Comparing the Policy of Aboriginal Assimilation: Australia, Canada, and New Zealand.* Vancouver: UBC Press.

Australian Bureau of Statistics. 2002. Deaths. Cat no. 3302.2. Canberra: ABS.

Australian Bureau of Statistics. 1997. Occasional Paper: *Mortality of Aboriginal and Torres Strait Islander Australians.* Cat no. 3315.0. Canberra: ABS.

Australian Bureau of Statistics. 1998. *1996 Census of Population and Housing: Aboriginal and Torres Strait Islander People.* Cat no. 2034.0. Canberra: ABS.

Beavon, D. and Cooke, M. 2003. "An Application of the United Nations Human Development Index to Registered Indians in Canada 1996." In White, J.P, Maxim, P., and Beavon, D. (Eds). *Aboriginal Conditions: Research as Foundation for Public Policy.* Vancouver: UBC Press.

Bennett, S. 2004. "The 1967 Aborigines Referendum." In Australian Bureau of Statistics. *2004 Year Book Australia.* Cat. no. 1201.0. Canberra: ABS.

Blakely, T., Tobias, M., Robson, B., Ajwani, S., Bonne, M., and Woodward, A. 2005. "Widening ethnic mortality disparities in New Zealand 1981–99." *Soc Sci Med.* 61: 2233-2251.

Bramley, D., Herbert, P., Jackson, R., and Chassi, M. 2004. "Indigenous Disparities in Disease-Specific Mortality: A Cross-Country Comparison: New Zealand, Australia, Canada, and the United States." *The New Zealand Medical Journal,* 117 (1207, 1–16.

Castles, I. (1999). "Reporting on human development: Lies, damned lies and statistics." In Castles, I. (Ed.). *Facts and fancies of human development.* Canberra: Academy of Social Sciences in Australia. 55–81.

Cooke, M., Beavon, D., and McHardy, M. 2004. "Measuring the Well-Being of Aboriginal People: An Application of the United Nations Human Development Index to Registered Indians in Canada, 1981–2001" in White, J.P., Maxim, P., and Beavon, D. (Eds.). *Aboriginal Policy Research: Setting the Agenda for Change,* Vol. 1. Toronto: Thompson Educational Publishing, Inc. 47–70.

Commonwealth of Australia. 1993. *Native Title Act 1993.* Retrieved 29 Apr. 2005. <**http://scaletext. law.gov.au/html/pasteact/2/1142/top.htm**>.

Clatworthy, S.J. 2003 "Impacts of the 1985 Amendments to the Indian Act in First Nations Populations." In White, J.P., Maxim, P., and Beavon, D. (Eds.) *Aboriginal Conditions.* Vancouver: UBC Press. 63–90

Cornell, S. 2004. "Indigenous Jurisdiction and Daily Life: Evidence from North America." Paper Presented at the National Forum on Indigenous Health and the Treaty Debate, University of New South Wales, Sydney.

Dow, C. and Gardiner-Garden, J. 1998. "Indigenous Affairs in Australia, New Zealand, Canada, United States of America, Norway and Sweden." Parliament of Australia Parliamentary Library Background paper 15 1997–98. <**www.aph.gov.au/library/pubs/bp/1997-98/98bp15.htm**>.

Eschbach, C. 1993 "Changing Identification among American Indians and Alaska Natives." *Demography.* 30(4): 635–652.

Fleras, A. and Elliott, J.L. 1992. *The Nations Within: Aboriginal–State Relations in Canada, the United States, and New Zealand.* Toronto: Oxford University Press.

Fukuda-Parr, S. 2003. "Rescuing the Human Development Concept from the HDI: Reflections on a New Agenda." In Fukuda-Parr, S. and Shiva Kumar, A.K. (Eds.) *Readings in Human Development: Concepts, Measures and Policies for a Development Paradigm.* New Delhi: Oxford University Press.

Gray, M.C. and Auld, A.J. (2000) *Towards an Index of Relative Indigenous Socioeconomic Disadvantage.* Discussion Paper 196. Centre for Aboriginal Economic Policy Research. Canberra: Australian National University. .

Guimond, E. 2003. "Changing Ethnicity: The Concept of Ethnic Drifters." In White, J.P., Maxim, P., and Beavon, D. (Eds.) *Aboriginal Conditions.* Vancouver: UBC Press. 91–107.

Guimond, E., Kerr, D., and Beaujot, R. 2004. "Charting the Growth of Canadian Aboriginal Populations: Problems, Options and Implications." *Canadian Studies in Population.* 31(1): 33-82.

High Court of Australia. 1992. *Mabo and Others v. Queensland* (No. 2) (1992) 175 CLR 1 F.C. 92/014.

Hill, K., Barker, B., Vos, T. 2007. "Excess Indigenous mortality: Are Indigenous Australians more severely disadvantaged than other Indigenous populations?" *International Journal of Epidemiology.,* Advance Access. Published 3 April 2007.

Hopkins, M. 1991 "Human Development Revisited: A New UNDP Report." *World Development.* 19 (10): 1469–1473.

Hull, J. 2005. *Post-Secondary Education and Labour Market Outcomes Canada, 2001.* Strategic Research and Analysis Directorate. Ottawa: INAC.Indian and Northern Affairs Canada. 2003. Basic Departmental Data, 2002. First Nations and Northern Statistics Section, Corporate Information Management Directorate, Information Management Branch. Ottawa: INAC.

Jolly, R. 2000. "Misrepresenting the *Human Development Report* and misunderstanding the need for re-thinking global governance." *World Economics,* 1(3): 1–15.

Kunitz, S.J. 1990. "Public Policy and Mortality among Indigenous Populations of Northern America and Australasia." *Population and Development Review.* 6(4): 647–672.

Lavoie, J. 2004."Governed by Contracts: The Development of Indigenous Primary Health Services in Canada, Australia and New Zealand." *Journal of Aboriginal Health.* 1(1): 6–24.

Maaka, R. and Fleras, A. 2005. *The Politics of Indigeneity: Challenging the State in Canada and Aotearoa New Zealand.* Dunedin: University of Otago Press.

Omram, A.R. 1971. "The epidemiologic transition." *Milbank Memorial Fund Quarterly.* 49: 509–538.

Ponting, J.R. and Gibbins, R. 1980. *Out of Irrelevance: A Socio-political introduction to Indian Affairs in Canada.* Toronto: Butterworths.

Pratt, A. and Bennett, S. 2004 *The end of ATSIC and the future administration of Indigenous Affairs.* Current Issues Brief No. 4 2004-05. Canberra: Parliament of Australia Parliamentary Library.

Roemer, M.I. 1985. "Social Policies and Health Care Systems: Their Effects on Mortality and Morbidity in Developed Countries." In Vallin and Lopez, (Eds.). 1985. *Health Policy, Social Policy, and Mortality:Proceedings of a Seminar at Paris, France, 28 February–4 March 1983.* Liège: Ordina Editions. 541–52.

Sen, A. 2003. "Development as Capability Expansion." In Fukuda-Parr, S. and Shiva Kumar AK. Editors. *Readings in Human Development: Concepts, Measures and Policies for a Development Paradigm.* New Delhi: Oxford University Press.

Snipp, C.M. 1992. "Sociological Perspectives on American Indians." *Annual Review of Sociology.* 18: 351–371.

Statistics Canada.2003.Aboriginal Peoples of Canada. Retrieved 1 Jan. 2006.<**www12.statcan.ca/ English/census01/producets/analytic/companion/abor/canada.cfm**>.

Statistics New Zealand. 2004. New Zealand Life Tables (2000–2002). Retrieved 1 Jan. 2006. <**www. stats.govt.nz/products-and-services/info-releases/nz-life-table-info-releases.htm**>.

Statistics New Zealand. 1999. New Zealand Life Tables (1995–97). Retrieved 1 Jan. 2006.<**www. stats.govt.nz/products-and-services/info-releases/nz-life-table-info-releases.htm**>.

Statistics New Zealand. 2005. Change in Ethnicity Question–2001 Census of Populations and Dwellings. Retrieved 1 Jan. 2006. <**www.stats.govt.nz/census/change-in-ethnicity-question.htm**>.

Taylor, J. and Bell, M. 1996. "Population Mobility and Indigenous Peoples: the View from Australia," *International Journal of Population Geography.* 2(2): 153–169.

Taylor, J. 1998. "Measuring Short-Term Population Mobility Among Indigenous Australians: Options and implications." *Australian Geographer.* 29(1): 125–137.

Te Puni Kokiri. 1991. Maori Living in Urban and Rural New Zealand. Retrieved 1 Jan. 2006. <**www.tpk.govt.nz/maori/population/rural.asp**>.

Trovato, F. 2001. "Aboriginal Mortality in Canada, the United States and New Zealand." *Journal of Biosocial Science.* 233: 67–86

ul Haq, M. 2003. "The Human Development Paradigm." In Fukuda-Parr, S. and Shiva Kumar, A.K. (Eds.) *Readings in Human Development: Concepts, Measures and Policies for a Development Paradigm.* New Delhi: Oxford University Press.

United Nations Development Programme. 2003. *Human Development Report 2003.* New York: Oxford University Press.

US Census Bureau. 1994. 1990 Census of Population—Subject Reports: Education in the US. Washington, D.C.: US Government Printing Office.

US Census Bureau. 2000. Census 2000 Summary File 4 (SF 4). Washington, D.C.: US Government Printing Office.

US. Census Bureau. 2000b. Racial and Ethnic Classifications Used in Census 2000 and Beyond. Retrieved 1 Jan. 2006. <**www.census.gov/population/www/socdemo/race/racefactb.html**>.

Waldram, J.B., Herring D.A., and Young, T.K. 1995. *Aboriginal Health in Canada: Historical, Cultural, and Epidemiological Perspectives.* Toronto: University of Toronto Press.

White, J.P., Beavon, D., and Spence, N. 2004. *Permission to Develop: Treaties, Case Law and Regulations.* Toronto: Thompson Educational Publishing, Inc.

Part Three:
The Community Well-being Index (CWB)

6

The Community Well-being Index (CWB): Well-being in First Nations Communities, Present, Past, and Future[1]

Erin O'Sullivan and Mindy McHardy

Introduction

The Community Well-being Index (CWB) was developed as a complement to the Registered Indian Human Development Index (HDI). While the HDI measures the well-being of Registered Indians at the national and regional levels, the CWB measures well-being at the community level. The CWB combines indicators of educational attainment, income, housing conditions, and labour force activity from the Census of Canada to produce well-being "scores" for individual communities. These scores permit the assessment of variations in well-being among First Nations communities, differences in well-being between First Nations and other Canadian communities, and changes in well-being patterns over time.

The Community Well-being Index (CWB)

The CWB index combines several indicators of well-being into a single number, or CWB score. A score is generated for each community in Canada,[2] allowing an "at-a-glance" look at the relative well-being of those communities. CWB scores may fall anywhere between 0 and 100 (with 100 being the highest).[3]

The CWB index consists of four equally weighted components:[4]

1) Education

This component is comprised of two indicators: functional literacy and "high school plus." The former is afforded a weight of 2/3 of the education component, and is operationalized as the percentage of a community's population, 15 years and over, that has completed at least a grade 9 education. The latter is defined as the percentage of the population, 20 years and over, that has obtained at least a secondary school education.

2) Labour Force

This component is also comprised of two indicators: labour force participation and employment rate. The former is operationalized as the percentage of the population, 20 years and over, that is involved in the labour force. Employment rate refers to the employed labour force expressed as a percentage of the total labour force, aged 15 and over.

3) Income

This component is defined as *income per capita*—a community's total income divided by its total population. To make them amenable to inclusion in the CWB index, per capita income values had to be converted into income scores running from 1 to 100. The following formula was used to this end:

$$\left(\frac{\text{Log (income per capita)} - \text{Log (2,000)}}{\text{Log (40,000)} - \text{Log (2,000)}} \right) \times 100$$

The theoretical minimum and maximum ($2,000 and $40,000, respectively), were derived from the actual range of income per capita across Canadian communities. The log function was incorporated into the income component to account for the *diminishing marginal utility of income*. According to this principle, those who occupy lower income strata benefit more from additional income than those at higher income levels.

4) Housing

This component is comprised of indicators of both housing quantity and quality. The former is operationalized as the percentage of the population living in dwellings that contain no more than one person per room. The latter is defined as the percentage of the population living in dwellings that are not in need of major repairs.

Limitations of the CWB Index

As an adaptation of the HDI, the CWB reflects an attempt to capture non-monetary aspects of well-being. Nevertheless, owing to the limited scope of the Census data on which it is based, the CWB does emphasize economic aspects of well-being. This emphasis is always problematic, as things such as physical and psychological health are equally important to well-being. Many would argue, however, that it is an even greater problem when one is considering First Nations. For example, some suggest that Aboriginal culture puts less emphasis on the accumulation of material wealth and that identifying First Nations communities as "good" or "bad" on the basis of modern economic indicators has assimilatory undertones. Relatedly, some contend that programs aimed at developing First Nations communities economically can have negative social effects that economic analyses alone cannot detect.

In addition to affording excessive importance to economics, indicators such as income and labour force activity do not capture fully the reality of the economic situation among Aboriginal people. Many First Nations are involved in traditional economic pursuits, which, although contributing to their material well-being, are not manifested in monetary income or paid employment.

While a useful tool, then, the CWB is not a comprehensive model of well-being. Its components were chosen based on the widespread acceptance of their importance and their availability across Census years, and do not preclude the importance of other aspects of well-being. The CWB must be regarded as only a first step, albeit an important one, towards understanding well-being in First Nations communities. See Chapter 2 for a rigorous discussion of these issues.

First Nations Community Well-being: The Present (2001)

The Data

The most recent CWB was constructed using data drawn from the 2001 census of Canada.[5,6,7] Readers should be aware that any references to the "current" state of well-being in Canada's First Nations communities are actually references to that state of well-being as of 2001.

As indicated above, the CWB is calculated at the community level. Communities are defined in terms of Census subdivisions (CSDs). CSD is the term applied to municipalities (as determined by provincial legislation) or their equivalent (i.e. Indian reserves, Indian settlements, and unorganized territories) (Statistics Canada, 2002: 224).

In this study, CSDs are categorized as either First Nations or other Canadian communities. The distinction is based on a listing of First Nations communities that was developed by Indian and Northern Affairs Canada (INAC, 2001) and employed by Statistics Canada to produce on-reserve population counts from the 2001 census.

INAC's complete list of First Nations communities includes:

- Land reserved under the *Indian Act*;
- Land set aside for the use and benefit of Indian people;
- Areas where activities on the land are paid for or administered by INAC or;
- Areas listed in the Indian Lands Registry System held by Lands and Trust Services at INAC.

The list includes all CSDs of the following types: Reserves (R), Indian Government Districts (IGD), Indian Settlements (S-E), Terre Reservées (TR), Nisga'a Lands (NL), Nisga'a Villages (NVL), and Teslin Lands (TL). A selection of the following CSD types are also classified as First Nations: Chartered Community (CC), Hamlet (HAM), Northern Hamlet (NH), Northern Village (NV), Settlement (SET), Town (T), and Village (VL).

Figure 6.1: First Nations and Other Canadian Communities Average CWB Scores, 2001

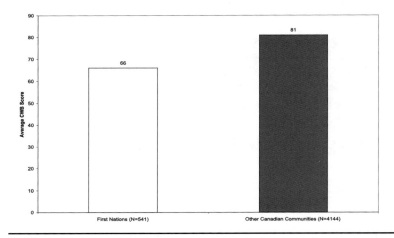

Figure 6.2: CWB Distributions, First Nations and Other Canadian Communities, 2001

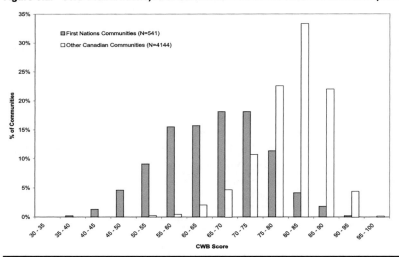

These analyses are based on 541 First Nations and 4,144 other Canadian communities. They represent all CSDs with populations of at least 65, that were free of data quality issues, and that participated in the 2001 Census. Readers should be aware that 30 First Nations communities, with a combined estimated Registered Indian population of 30,000 to 35,000, chose not to participate in the 2001 Census.

Note that other types of Aboriginal communities such as Inuit and Metis communities are categorized, in this study, as "other Canadian communities." A separate study of Inuit communities, which compares them to First Nations and non-First Nations communities is provided in Chapter 7.

Table 6.1:   Number of Communities by Type and Region, 2001

Region	First Nations Communities	Other Canadian Communities	Total
Maritimes	29	795	842
Quebec	35	1,306	1,341
Ontario	59	425	484
Manitoba	65	211	276
Saskatchewan	91	715	806
Alberta	57	334	391
British Columbia	170	316	486
North	35	42	77
Total	541	4,144	4,703

Figure 6.3:   Gaps in Community Well-being, by CWB Components, 2001

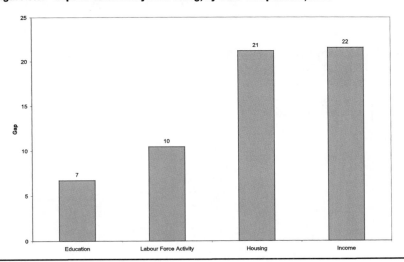

Results—First Nations Community Well-being, a National Overview, 2001

As indicated earlier, interpretation of the CWB is very straightforward. The scale runs from 0–100, with zero being the lowest score and 100 being the highest. As is illustrated in **Figure 6.1**, the average CWB score for First Nations is 66 while the average score for other Canadian communities is 81—a difference of 15 points on the 100-point CWB scale.

Figure 6.2 illustrates the distribution of First Nations and other Canadian communities. The disparity between First Nations and other Canadian communities is quite clear, with the latter concentrated at the high end of the CWB range, and the former at the middle and lower end. Nearly 50% of First Nations communities

Figure 6.4: Average CWB Scores for First Nations and Other Canadian Communities by Region, 2001

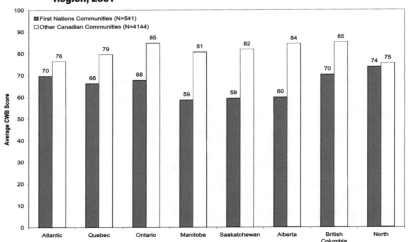

Figure 6.5: CWB Distributions of First Nations and Other Canadian Communities in Alberta, 2001

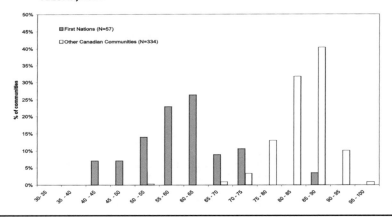

occupy the lower half of the index range (between 35 and 65). Conversely, less than 3% of other Canadian communities fall within this range. While about 94% of First Nations have CWB scores lower than the average score for other Canadian communities (81), only about 3% of other Canadian communities have CWB scores lower than the average score for First Nations (66). Perhaps most strikingly, only 1 of the top 100 Canadian communities is a First Nation while 92 of the lowest-scoring communities are First Nations.[8]

Figure 6.3 (page 115) illustrates the differences between First Nations and other Canadian communities on the four components of the CWB Index. The housing and income components exhibit the greatest differences. These two components

Figure 6.6: CWB Distributions of First Nations and Other Canadian Communities in the North, 2001

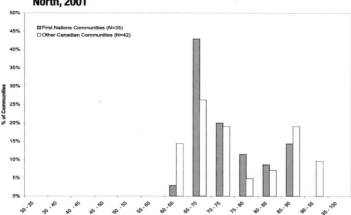

account for more than two-thirds of the current disparity in well-being between First Nations and other Canadian communities.[9]

For reference, **Table 6.1** provides the number of First Nations and other Canadian communities in each region.

As illustrated in **Figure 6.4**, average CWB scores vary from region to region, as does the well-being gap between First Nations and other Canadian communities. The widest disparity between First Nations and other Canadian community CWB scores exists in Alberta, while the smallest disparity exists in the North. CWB distributions in these two regions are illustrated in **Figures 6.5** and **6.6**, respectively.

Map 1 (page 144) groups First Nations communities into three strata. These strata are based on the mean and standard deviation of the average CWB for score for all 541 First Nations. The "Average" stratum includes all communities whose scores fall within one standard deviation (9.925) above or below the average First Nations CWB score (66). First Nations whose scores fall above and below the limits of this stratum are categorized as "Above Average" and "Below Average," respectively. The ranges[10] of the three strata are as follows: 0–55 = Below Average, 55–75 = Average, and 75–100 = Above Average.

The map demonstrates that communities with higher well-being are concentrated around the outer edge of Canada, and emphasizes the prevalence in the Prairie provinces of lower-scoring First Nations.

The Data

To assess well-being trends in First Nations and other Canadian communities across time, we constructed CWB indices for 1981, 1991, 1996, and 2001.[11] Owing to differences in the ways key variables were measured in the 1986 Census, and

Table 6.2: Census Database Details 1981–2001

Census Year	CSDs for which CWB Score was Calculated[1]	Incompletely Enumerated Reserves	CSDs Excluded Owing to Data Quality	CSDs with Population 65 and Over		CSDs included in 1981–2001 Time Series Analyses	
				First Nations[2]	Other Canadian Communities	First Nations	Other Canadian Communities
1981	5,509	8[3]	0	458	4,731		
1991	5,693	78	51	485	4,697	318	3,171
1996	5,585	77	49	541	4,579		
2001	5,188	30	98	541	4,144		

Notes:

1. Includes all CSDs present on the 2B micro-databases.

2. As indicated above, for the purposes of the time series analyses, CSDs were divided into First Nations and other Canadian communities based on INAC's 2001 geography hierarchy. For the purposes of this table, however, the 1996 INAC hierarchy was used to identify the number of First Nations in 1996. As the 1996 hierarchy is the earliest one that exists, it was also used to identify the number of First Nations in 1991. Six CSDs in the 1991 database, which did not exist in 1996 but which were INAC legal reserve CSD 'types' (five 'R' and one 'S-E') have also been counted as First Nations for the purposes of this table.

3. Counts are available for these CSDs (which include Kahnawake 4, Webequie, Wunnumin 2, Kingfisher 1, Peigan 147, Cowicha 1, Theik 2, and Cowicahn 9), but the numbers were actually imputed. Since the "donor cases" were chosen from outside the reserves in question, data for these CSDs do not reflect their conditions accurately. Beginning in 1986, missing data were replaced by values from donor cases within the same reserve, improving the veracity of on-reserve data.

Table 6.3: Average CWB Scores for First Nations and Other Canadian Communities in Canada, 1981–2001 (Numbers are rounded)

Census Year	Average CWB Score		Difference
	First Nations (N=318)	Other Canadian Communities (N=3,171)	
1981	52	73	21
1986	NO DATA		
1991	57	77	19
1996	62	77	16
2001	64	80	15

Note: Numbers Presented in table are rounded

to the large number of First Nations communities that did not participate in that Census, 1986 CWB scores are not available.

In most respects, the methods used to create this 1981–2001 series of CWB indices are identical to those used to create the single-year (or cross-sectional) CWB index described in the previous section. The time series indices differ, however, in two ways. Both of these differences were implemented to make the indices comparable across time.

First, to account for inflation, the income components of the indices were adjusted using the Consumer Price Index (CPI) (Statistics Canada, 2004). These adjustments, which are described in detail below, permit the comparison of income values from the 1981, 1991, 1996, and 2001 censuses.

Where 1992=100, the CPI value for 1980 is 52.4, for 1990 is 93.3, and for 2000 is 113.5.[12] These values were transformed to make 1995=100, establishing income values from the 1996 census as a "baseline." To render them comparable to this baseline, 1981, 1991, and 2001 income data were multiplied by 1.989, 1.117, and 0.918, respectively.

The second adjustment to the 1981–2001 series of CWB indices involved the exclusion of communities deemed "inconsistent" across time. CSDs themselves can change over time. For example, a CSD may gain a large portion of land and its associated population. In other cases, a block of population belonging to one CSD may be reassigned to another. In order to legitimately compare a community across time, one must be sure that one is assessing the same entity. To illustrate, consider the result if a very wealthy community was absorbed by a less affluent one between Census years: the overall well-being of the latter will appear to have improved even though the population of which it was originally comprised may not have improved at all—it may have even declined.

As such, analyses of CWB trends between 1981 and 2001 are based upon only those 318 First Nations and 3,171 other Canadian communities deemed as "consistent entities" from 1981 through 2001.[13] The criteria we used to designate a CSD as consistent are as follows:

1) The CSD existed in each Census year.[14]

2) The CSD did not gain or lose, owing to boundary changes, more than 5% of its population.[15]

3) The CSD had a CWB score in each Census year.

4) The CSD had a population of at least 65 in each Census year.

Summaries of each of the Census data sets and comparability analyses are provided in **Table 6.2**.

It is important to recognize that, as our analyses are based on a subset of CSDs, one must not assume that our results are representative of all First Nations and other Canadian communities.

It is perhaps also prudent to emphasize that the 2001 CWB data included in this series are necessarily different from those presented in the previous section, which looked at 2001 alone. Specifically, the cross-sectional 2001 data included raw income scores rather than scores adjusted to account for inflation. Additionally, the cross-sectional 2001 data included communities deemed inconsistent across time.

Results—First Nations Community Well-being, a National Overview, 1981–2001

As demonstrated in **Table 6.3** (page 118) and **Figure 6.7**, the average CWB score for both First Nations and other Canadian communities increased between each Census and the well-being "gap" between the two community types decreased.

Figure 6.7: Average CWB Scores for First Nations and Other Canadian Communities, 1981–2001

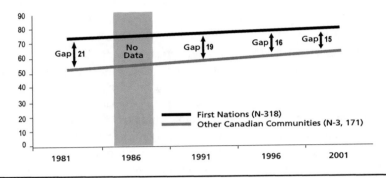

Figure 6.8: First Nations' CWB Distributions 1981–2001

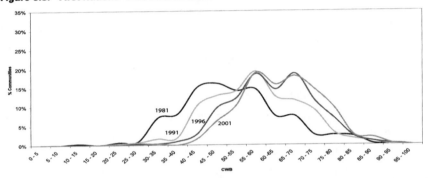

Figure 6.9: Other Canadian Communities' CWB Distributions 1981–2001

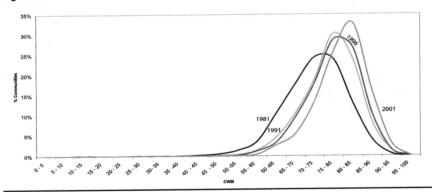

Notably, most of the absolute and relative gains experienced by First Nations appear to have occurred between 1991 and 1996. The gap decreased by less than a point between each of the 1996–2001, 1981–1986, and 1986–1991 intercensal periods (as we do not have CWB scores for 1986, we must assume that the gap decreased equally in each of the two latter periods).

Figure 6.10: Changes in CWB Scores for First Nations and Other Canadian Communities, 1981–2001

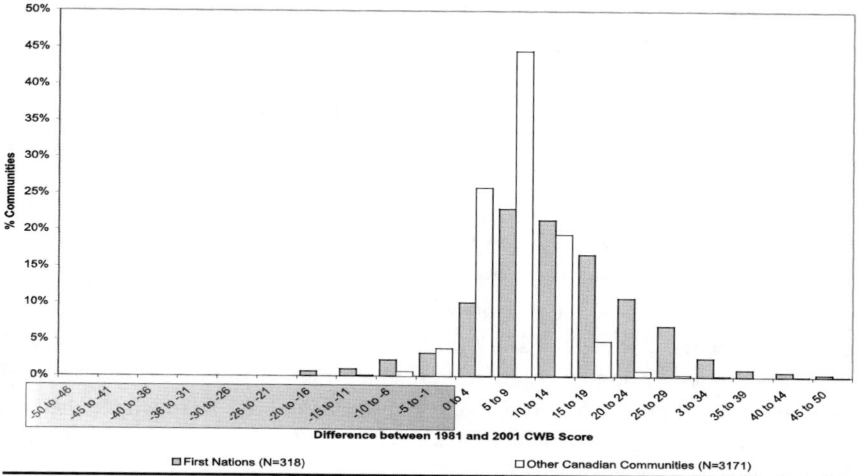

Difference between 1981 and 2001 CWB Score

☐ First Nations (N=318)   ☐ Other Canadian Communities (N=3171)

Figure 6.8 shows the distributions of First Nations' CWB scores for 1981, 1991, 1996, and 2001. **Figure 6.9** shows these distributions for other Canadian communities. The graphs demonstrate several things. First, CWB scores in both First Nations and other Canadian communities increased steadily over time. Second, the relatively consistent shapes[16] of the distributions and their wholesale shifts to the right of the graph suggests that scores have increased "across the board" for both community types. It was not the case, for example, that the mean CWB of First Nations was drawn upwards by the removal of a few communities to the extreme high end of the CWB continuum. Third, CWB scores were consistently lower for First Nations communities. Finally, scores for both types of communities spanned a wide range of the CWB continuum in each Census year, with a greater amount of variation being found in First Nations communities.

In addition to changes in the averages and distributions of the CWB, it is important to examine the changes in individual communities' scores across time. This permits us to distinguish between a scenario wherein all communities experience a "slow but steady" increase in well-being over time and a scenario wherein communities experience erratic periods of "boom and bust."[17]

Figure 6.10 demonstrates changes in CWB scores for individual communities between 1981 and 2001. The x-axis represents the change in a community's CWB score between the two Census years (literally, its 2001 CWB score minus its 1981 CWB score). Where the number is positive, the community's CWB score has increased. Where the number is negative, the community's score has decreased. For ease of interpretation, the area of the graph containing negative numbers has the numbers on the x-axis shaded in grey. The graph demonstrates that most Canadian communities, both First Nations and otherwise, improved between 1981 and 2001. Only 22 (7%)[18] First Nations and 141 (4%) other Canadian communities had a lower CWB score in 2001 than in 1981.

Figure 6.10 also reveals that the pattern of change for First Nations differed from that of other Canadian communities. The bulk of the curve for First Nations is slightly farther to the right than that for other Canadian communities, suggesting that First Nations communities, on the whole, improved more. Congruously, the mean change was 12 for First Nations but only 7 for other Canadian communities. As importantly, however, the First Nations curve is much "flatter,"[19] indicating that the amount of change varied more across First Nations than across other Canadian communities.

Another means of analysing changes in individual communities is illustrated in **Table 6.4**. The table contains one "change matrix" for First Nations and another for other Canadian communities. CWB scores in both 1981 and 2001 are collapsed into 5 levels: 0–20, 20–40, 40–60, 60–80, and 80–100. The CWB 1981 levels lie on the vertical axes, while the 2001 levels lie on the horizontal axes. Each cell represents the proportion of communities which moved from its corresponding CWB stratum in 1981 to its corresponding stratum in 2001. To illustrate, the cell in **Table 6.4** that is located at the point where "20–40" on the vertical axis (in the First Nations segment of the table) and "40–60" on the horizontal axis interact, represents the percentage (11%) of First Nations whose CWB score moved from between 20 and 40 in 1981 to between 40 and 60 in 2001.

One benefit of this type of analysis is that it provides a good "at a glance" representation of how well-being in First Nations and other Canadian communities has changed over time. The diagonal lines of shaded cells include those CSDs which occupied the same CWB stratum in both Census years. The cells above the diagonals include CSDs whose CWB scores have moved to a higher stratum between the Census years in question. The cells below the diagonals include CSDs whose CWB scores have moved to a lower stratum.

Like **Figure 6.10**, this table indicates that a decline in well-being, both in First Nations and other Canadian communities, was the exception rather than the rule, and that improvement between 1981 and 2001 was more common among First Nations communities. On the one hand, 55% of First Nations occupied a higher CWB stratum in 2001 than in 1981, compared to 41% of other Canadian communities. On the other hand, 43% of First Nations and 58% of other Canadian communities occupied the same CWB stratum in both Census years. A slightly larger percentage of First Nations declined (2% vs. 1% of other Canadian communities), but the difference is negligible. Overall, these numbers indicate that well-being improved gradually in Canadian communities between 1981 and 2001, and at a faster rate among First Nations.

Components of the CWB, Canada, 1981–2001

Between 1981 and 2001, First Nations scores increased across all components of the CWB index, both in absolute terms and relative to other Canadian communities. The greatest gains were seen in the education component. The education score for

Table 6.4:   CWB Change Matrices for First Nations and Other Canadian Communities, 1981–2001

			CWB 2001				
			0–20	20–40	40–60	60–80	80–100
First Nations (N=318)	CWB 1981	0–20			1 (0.3%)		
		20–40		1 (0.3%)	35 (11%)	18 (5.7%)	
		40–60			77 (24.2%)	112 (35.2%)	1 (0.3%)
		60–80			5 (1.6%)	52 (16.4%)	7 (2.2%)
		80–100				2 (0.6%)	7 (2.2%)
Other Canadian Communities (N=3,171)	CWB 1981	0–20			1 (0.0%)		
		20–40				3 (0.1%)	
		40–60			12 (0.4%)	167 (5.3%)	5 (0.2%)
		60–80			3 (0.1%)	1,313 (41.4%)	1,113 (35.1%)
		80–100				27 (0.9%)	527 (16.6%)

Figure 6.11: First Nations' Gains and Gap Reduction in the Components of the CWB, 1981–2001

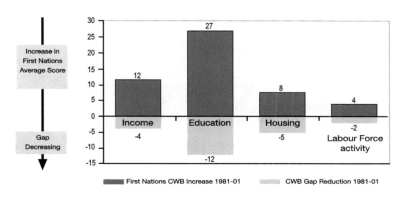

First Nations increased by 27 points. This gain is more than that seen in the other three CWB components combined. The gap between the education score for First Nations and that calculated for other communities decreased by 12 points between 1981 and 2001. This reduction is greater than that seen in the other three CWB components combined.[20] As is illustrated in **Figure 6.11** (page 123), the second largest absolute gains were seen in income (12 points), followed by housing (8 points), and labour force activity (4 points). The second largest gap reduction

Figure 6.12: CWB Component "Gaps" 1981–2001

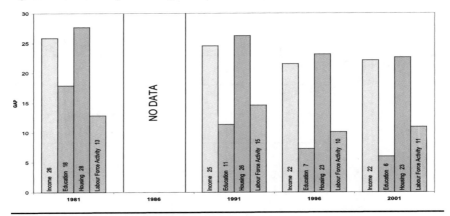

Figure 6.13: First Nations' CWB Scores by Region, 1981–2001

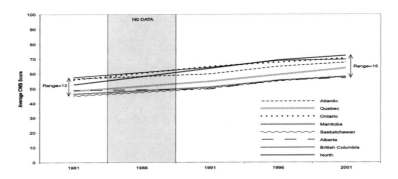

Source: Derived from Appendix Table 1

Figure 6.14: Other Canadian Communities' CWB Scores by Region, 1981–2001

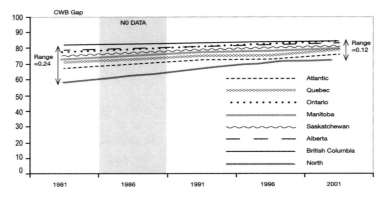

Source: Derived from Appendix Table 2

occurred in housing (5 points), followed by income (4 points), and labour force activity (2 points).

The large gains in education are evident in **Figure 6.12**, which shows the gaps between First Nations and other Canadian communities in the CWB components for 1981, 1991, 1996, and 2001. In each Census year, the largest gaps existed in the housing component, closely followed by the income component. The gap in the labour force activity component was consistently about half as large. However, the education gap, which was about two-thirds the size of the housing and income gaps in 1981, had shrunk to less than one third their size by 2001.

First Nations Community Well-being, a Regional Breakdown, 1981–2001[21]

Readers should interpret regional CWB statistics with caution. As we discussed in an earlier section of this report, our analyses are based on the subset of communities that existed in a relatively consistent manner between 1981 and 2001. Excluding communities which did not meet this criterion may have introduced bias. Given that the number of communities per region is much smaller than the aggregate analysis, such bias may be exacerbated. Moreover, regional boundaries are somewhat arbitrary. Cross-sectional analyses of 2001 CWB scores, presented earlier, indicate that First Nations' well-being follows certain geographic patterns, but that these patterns do not conform closely to regional borders. Essentially, while regional analyses provide a good general indication of the dispersion of well-being across the country, data limitations must be remembered and regional differences should not be overemphasized.

Figures 6.13 and **6.14** plot changes in regional CWB averages for First Nations and other Canadian communities, respectively. These graphs demonstrate that the average CWB scores for both types of communities increased across regions each Census year.

These figures also demonstrate that, while regional scores for other communities converged between 1981 and 2001, regional scores for First Nations diverged slightly. In other words, the disparity in well-being between First Nations across regions of Canada increased between 1981 and 2001.

Figure 6.13 also demonstrates that the well-being of First Nations varied from region to region in a fairly consistent manner between 1981 and 2001. Consistently, average CWB scores were highest in British Columbia, Ontario and the Atlantic region, and lowest in the Prairies. First Nations in the North, whose average score was middling in 1981, rose to be the highest in 2001. Quebec First Nations, whose score was comparable to those of the Prairie provinces in 1981, had become more middling by 2001.

The largest increase in First Nations' CWB score occurred in the North (19 points), while the smallest occurred in Alberta (almost 8 points). Increases in First Nations' CWB scores in the other regions were as follows: Quebec (15), Ontario

Figure 6.15: CWB Gaps by Region, 1981–2001

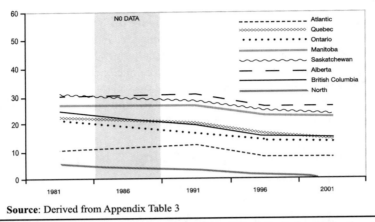

Source: Derived from Appendix Table 3

(14), Saskatchewan (13), British Columbia (12), Manitoba (11), the Atlantic region (11).

Figure 6.15 illustrates changes in the gaps between First Nations and other communities, by region, between 1981 and 2001. This graph demonstrates that, with the exception of Alberta and the Atlantic region, the regional gaps between First Nations and other communities decreased with each Census year (the gap increased very slightly in Alberta and somewhat more in the Atlantic region between 1981 and 1991, though gaps in both regions decreased in the overall 1981–2001 period).

Regional differences in the disparity between First Nations and other communities were also quite consistent across time. The smallest gaps were found in the North and the Atlantic region, to a certain extent owing to the lower CWB scores of non-First Nations communities in those regions. Middling gaps were found in Ontario, British Columbia, and Quebec. The largest disparities between First Nations and other communities were found in the Prairie provinces.

As mentioned above, the disparities between First Nations and other Canadian communities decreased in all regions between 1981 and 2001. The largest reduction occurred in British Columbia (almost 10 points), while the smallest occurred in the Atlantic region (about 3 points). Gap reductions in the other regions were as follows: Ontario (8), Quebec (8), Saskatchewan (7), the North (5), Manitoba (4), Alberta (4).

Overall it may be said that while there were clear regional patterns in First Nations' CWB scores and gaps in 1981, 1991, 1996, and 2001, regional patterns of changes in scores and gaps between Census years were less pronounced.[22]

Figure 6.16: CWB Score Change 1981–2001 by 1981 CWB Score Strata

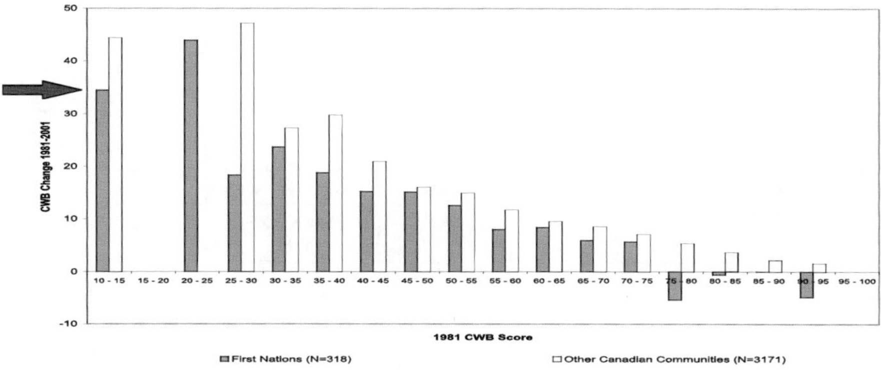

⊞ First Nations (N=318)   □ Other Canadian Communities (N=3171)

The Importance of "Initial Scores"

Analyses of 1981–2001 CWB data revealed two interesting patterns. These patterns provide insight into both past and future CWB trends. Consequently, we decided to highlight the patterns in this separate section.

The patterns, in brief, are as follows:

a) As communities' CWB scores at the outset of an intercensal period (i.e. their "initial scores") increased, the amount of improvement they experienced during the intercensal period decreased.

b) Within categories of "initial scores," First Nations improved less than other Canadian communities.

These patterns were evident almost uniformly across intercensal periods.[23] The patterns were also evident across all components of the CWB index[24] except for education. While improvement in education decreased as initial education scores increased, First Nations and other communities with similar initial scores generally improved at a similar rate.

Using the 1981–2001 inter-censal period as an example, **Figure 6.16** illustrates these patterns in the CWB scores of First Nations and other Canadian communities. The 1981 CWB scores, divided into 20 equidistant groups, fall on the x-axis. On the y-axis is the average change in CWB score that communities within each 1981 CWB stratum experienced between 1981 and 2001. For example (as indicated by the arrow), the average amount of change experienced by First Nations whose 1981 CWB score fell between 10 and 15 was about 35 points on the 100-point CWB scale.

The decline in bar heights from left to right demonstrates that improvement between 1981 and 2001 decreased as 1981 scores increased: communities with lower scores in 1981 improved more between 1981 and 2001 than did communi-

Table 6.5: **Regression Analysis: Examining Determinants of Change in CWB Scores Between 1981 and 2001**

Predictors of CWB Score Change 1981–2001	R	R²		B (slope)
1981 CWB Score only (Model 1)	0.630	0.397		-0.342
First Nations status only (Model 2)	0.287	0.082		0.057
1981 CWB Score with First Nations status added (Model 3)	0.637	0.406	1981 CWB Score	-0.379
			First Nations status	-0.023

ties with higher scores in 1981. Each 1981 CWB score stratum contains a pair of bars. In each stratum, the grey bar representing the average change between 1981 and 2001 for First Nations is shorter than the white bar which represents the average change between 1981 and 2001 for other Canadian communities. This indicates that, within categories of "initial scores," First Nations improved less than other Canadian communities.

What Do These Patterns Say About CWB Trends in the Past?

Almost uniformly, our analyses of the CWB index indicate that First Nations well-being increased between 1981 and 2001 and that the gap between First Nations and other communities narrowed. What those analyses did not determine, however, was why First Nations improved more than other communities.

An attractive explanation is that something was "going on" in First Nations communities that allowed them to progress faster than other communities. That is, we could assume that the correlation between First Nationhood and CWB improvement (i.e. First Nations improved more) was actually a causal link (i.e. First Nations improved more because they were First Nations).

The patterns revealed in **Figure 6.16** (page 127), however, negate this supposition. First, the graph demonstrates that in both First Nations and other communities, improvement in well-being scores decreased as initial scores increased. Since CWB scores were generally lower among First Nations communities, their average score would necessarily have increased more than that of other Canadian communities. In other words, the relationship between "First Nationhood" and improvement in well-being is largely spurious.

The relationship is not entirely spurious; but what impact First Nationhood had on improvement in well-being was not favourable. Within the strata of 1981 CWB scores, First Nations improved less than other communities, indicating that First Nationhood had a negative impact on CWB improvement.

The regression analyses presented in **Table 6.5** will help clarify these claims. As indicated by the R-Square values of the three different "models," 1981 CWB scores

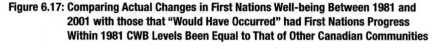

Figure 6.17: Comparing Actual Changes in First Nations Well-being Between 1981 and 2001 with those that "Would Have Occurred" had First Nations Progress Within 1981 CWB Levels Been Equal to That of Other Canadian Communities

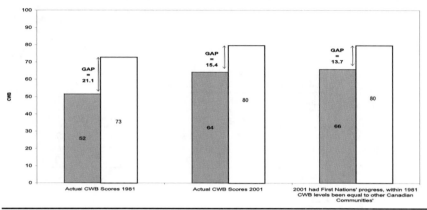

alone accounted for about 40% of the variation in CWB change between 1981 and 2001. Alone, First Nations status accounted for only about 8%. Adding the latter to the first model improved its ability to account for variation in 1981–2001 CWB change only minutely. These results suggest that little of the difference between communities' 1981 and 2001 CWB scores was related to whether or not they were First Nations.

The B values, or "slopes," demonstrate that what influence First Nationhood had on CWB improvement between 1981 and 2001 was negative. When examined in isolation (Model 2), First Nationhood appears to have a weak but positive relationship with the amount of improvement communities experienced between 1981 and 2001. When one "controls" for communities' initial scores by introducing 1981 CWB scores into the model (Model 3), however, that relationship is reversed: First Nations improved slightly less than other Canadian communities.

Essentially, despite the increase in First Nations well-being between 1981 and 2001 and the fact that the disparity between First Nations and other Canadian communities decreased, we cannot claim that First Nations progressed faster, or even as fast, as other communities. Put another way, had First Nations' progress really been equal to that of other communities, their average score would have increased more, and the gap would have narrowed more appreciably.

Figure 6.17 is illustrative. The first two sets of bars represent the actual average CWB scores for First Nations and other Canadian communities in 1981 and 2001, respectively. In the final set of bars, the First Nations score for 2001 has been adjusted to represent what the First Nations score "would have been" had First Nations progressed at the same rate as other communities within their respective 1981 CWB score strata.[25] Had that been the case, the CWB gap would have decreased by about 7.4 points on the 100-point CWB scale, slightly more than the actual decrease of about 5.7 points.

Table 6.6: Summary of Regression Equations Used to Generate Projections

Period	Indicator	Regression Equation *where* x = change between year A and year B, and y = score year A	
		First Nations (N = 318)	Other Canadian Communities (N = 3,171)
1981–2001	CWB	x = 38.0 + -0.494 (y)	x = 32.3 + -0.350 (y)
	Income	x + 30.4 + -0.529 (y)	x = 36.5 + -0.466 (y)
	Education	x = 47.2 + -0.479 (y)	x = 38.4 + -0.388 (y)
	Housing	x = 51.9 + -0.706 (y)	x = 66.3 + -0.705 (y)
	Labour Force Activity	x = 58.7 + -0.832 (y)	x = 15.2 + -0.167 (y)
		First Nations (N = 399)	Other Canadian Communities (N = 3,454)
1991–2001	CWB	x = 20.9 + -0.247 (y)	x = 20.4 + -0.228 (y)
	Income	x = 14.0 + -0.187 (y)	x = 22.6 + -0.288 (y)
	Education	x = 27.8 + -0.280 (y)	x = 27.3 + -0.299 (y)
	Housing	x = 30.9 + -0.397 (y)	x = 48.4 + -0.519 (y)
	Labour Force Activity	x = 33.9 + -0.455 (y)	x = 18.0 + -0.217 (y)
		First Nations (N = 470)	Other Canadian Communities (N = 3,643)
1996–2001	CWB	x = 12.1 + -0.160 (y)	x = 15.6 + -0.174 (y)
	Income	x = 9.3 + -0.139 (y)	x = 19.8 + -0.248 (y)
	Education	x = 14.5 + -0.157 (y)	x = 20.6 + -0.241 (y)
	Housing	x = 22.8 + -0.315 (y)	x = 42.2 + -0.455 (y)
	Labour Force Activity	x = 28.0 + -0.395 (y)	x = 19.1 + -0.221 (y)

What Do These Patterns Say About CWB Trends in the Future?

As the implications of the patterns we have described are borne out in our projections, little needs to be said about them here. In brief, the fact that improvement declines as initial scores increase suggests that well-being will eventually "plateau." The fact that within the strata of initial scores, First Nations improved less than other communities, suggests that First Nations will plateau at a lower level of well-being than other Canadian communities.

First Nations Community Well-being: the Future (2001–2041)—Projection Methodology

We cannot know for certain how well-being among First Nations will develop. Innumerable unexpected factors may emerge to alter the course of First Nations history. We can, however, ascertain what implications previous CWB patterns have for the future progress of First Nations well-being. In simple terms, what is the future of First Nations well-being, if things continue on their present course?

Without any clear indication of which intercensal period best represents how First Nations will fare in the future,[26] it is prudent to produce several projections based on different intercensal periods. We used the 1981–2001 period, the 1991–2001 period, and the 1996–2001 periods,[27,28] to produce projections for the CWB and its components through 2041. Producing multiple projections also allows us to minimize the impact of any random variation that may appear in any individual intercensal period.

In the previous section, we discussed the impact of communities' initial scores on how much their scores are likely to change. To account for this impact in our projections, we employed regression equations. These equations summarize the relationship between communities' scores at the beginning of a period and how much they changed by the end of the period. They allowed us to estimate how much communities' scores would be expected to increase in the future, given their scores in 2001.

Our methodology is described in detail below, using projections of the CWB index based on the 1981–2001 period as an example.

The following regression equation describes the relationship between First Nations communities' 1981 CWB scores and the amount of change those communities incurred between 1981 and 2001.

*Change 1981 to 2001 = 38 + (-.494 * 1981 CWB Score)*[29]

The corresponding regression equation for other communities is:

*Change 1981 to 2001 = 32.3 + (-.350 * 1981 CWB Score)*

To calculate 2021[30] CWB scores for First Nations, we added to their 2001 CWB scores 38 minus 0.494 multiplied by their 2001 CWB scores. To calculate First Nations 2041 CWB scores, we repeated the process, this time multiplying the 0.494 by communities' 2021 CWB scores.

To calculate 2021 CWB scores for other Canadian communities, we added to their 2001 CWB scores 32.3 minus 0.350 multiplied by their 2001 CWB scores. To calculate other Canadian communities' 2041 CWB scores, we repeated the process, this time multiplying the .350 by communities' 2021 CWB scores.

In all, we completed 15 projections. They are detailed in **Table 6.6**.

A Word of Caution

A simple and popular method of projecting trends into the future is to extrapolate changes in group averages. That is, since First Nations' average CWB score increased by 13 between 1981 and 2001, we could assume that it would increase by the same 13 between 2001 and 2021 and in every subsequent 20-year period.

In the case of the CWB, this method would implicitly assume that some inherent quality in First Nations allowed them to improve at a faster rate than

Figure 6.18: 2001–2041 CWB Projections Based on Trends Observed in the 1981–2001 Intercensal Period

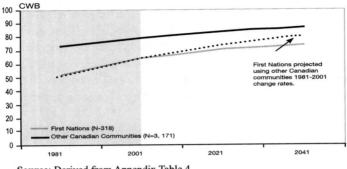

Source: Derived from Appendix Table 4

other communities. Such an assumption is unwarranted, however, given the relationship we uncovered earlier between initial scores, changes in scores, and First Nations community status. Consequently, we utilized a more complex projection method which accounted for that relationship.

This more complex projection method, however, contains its own assumptions. Specifically, our method assumes that the aforementioned negative relationship between initial scores and improvement and between First Nationhood and improvement are "real" and not by-products of factors unknown.

For example, as the positive one was revealed to be, the negative relationship we discovered between First Nationhood and well-being improvement may be spurious. Perhaps communities within the strata of initial scores tended to improve more if they were closer to highways. First Nations might appear to improve less simply because they tended to be located farther from highways, even though First Nations near highways improved just as much as other Canadian communities near highways and other Canadian communities removed from highways improved just as little as their First Nations neighbours.

The possibility of such an effect might prompt readers to wonder why we didn't investigate the matter, and, if such an effect existed, account for it in our projection model. The answer is simple: research is an iterative, cumulative, long-term process. The factors that one might examine for influence on the trajectory of First Nations well-being are innumerable, and investigation is bounded only by researchers' imaginations (and, of course, data availability!).

No matter what method was used, we could not claim to have the definitive "answer" to what affects First Nations well-being, or how it will progress in the future. Our projection method accounts for the patterns we have discovered in the CWB data thus far. As additional patterns are discovered, better methods of projection may be developed. At this point in time, however, we may state confidently that our method of projecting well-being into the future reflects our current level of understanding of how First Nations well-being evolved in the past.

Projection Results, 2001–2041[31]

The results of our projection models are reported in absolute terms. That is, we often refer to what will happen. This mode of expression was chosen for its clarity and brevity. Our projections are merely "educated guesses," however, and should not be interpreted as concrete claims.

The CWB Index, Canada, 2001–2041

Figure 6.18 illustrates our projection of the CWB index based on the 1981–2001 intercensal period. Past CWB scores have been shaded in grey to distinguish them from projected scores.

The graph indicates that by 2041, the average CWB score for First Nations communities will be about six points below the level seen in other Canadian communities in 2001. Moreover, the amount of improvement in the First Nations average decreases steadily between 2001 and 2041, implying that improvement will "level off" when First Nations have achieved only a moderate level of well-being.

In addition, the gap between First Nations and other Canadian communities, while slightly narrower in 2041 than in 2001, is still very much in evidence. The CWB gap narrows by only about 3 points over the 40-year projected period and remains 13 points wide in 2041.

As indicated earlier, within categories of initial conditions, First Nations improved less, on average, than other Canadian communities. The effect of this disparity is demonstrated in the dashed grey line of **Figure 6.18**. The line represents what the projection for First Nations would have looked like had First Nations changed at the same rate as other Canadian communities within initial conditions strata between 1981 and 2001.[32] Had this been the case, First Nations would have achieved a substantially higher level of well-being by 2041.

As also noted earlier, we simply do not know which of the intercensal periods best represents what we will see in the future. **Figures 6.19** and **6.20** (both on page 134) are based on the rates of change observed between 1991 and 2001, and 1996 and 2001, respectively.

Projections of the CWB index based on the 1991–2001 period (**Figure 6.19**) yield the largest absolute and relative increases for First Nations. While the well-being gap is expected to be about eight points wide in 2041, this projected gap is approximately half the size of the current one. Moreover, the projected 2041 CWB score for First Nations will still not have achieved the level observed in other Canadian communities in 2001.

Figure 6.19 also demonstrates the similarity between the actual First Nations projection and the hypothetical projection based on the regression line for other Canadian communities. This similarity demonstrates that, within the strata

Figure 6.19: 2001–2041 CWB Projections Based on Trends Observed in the 1991–2001 Intercensal Period

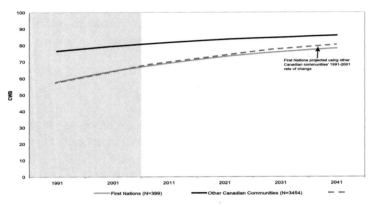

Source: Derived from Appendix Table 5

Figure 6.20: 2001–2041 CWB Projections Based on Trends Observed in the 1996–2001 Intercensal Period

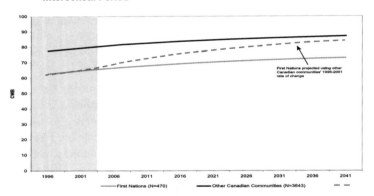

Source: Derived from Appendix Table 6

Figure 6.21: Projecting Well-being in First Nations and Other Canadian Communities: A Summary

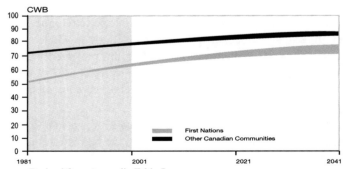

Source: Derived from Appendix Table 7

of 1991 scores, First Nations improved only slightly less than other communities between 1991 and 2001.

Projections based on the 1996–2001 period (**Figure 6.20**) are very similar to the ones based on the 1981–2001 period. Progress in First Nations' well-being quickly plateaus and the CWB gap remains virtually unchanged by 2041. Again, the dashed grey line represents a hypothetical projection of First Nations well-being. The line depicts how we would have projected First Nations well-being had their 1996–2001 rate of change been identical to that of other Canadian communities. Had this been the case, the well-being gap projected for 2041 would have been about 80% smaller.

The following graph is a summary of the previous three projections. We have included it for a very important reason: it highlights the variability in those projections. We cannot foresee the future of First Nations well-being. We can only extrapolate previous data trends, and can only guess at which trends best approximate what we will see in the future.

As **Figure 6.21** demonstrates, there is a gap of about 5 points between our highest and lowest estimates of First Nations 2041 CWB scores. The gap between our highest and lowest estimates for other Canadian communities is only about 1.5 points wide. Uniformly, however, our projections indicate that progress in First Nations will begin to level off, and that a gap between the average CWB score for First Nations and that of other Canadian communities will remain in 2041.

Components of the CWB, Canada, 2001–2041

In the interest of brevity, we have summarized our projections of the CWB components. As in **Figure 6.21**, the projections based on the 1981–2001, the 1991–2001, and the 1996–2001 periods have been combined to form ranges of possible futures for First Nations and other Canadian communities.

Income

The projections for the income component of the CWB are illustrated in **Figure 6.22** (page 136). It indicates that the First Nations income score will increase between 8 and 15 points between 2001 and 2041. The income gap in 2041 is expected to be anywhere from 13 to 24 points wide. This range is not directly comparable to the 1981 income gap of 26, given that some of the communities used to produce our projections from the 1991–2001 and 1996–2001 time periods were not included in our 1981–2001 analyses. Still, we can claim in general terms that the income gap may be reduced by as much as 50% or almost not at all by 2041. Whatever the case, our projections indicate that the income disparity between First Nations and other communities will persist through 2041. The fact that First Nations' income improvement has begun to plateau by that time suggests that the gap will persist for some time after.

Figure 6.22: Income Projections for First Nations and Other Canadian Communities 2001–2041: A Summary

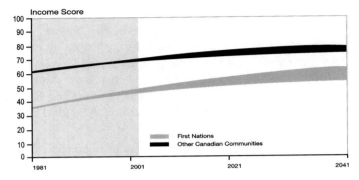

Source: Derived from Appendix Table 8

Figure 6.23: Education Projections for First Nations and Other Canadian Communities 2001–20041: A Summary

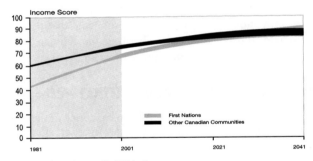

Source: Derived from Appendix Table 9

Figure 6.24: Housing Projections for First Nations and Other Canadian Communities 2001–2041: A Summary

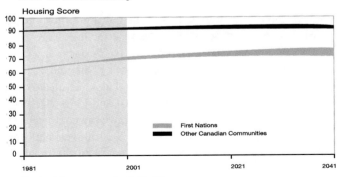

Source: Derived from Appendix Table 10

Education

The projections for the education component of the CWB are illustrated in **Figure 6.23**. Between 2001 and 2041, the First Nations average education score is expected to increase between 17 and 22 points. All of our projections indicate that, by 2041, the education gap between First Nations and other Communities will effectively be closed. Some of our estimates actually predict that First Nations' education scores will surpass that of other Canadian communities. Again, it is important to remember that the education indicator emphasizes achievement at the lower end of the education continuum. Differences in educational attainment between First Nations and other Canadian communities in the higher echelons of education are not captured.

The projections for the housing component of the CWB index are illustrated in **Figure 6.24**. The First Nations average housing score is expected to increase between 1 and 6 points by 2041. The gap between First Nations and other communities is expected to remain between 16 and 22 points wide. The plateau of First Nations progress is very evident in the housing component. All of our projections indicated that little improvement will occur between 2021 and 2041 (never much more than a single point). This suggests that the 2041 housing gap, even the smallest one predicted by our projections, will not reduce much further in the years beyond 2041.

Labour Force Activity

Projections for the labour force activity component of the CWB index are illustrated in **Figure 6.25** (page 138). The labour force activity gap in 2041 is expected to be between 8 and 15 points wide. The "plateau effect" for First Nations was evident in all our projections of labour force activity. This suggests that the labour force activity gap, whatever it may be in 2041, will reduce little in the years that follow.

It should be noted that projections using the 1991–2001 intercensal period yielded higher estimates for First Nations well-being, in terms of both the CWB and its components, than projections based on the 1981–2001 and 1996–2001 periods. Labour force activity was an exception. The largest absolute increase in the First Nations labour force activity score was generated by the projections based on the 1991–2001 period, but the projections based on the 1996–2001 period indicated a greater gap reduction between First Nations and other communities.

Figure 6.25: Labour Force Activity Projections for First Nations and Other Canadian Communities, 2001–2041: A Summary

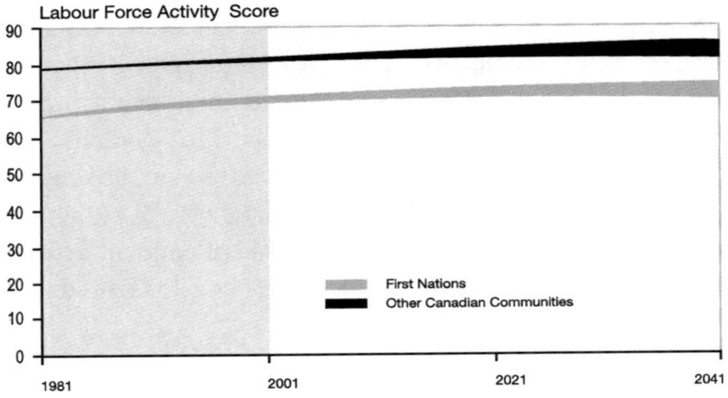

Source: Derived from Appendix Table 11

Summary of Results

First Nations Community Well-being: The Present (2001)

As of 2001, First Nations communities have, on average, substantially lower CWB scores than other Canadian communities. CWB scores vary considerably across First Nations communities. First Nations' average CWB scores vary across regions of Canada, as do disparities in average CWB scores between First Nations and other Canadian communities. The largest disparities between First Nations and other communities exist in the income and housing components of the CWB.

First Nations Community Well-being: The Past (1981–2001)

Average CWB scores for both First Nations and other Canadian communities have increased since 1981 and the well-being gap between the two types of communities has narrowed. The largest disparities between First Nations and other Canadian communities were found consistently in the housing and income components of the CWB. First Nations scores, both absolutely and relative to those of other communities, increased in all four components of the CWB index since 1981. First Nations experienced their greatest gains, by far, in education.

Regional disparities in First Nations' CWB scores were fairly consistent between 1981 and 2001. Scores in Ontario, British Columbia, the North, and the Atlantic region were fairly similar, while scores in the Prairies were noticeably lower. Gaps between First Nations and other Canadian communities were smallest in the North and the Atlantic region, mid-range in Quebec, Ontario, and British Columbia, and largest in the Prairies. First Nations well-being improved across regions between 1981 and 2001. Degree of improvement varied across regions, but not in a markedly systematic way.

On average, the higher a community's score at the outset of a given intercensal period, the less it improved during that period. On average, First Nations improved less during each inter-censal period than did other Canadian communities whose scores at the outset of the period were comparable. These patterns indicate that the reduction in the CWB gap between First Nations and other Canadian communities between 1981 and 2001 was driven by the large proportion of First Nations whose very low CWB scores predisposed them to a large amount of improvement. The patterns also suggest that improvement in First Nations well-being will slow down in the future and that First Nations' average CWB score will plateau at a level below that of other Canadian communities.

These patterns were consistent across inter-censal periods, almost uniformly across regions, and were evident in all components of the CWB except for education.

First Nations Community Well-being: The Future (2001–2041)

Overall, our projections of the CWB suggest that increases in First Nations' average CWB score will slow down and that a significant gap will remain between First Nations and other communities in 2041. Significant gaps are also predicted to remain in all components of the CWB except for education.

Projections of the CWB varied with the intercensal period upon which they were based. Generally, projections using the 1991–2001 intercensal period yielded higher estimates for First Nations well-being, both in terms of the CWB and its components, than projections based on the 1981–2001 and 1996–2001 periods.

Conclusion

That well-being in First Nations communities improved between 1981 and 2001 and First Nations achievements, particularly in the area of education, should not be down-played. Despite these successes, however, a significant well-being gap between First Nations and other Canadian communities remains.

Moreover, First Nations' continued progress cannot be taken for granted. According to the evidence in hand, maintenance of the status quo in First Nations communities means that, to at least some extent, the well-being gap is here to stay.

That being said, the evidence in hand is, as always, contestable. The CWB is an important first step in understanding the disparity in well-being between First Nations and other communities, but it does not represent "the final word" on First Nations community well-being. Future research into the determinants of First Nations well-being is necessary. Such research will not only provide insight into the factors that impact well-being, but will demonstrate what factors might be included in a more comprehensive model of First Nations well-being.[33] Additional research will also allow us to predict the future trajectory of First Nations well-being with greater accuracy. Incorporating the effects of "initial scores" into our projection model likely produced more accurate predictions than a simplistic extrapolation of mean changes would have. Still, much more must be learned about the dynamics of First Nations well-being before definitive forecasts of future trends will be possible.

Endnotes

1 This chapter is an amalgam of the following articles: McHardy, M., and O'Sullivan, E., 2004. "First Nations Community Well-being in Canada: The Community Well-being Index (CWB), 2001." INAC. Catalogue no. R2-334/2001E; O'Sullivan, E. and McHardy, M. 2004. "The Community Well-being (CWB) Index: Disparity in Well-being Between First Nations and Other Canadian Communities Over Time." INAC, Catalogue no. R2-349/2004E; O'Sullivan, E. and McHardy, M. 2004. "The Community Well-being (CWB) Index: Well-being in First Nations Communities, 1981–2001 and into the Future." INAC, Catalogue no. R2-441/2006E. These articles were published individually by the Strategic Research and Analysis Directorate of Indian and Northern Affairs Canada and are available online at <**www.ainc-inac.gc.ca/pr/ra/pub4_ e.html**>.

2 Excluding communities that did not participate in the Census, had data quality issues, or had populations of less than 65.

3 In previous publications, the CWB scale ran from 0 through 1. It has been re-scaled here for ease of interpretation. This re-scaling has no substantive impact on analyses of the CWB. Effectively, CWB and component scores were multiplied by 100. For example, a CWB score of 0.85 was multiplied by 100, producing a re-scaled score of 85. Other articles in this volume do not multiple by 100 and list CWB as a value between 0 and 1.

4 Unless otherwise noted, the indicators comprising each component of the CWB are equally weighted.

5 Census data on Indian reserves and in remote areas were collected from 100% of households. In other areas, data collected from a random 20% sample of households were weighted to make them representative of the total population in those areas.

6 Missing information on individual records was imputed during processing of the Census data. Each missing value was replaced by the corresponding entry for a "similar" record.

7 The original data source for the CWB was a selection of un-rounded, unsuppressed individual-level data which was accessed through a memorandum of understanding between INAC and Statistics Canada.

8 To put these values in context, note that First Nations communities make up approximately 13% of all Canadian communities.

9 While numerous factors may contribute to CWB disparities between First Nations and other communities, it is especially important to point out the likely impact of the Aboriginal age structure on income in First Nations communities. The Aboriginal population is significantly younger than the population of other Canadians. Consequently, a greater proportion of Aboriginal people are in the beginning phases of their careers in employed work. Since salary tends to increase with seniority, the lower incomes seen in First Nations communities are at least partly attributable to the youthfulness of the Aboriginal population.

10 These ranges are approximations that have been rounded in the interest of brevity.

11 In 1991, 1996, and 2001, Census data on Indian reserves and in remote areas were collected from 100% of households. In other areas, data collected from a random 20% sample of households were weighted to make them representative of the total population in those areas (Statistics Canada, 2002:279; Statistics Canada, 1999:356; Statistics Canada, 1992:32). In 1981, while data were generally collected from 100% of households in remote areas, reserves were not singled out for 100% sampling (Statistics Canada, 1984:18).

12 As income represents one's total income in the full year prior to the Census year, income values are adjusted using inflation rates from the years preceding any given census year.

13 Note, however, that CWB scores for "inconsistent" CSDs have still been calculated, and may be useful for specific types of analyses.

14 Typically, a CSD was identified across time by its CSD code. In a small number of cases, a CSD code changed without affecting the population associated with that name and number. In these cases, the "old" and "new" CSDs are regarded as a single entity.

15 Population changes resulting from births, deaths, and migration are not bases for the exclusion of communities from our analyses.

16   The distributions for First Nations are considerably less "smooth" than those for other Canadian communities. This is attributable to the much smaller number of First Nations being analysed. No clear evidence of a bimodal distribution, for example, was found.

17   For example, imagine we are measuring well-being in only two communities: Community A and Community B. In 1981, Community A had a score of 0 and Community B had a score of 1. The average score for these two communities in 1981 was, therefore, 0.5. In 2001, the average score for these 2 communities was still 0.5, suggesting that well-being remained stable for these communities between 1981 and 2001. When we look at the individual communities' scores, however, we see that, in 2001, Community A had a score of 1 while Community B's score had dropped to zero. The extreme "boom and bust" pattern of these communities was masked by the consistency of their average score across time.

18   Notably, however, a few First Nations seem to have declined substantially. It is possible that these declines are illusory. The method of imputing missing data in 1981 did not require that missing data for reserve residents be replaced by the values from a "donor case" in the same reserve. Consequently, missing data in reserves may have been replaced with data from residents of non-reserve communities. Given the lower well-being among First Nations, it is possible that this sort of imputation inflated the 1981 scores of some First Nations communities. If so, when more accurate scores were computed in later Census years, these communities will have appeared to have declined. There is, unfortunately, no documentation available that can either confirm or deny this speculation. We do, however, wish to acknowledge the possibility and to suggest that readers consider steeply declining First Nations with caution.

19   The standard deviation of the change in CWB scores between 1981 and 2001 was .10293 for First Nations and .04826 for other Canadian communities.

20   When considering the improvements in First Nations education, it is important to keep in mind how education is defined in this study. The education indicator emphasizes achievement at the lower end of the education continuum (literacy and high school "plus"). Differences in educational attainment between First Nations and other Canadian communities in the higher echelons of education are not captured.

21   Data tables related to this section are provided in Appendix 1.

22   The fact that Manitoba and Alberta seem to have been doubly disadvantaged by lower CWB scores and less improvement is worthy of consideration, however.

23   As will be detailed later, we examined the 1981–2001, 1991–2001, and 1996–2001 periods.

24   The strength of the relationships varied.

25   To produce this estimate, we recalculated the average 2001 CWB score for First Nations using the regression equation that defines the relationship between 1981 CWB score and change in CWB score between 1981 and 2001 for other Canadian communities. The complete adjustment equation is as follows: First Nations CWB 2001 = First Nations CWB 1981 + (0.323 + (-0.35 * First Nations CWB 1981)).

26   For example, if the evolution of well-being follows a long-term trajectory, patterns of change since 1981 may be the most appropriate bases for our well-being projections. Alternately, the deceleration of First Nations progress following 1996 may have marked the beginning of a new trend in First Nations development.

27   Projections based on 1981–2001 CWB changes are based on 318 First Nations and 3,171 other communities that were deemed comparable between 1981 and 2001. Projections based on 1991–2001 CWB changes are based on 399 First Nations and 3,454 other communities that were deemed comparable between 1991 and 2001. Projections based on 1996–2001 CWB changes are based on 470 First Nations and 3,643 other communities that were deemed comparable between 1996 and 2001.

28   Projections based on these time periods assume that well-being progresses in 20-, 10-, and 5-year cycles, respectively.

29   In simple terms, this equation means that each community had a base increase of 0.380 between 1981 and 2001. 0.494 multiplied by the community's 1981 CWB score is the amount that is subtracted from the base amount of 0.380. We can see that the higher a First Nations' CWB score was in 1981, the less it would have improved by 2001.

30 Since this projection is based on the 20-year period between 1981 and 2001, CWB scores are projected in 20-year intervals. Correspondingly, for projections based on the 1991–2001 and 1996–2001 periods, CWB scores were projected in 10- and 5-year intervals, respectively.

31 Data tables related to this section are provided in Appendix 1.

32 Literally, we replaced the regression equation that described the relationship between First Nations 1981 CWB scores and changed in those scores with the equation that describes the relationship between other Canadian communities' 1981 CWB, and changes in those scores.

33 Fortunately, the CWB index is itself a powerful research tool that can be used to this end. It may be employed as a dependent and even an independent variable in a myriad of research projects, providing an efficient means of identifying determinants of well-being.

References

Indian and Northern Affairs Canada. 2002. "2001 Census Linkage Files," Corporate Information Management Directorate, First Nations and Northern Statistics Section. Ottawa: INAC.

_____. 2001. "Band Classification Manual." Corporate Information Management Directorate. Ottawa: INAC. <**www.ainc-inac.gc.ca/pr/pub/fnnrg/2001/bandc_e.pdf**>.

Statistics Canada. 2004. "Consumer Price Index, Historical Summary." Ottawa: Statistics Canada. February 17, 2004. <**www.statcan.ca/english/Pgdb/econ46.htm**>

Statistics Canada. 2002. *2001 Census Dictionary. 2001 Census of Canada.* Catalogue No. 92-378-XPE. Ottawa: Industry Canada.

Statistics Canada. 1999. *1996 Census Dictionary. 1996 Census of Canada.* Catalogue No. 92-351-UPE. Ottawa: Industry Canada.

Statistics Canada. 1992. *1991 Census Handbook. 1991 Census of Canada.* Catalogue No. 92-305E. Ottawa: Supply and Services Canada.

Statistics Canada. 1984. *Census of Canada, 1981, Summary Guide: Sample Population.* Catalogue No. 99-903. Ottawa: Supply and Services Canada.

Appendix—Map

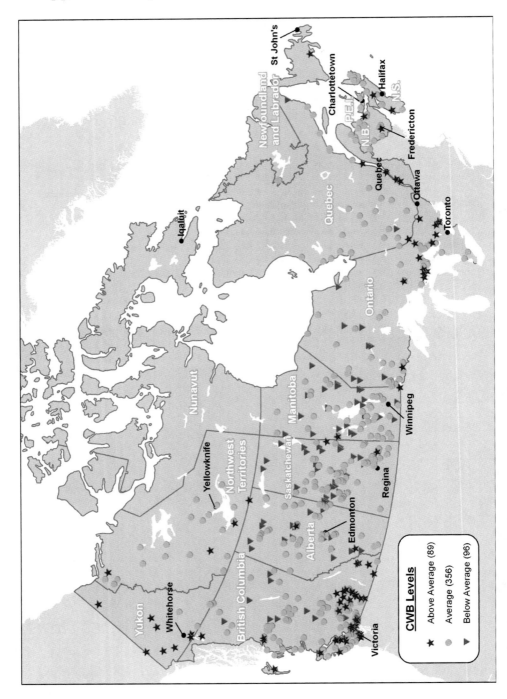

Appendix—Data Tables Related to Selected Figures

Appendix Table 1: First Nations' CWB Scores by Region, 1981–2001

	1981	1986	1991	1996	2001
Atlantic (N=15)	57	58	60	65	68
Quebec (N=21)	49	52	55	59	64
Ontario (N=23)	56	60	65	67	70
Manitoba (N=40)	46	49	51	55	58
Saskatchewan (N=73)	45	48	50	55	58
Alberta (N=27)	49	49	50	55	57
British Columbia (N=97)	58	61	64	69	70
North (N=22)	53	58	64	69	72

Appendix Table 2: Other Canadian Communities' CWB Scores by Region, 1981–2001

	1981	1986	1991	1996	2001
Atlantic (N=654)	67	70	72	73	75
Quebec (N=1,030)	71	73	75	76	79
Ontario (N=220)	78	80	82	82	84
Manitoba (N=194)	73	75	78	78	80
Saskatchewan (N=744)	76	77	78	80	81
Alberta (N=272)	79	80	80	82	83
British Columbia (N=122)	82	83	84	84	85
North (N=35)	58	62	67	71	73

Appendix Table 3: CWB Gaps by Region: 1981–2001 (See Figure 6.15)

	1981	1986	1991	1996	2001
Atlantic	10	11	12	8	8
Quebec	22	21	20	16	15
Ontario	21	19	17	14	14
Manitoba	27	27	26	23	22
Saskatchewan	30	29	28	25	23
Alberta	30	30	30	26	26
British Columbia	25	22	19	16	15
North	5	4	3	2	0

Appendix Table 4: 2001–2041 CWB Projections Based on Trends Observed in the 1981–2001 Intercensal Period (See Figure 6.18)

	1981	2001	2021	2041
First Nations (N=318)	52	64	70	74
Other Canadian Communities (N=3,171)	73	80	84	87
First Nations projected using other communities' 1981–2001 rate of change	52	64	74	80

Appendix Table 5: **2001–2041 Projections Based on Trends Observed in the 1991–2001 Intercensal Period (See Figure 6.19)**

	1991	2001	2011	2021	2031	2041
First Nations (N=399)	58	64	69	73	76	78
Other Canadian Communities (N=3,454)	77	79	82	84	85	86
First Nations projected using other communities' 1991–2001 rate of change	58	64	70	75	78	81

Appendix Table 6: **2001–2041 CWB Projections Based on Trends Observed in the 1996–2001 Intercensal Period (See Figure 6.20)**

	1996	2001	2006	2011	2016	2021	2026	2031	2036	2041
First Nations (N=470)	63	65	66	68	69	70	71	72	72	73
Other Canadian Communities (N=3,643)	77	80	81	83	84	85	85	86	87	87
First Nations projected using other communities' 1996–2001 rate of change	63	65	69	73	76	78	80	82	83	84

Appendix Table 7: Projecting Well-being in First Nations and Other Communities: A Summary (See Figure 6.21)

	1981	1991	1996	2001	2006	2011	2016	2021	2026	2031	2036	2041
First Nations 1981–2001 (N=318)	52			64				70				74
First Nations 1991–2001 (N=399)		58		64		69		73		76		78
First Nations 1996–2001 (N=470)			63	65	66	68	69	70	71	72	72	73
Other Canadian Communities 1981–2001 (N=3,171)	73			80				84				87
Other Canadian Communities 1991–2001 (N=3,454)		77		79		82		84		85		86
Other Canadian Communities 1996–2001 (N=3,643)			77	80	81	83	84	85	86	86	87	87

Appendix Table 8: Income Projections for First Nations and Other Canadian Communities, 2001–2041: A Summary (See Figure 6.22)

	1981	1991	1996	2001	2006	2011	2016	2021	2026	2031	2036	2041
First Nations 1981–2001 (N=318)	36			47				53				55
First Nations 1991–2001 (N=399)		42		48		53		57		60		63
First Nations 1996–2001 (N=470)			45	48	51	53	55	57	58	59	60	61
Other Canadian Communities 1981–2001 (N=3,171)	61			69				74				76
Other Canadian Communities 1991–2001 (N=3,454)		66		69		72		74		75		76
Other Canadian Communities 1996–2001 (N=3,643)			66	69	72	74	75	77	77	78	78	79

Appendix Table 9: Education Projections for First Nations and Other Canadian Communities, 2001–2041: A Summary (See Figure 6.23)

	1981	1991	1996	2001	2006	2011	2016	2021	2026	2031	2036	2041
First Nations 1981–2001 (N=318)	42			69				83				91
First Nations 1991–2001 (N=399)		57		69		77		83		88		91
First Nations 1996–2001 (N=470)			65	69	73	76	78	81	82	84	85	86
Other Canadian Communities 1981–2001 (N=3,171)	60			75				84				90
Other Canadian Communities 1991–2001 (N=3,454)		68		75		80		83		86		87
Other Canadian Communities 1996–2001 (N=3,643)			72	75	78	80	81	82	83	84	84	84

Appendix Table 10: Housing Projections for First Nations and Other Canadian Communities, 2001–2041: A Summary (See Figure 6.24)

	1981	1991	1996	2001	2006	2011	2016	2021	2026	2031	2036	2041
First Nations 1981–2001 (N=318)	63			70				73				73
First Nations 1991–2001 (N=399)		67		71		74		75		76		77
First Nations 1996–2001 (N=470)			70	71	71	72	72	72	72	72	72	72
Other Canadian Communities 1981–2001 (N=3,171)	90			93				94				94
Other Canadian Communities 1991–2001 (N=3,454)		92		93		93		93		93		93
Other Canadian Communities 1996–2001 (N=3,643)			93	93	93	93	93	93	93	93	93	93

Appendix Table 11: Labour Force Activity Projections for First Nations and Other Canadian Communities, 2001–2041: A Summary (See Figure 6.25)

	1981	1991	1996	2001	2006	2011	2016	2021	2026	2031	2036	2041
First Nations 1981–2001 (N=318)	66			70				70				71
First Nations 1991–2001 (N=399)		66		70		72		73		74		74
First Nations 1996–2001 (N=470)			70	70	71	71	71	71	71	71	71	71
Other Canadian Communities 1981–2001 (N=3,171)	79			81		81		82		82		84
Other Canadian Communities 1991–2001 (N=3,454)		80		81		81		82		82		82
Other Canadian Communities 1996–2001 (N=3,643)			79	81	82	83	84	84	85	85	85	86

7

Applying the Community Well-being Index and the Human Development Index to Inuit in Canada

Sacha Senécal, Erin O'Sullivan, Éric Guimond,
and Sharanjit Uppal

Introduction

Recent trends in Aboriginal research have placed much emphasis on examining the living conditions existing within Canada's Aboriginal populations and communities. This interest has generated a great deal of research, as we have outlined in the preceding chapters. This research has included investigations of well-being[1] which have measured and compared the well-being of First Nations in Canada with that of other Canadians and have assessed disparities over time using an extension of the United Nations Development Programme's (UNDP) Human Development Index (HDI) (See Chapter 3). Of particular interest is the challenge to produce a measure of the well-being of populations residing within communities. To tackle the issue, researchers have developed the First Nations Community Well-Being Index (CWB) (See Chapter 6).

These initial research developments have proved very influential in the policy research environment in Canada and have been widely integrated in the body of knowledge of Aboriginal living conditions. They have also lead to several questions which warrant further research. Amongst the key issues raised was the inclusion of other types of Aboriginal populations and communities, such as Inuit and Inuit communities within the larger grouping of "other Canadians" to which First Nations were compared. It is also interesting to look at such Aboriginal communities and the peoples in those communities types in relation to one another and in relation to other Aboriginal and non-Aboriginal communities. Widening the scope of our analysis will push forward our understanding of Aboriginal well-being. This is particularly true for the Inuit, as they are often left out of policy research and policy development. They represent a small proportion of the Canadian population and they tend to live in very remote areas of the country. Inuit numbers are often "drowned" in the sea of First Nations numbers, which vastly surpass them. As a result, the specificity of Inuit issues, even in cases where research is focused on the wider "Aboriginal" concept, is often not clearly assessed.

This chapter will address this issue by providing an extension of the CWB and HDI with a specific focus on Inuit residing in four regions of the Canadian North.

Inuit Population and Inuit Communities in Canada

Of the 976,305 individuals who identified themselves as Aboriginal[2] in the 2001 Census, about 5% or 45,070 reported that they were Inuit (Statistics Canada, 2003a). The majority (83%) of Inuit are living in communities situated in the Canadian Arctic. About half of the population lives in Nunavut, while Quebec's northern portion (Nunavik) is home to 19%. The northern coastal and south-eastern areas of Labrador and the Inuvialuit region in the northwest corner of the Northwest Territories are home to most of the remainder of the Inuit population with 7%, in each of these regions (Health Canada, 2004).

The Inuit Tapiriit Kanatami (ITK) is the national Inuit organization in Canada representing the four Inuit regions located in two provinces and two territories and living within four land claim areas—Nunatsiavut (Labrador), Nunavik (northern Quebec), Nunavut, and the Inuvialuit region in the Northwest Territories.[3] ITK represents the interest of those Inuit living in one of the 53 communities dispersed throughout these regions: 6 in Labrador,[4] 14 in Nunavik, 27 in Nunavut and 6 in the Northwest Territories.

This chapter uses two distinct approaches to explore the Inuit reality. In the first section dealing with the HDI of Inuit-inhabited areas, a geographic-based model is used to identify areas of the North which contain large portions of Inuit inhabitants. Limitations in basic data source have prevented us from being able to perfectly match the land claims areas. As such, these areas do not match perfectly the Inuit land claims areas but are fairly close. The second portion of the chapter will apply the CWB concepts to 51 selected Inuit communities representing all of Canada's Inuit communities with a population size of 65 and over. This was the population utilized in the CWB assessment of other Aboriginal populations in Canada (see Chapter 6).

The Inuit Human Development Index

The Strategic Research and Analysis Directorate (SRAD) at Indian and Northern Affairs Canada (INAC) introduced an application of the United Nations Development Programs Human Development Index to the Registered Indian Population of Canada (Beavon & Cooke, 2003). This was considered an important first step in measuring the relative well-being of Aboriginal and non-Aboriginal populations and in allowing to monitor improvements associated with well-being experienced over time by this important part of the Aboriginal populations of Canada. This measure, focused on educational attainment, average annual income, and life expectancy illustrated the gaps between Registered Indians, a sub-portion of the total Aboriginal populations of Canada, and that other Canadians (Beavon &

Cooke, 2003). A further study looking at HDI scores from 1981 to 2001 has also illustrated that although the gap in overall HDI scores between these two populations declined somewhat during the period, large disparities still remained (Cooke, Beavon, and McHardy, 2004).

As part of this research, Registered Indians were compared with a reference population defined as "... Canadians who are not registered, and includes both non-registered First Nations, Inuit and Métis people, as well as non-Aboriginal people" (Cooke, Beavon, and McHardy, 2004, 6). This section will highlight the specific human development of the Inuit-inhabited areas of Northern Canada, thus partly bridging some of the limitations of previous efforts.

Applying the HDI to Inuit: Challenge and Solution

While applying the methodology developed for the Registered Indian population to the Inuit seems like a logical and straightforward idea, in fact such an application is more complicated than would appear. As is often the case when dealing with Inuit issues, data availability is again an impediment. Numerous data sources do not adequately cover the Canadian territories, which are home to a large portion of Inuit. Additionally, Aboriginal identity of individuals is not collected by most provincial and territorial vital statistics programs. Hence, basic Inuit demographic and health indicators, such as life expectancy at birth, cannot be estimated nationally through standard data sources and methodologies for the Inuit (Wilkins et al., forthcoming). There were previously no national estimates of life expectancy, a key component of the HDI, for the Inuit.

The SRAD, in partnership with the Health Analysis and Measurement Group at Statistics Canada, and the Health Information and Analysis Division at Health Canada have developed a geographic-based approach as a means to fill this important health data gap for Inuit.

With this geographic-based methodology, it becomes possible to calculate HDI components and scores for the areas identified as Inuit-inhabited. While the resulting scores do not represent all Inuit of Canada, and while non-Inuit are also included to some level within the calculation of the scores, the large concentration of Inuit in Northern areas of the country, combined with the fact that they represent the vast majority of the population of these areas, are more than supportive for applying this methodology, especially in the absence of adequate alternatives.

Methodology

In order to apply the UNDP methodology to the Inuit, an adaptation of the measures comprised in the international HDI had to be used because of data availability issues. This adaptation is similar to that required to calculate an HDI for Registered Indians and involves substituting the original HDI's per capita GDP and education indicators with appropriate measures from the Census (for an in-depth description of the methodology see Chapter 3).

Table 7.1: HDI and Component Measure Scores, Inuit, Registered Indians, and Other Canadians, 1991–2001

Indicator	Population	1991	1996	2001
Life Expectancy at Birth (years)	Inuit	67.8	67.7	67.1
	Registered Indians	70.6	72.2	72.9
	Other Canadians	77.9	78.5	78.7
Life Expectancy Index	Inuit	0.713	0.712	0.674
	Registered Indians	0.760	0.786	0.799
	Other Canadians	0.881	0.891	0.896
Proportion Completed Grade 9 or Higher[1]	Inuit	0.585	0.700	0.739
	Registered Indians	0.721	0.781	0.825
	Other Canadians	0.863	0.881	0.903
Proportion Completed High School or Higher[2]	Inuit	0.469	0.520	0.544
	Registered Indians	0.456	0.514	0.567
	Other Canadians	0.680	0.717	0.754
Educational Attainment Index	Inuit	0.546	0.640	0.674
	Registered Indians	0.633	0.692	0.739
	Other Canadians	0.802	0.826	0.853
Average Annual Income (Year 2000 Constant Dollars)[3]	Inuit	11,182	13,139	15,125
	Registered Indians	8,243	8,887	10,094
	Other Canadians	20,072	19,989	22,489
Income Index	Inuit	0.819	0.826	0.838
	Registered Indians	0.725	0.737	0.759
	Other Canadians	0.873	0.873	0.892
HDI Score	Inuit	0.693	0.726	0.738
	Registered Indians	0.706	0.739	0.765
	Other Canadians	0.852	0.863	0.880

Notes:

(1) The proportion completed high school or higher is estimated by the ratio of the population with a secondary school graduation certificate, some post-secondary or trades education, or some university with or without degree, to the population aged 19 years and over.

(2) The proportion completed grade 9 is the population aged 15 years and over completed grade 9 or higher, divided by the total population aged 15 years and over.

(3) The average annual income is the average income from all sources, for the total population with or without income, for the year before the Census enumeration, adjusted by the Statistics Canada Consumer Price Index to year 2000 constant Dollars.

Sources: Statistics Canada, custom tabulation, unpublished data, (Statistics Canada), 1995 and 1998; Rowe and Norris, 1995; Nault et al., 1993; Norris, Kerr, and Nault, 1996; DIAND, 1998; Verma, Michalowski, and Gauvin 2003; authors' calculations.

In order to extract adequate data on life expectancy for Inuit, a geographic approach was used. First, areas with a high proportion of Inuit residents were identified. For a given Census subdivision[5] (CSD), if the observed proportion of residents who were of Inuit identity was greater than or equal to a chosen cut-off point (33%), that census subdivision was then included in the list of Inuit-inhabited areas. The census subdivisions selected were then grouped into four regions: the Inuvialuit region (Northwest Territories, 6 communities), Nunavut (the entire territory, 28 communities), Nunavik (Quebec, 14 communities), and Nunatsiavut (Newfoundland and Labrador, 6 communities).[6]

Second, Census data and recorded deaths from death records are then used to compute life expectancy, education, and income per capita measures, for the Inuit-inhabited areas for the years 1991, 1996, and 2001 (for more details of the methodology, see Wilkins et al., forthcoming).

Results

Table 7.1 presents the basic HDI results for Inuit, Registered Indians, and other Canadians as well as the component scores from which the CWB scores are derived. In 2001, the Inuit of northern Canada were experiencing lower levels of Human Development than other Canadians[7] with an average score that was 0.14 lower. This placed the Inuit just below Registered Indians in terms of the overall HDI score for 2001.

Figure 7.1 (page 154) shows the average HDI scores for Inuit and other Canadians for 1991, 1996, and 2001. The pattern of HDI scores over time reveal that, while a reduction of the gap was observed between 1991 and 2001, this gap reduction is entirely based on the large increase of HDI scores between 1991 and 1996. So, while the Inuit HDI scores were going up between 1996 and 2001, it was not growing as fast as that of other Canadian. As a consequence, the HDI gap has actually been increasing since 1996.

While there are some clear cultural connections between all Inuit in the country, there are recent historical differences between the Inuit of each of the four land claims areas. Such differences are also reflected in living conditions as measured with the HDI. **Figure 7.2** (page 154) clearly illustrates that there are large disparities across the four Inuit regions with scores ranging from a low of 0.683 in Nunavik to a high of 0.802 in the Inuvialuit region.

To further understand the variations outlined in HDI scores between Inuit regions, one needs to look at which components seem to be responsible for these observed differences. **Figure 7.3** (page 155) shows that while all three components exhibit important differences from region to region, the education component is the component for which the largest variation is observed with Nunavik showing the lowest scores (0.683) while the Inuvialuit region has the highest (0.802). While the Inuvialuit region consistently shows the highest scores for all HDI components, Nunavik places last in education and life expectancy while Nunatsiavut has the lowest income score.

Figure 7.1: HDI Scores, Inuit and Other Canadians, 1991–2001

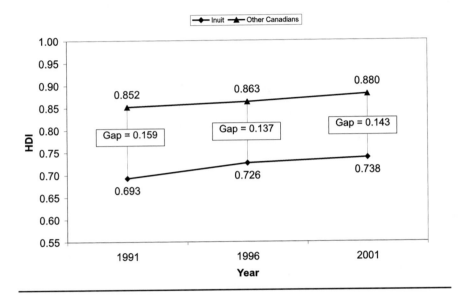

Figure 7.2: Average HDI scores by Inuit region, 2001

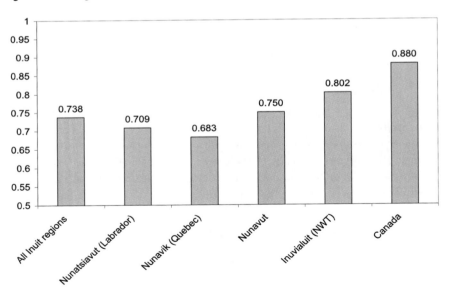

Figure 7.3: HDI Score by Inuit Region, 2001

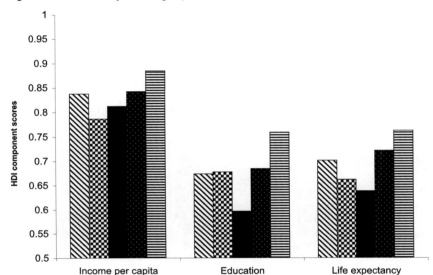

Given that the HDI is a composite index, there can be differences in the way that each component behaves over time. **Figure 7.4** (page 156) presents the average change over time[8] between 1991 and 2001 by HDI components and shows clear variations across components in the degree of change. Three very different patterns emerge: (1) gaps in income have remained similar to what they were in 1991; (2) Inuit have made significant gains in education level; and (3) the life expectancy gap is actually increasing between Inuit and other Canadians. The latter is a source for concern as it highlights the fact that Inuit have been experiencing slight declines in life expectancy in the 1991–2001 period (Wilkins et al., forthcoming). The importance of education is clearly outlined in this figure, as all of the overall gap reduction in HDI between 1991 and 2001 can actually be attributed to this component.

Discussion

Generally speaking, the levels of HDI in Inuit-inhabited areas have increased since 1991 and the gap between the population of these areas and other Canadians has decreased overall. However, this gap reduction occurred mostly between 1991 and 1996. Since 1996, the progress experienced in well-being in Inuit-inhabited areas has not been on par with that of other Canadians, which has lead to a slight gap increase between 1996 and 2001. One the one hand, when broken down into HDI components, this gap increase is mostly due to life expectancy scores which have failed to rise as quickly as that of other Canadians. Education, on the other hand, is one area where significant progress has been achieved. Levels of

Figure 7.4: HDI Component Change Over Time, 1991-2001

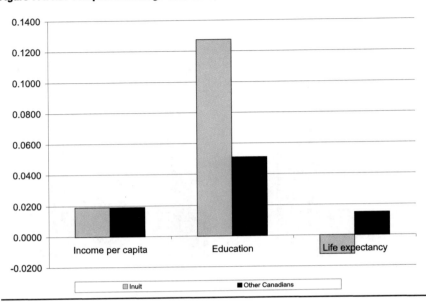

well-being as well as individual components have been shown to vary quite significantly from one Inuit-inhabited region to the next. Such differences can likely be associated with specific historical, political, and socio-economic issues which are associated with each land-claim area. Regional variations observed can further stress the need to look at issues on a region-by-region basis.

Inuit regions across the country are going through significant changes. Signing of land claim agreements, establishment of government structure, and economic development—to name a few—all have clear impacts on the populations. In the case of some of the Inuit-inhabited areas, these changes can lead to important migration of workers, such as a fairly large contingent of educated workers migrating from the south to Inuit-inhabited areas. The shifting pattern of Inuit versus non-Inuit population contained within each Inuit-inhabited area is likely one potential explanation for some of the patterns observed. Other research has illustrated the differences between Inuit and non-Inuit in the North (see Wilkins et al., forthcoming, for a review of key socio-economic indicators). Further research should be aimed at assessing the specific well-being of Inuit and non-Inuit living in Inuit land claims areas. Additionally, research aimed at Inuit living "in the south" could also help fill in some of the limitations of the research presented here.

As discussed in previous chapters, we have used here the term "well-being" to refer to the overall welfare of a population in a way more or less synonymous with the UNDP's "human development." It is worth mentioning that the broad measures used here do not necessarily provide a clear and complete picture of what is commonly meant by well-being. Most notably, subjective and qualitative dimensions associated with one's well-being are not easily addressed by such broad data-driven indicators. Additionally, important elements such as preservation of culture and language; relationship with one's family, community, or the land; and spirituality, as well as numerous additional aspects of overall well-being, are also not addressed here. Despite its limitations, the HDI does show that there are important and continuing differences in the average achievement of Inuit and other Canadians in life expectancy, income, and educational attainment. While these do not capture well-being in its entirety, they do represent important issues for research and policy development.

International Human Development Index Ranking of the Inuit

In its annual Human Development Report, the UNDP calculates several indicators of development and ranks countries according to their HDI scores. As part of the Registered Indian adaptation of the HDI, the SRAD has adjusted its HDI estimates to be able to estimate where the Registered Indian population would be placed among the countries ranked by the UNDP (See Beavon and Cooke, 2003, and Chapter 3 in this volume for more detail in terms of methodology. We have followed the same methodology).

Appendix Table 1 (pages 170–172) presents the ranking of Inuit, Registered Indians, and the reference population among the countries included in the Human Development Report 2003 (UNDP, 2003). The population living in the Inuit-inhabited areas rank approximately 60th, alongside countries such as Malaysia, Panama, Macedonia, and the Libyan Arab Jamahiriya. This ranking places these Inuit-inhabited areas at the top of countries considered to have "medium human development" by the UNDP; higher than that of the Registered Indians on-reserve, but lower than those living off-reserve.

The Inuit Community Well-being Index

In this book we present the collective research of the teams working on living conditions both from the Strategic Research Directorate at Indian and Northern Affairs and the First Nations Cohesion Project—Aboriginal Policy Research Consortium at The University of Western Ontario. This research has focused on individual First Nations communities. As such, the Community Well-Being Index (CWB) was developed as a complement to the Registered Indian Human Development Index (See Chapter 6 of this volume). While the HDI measures the well-being of Registered Indians at the national and regional levels, the CWB measures well-being at the community level. The CWB combines indicators of educational attainment, income, housing conditions, and labour force activity from the Census of Canada to produce well-being "scores" for individual communities.

As part of this research, First Nations communities were compared with "other Canadian Communities," which included Inuit and Métis communities (see

---

Housing in Inuit Communities: Quality and Quantity

The CWB housing score is comprised of two distinct measures: quantity and quality. The resulting scores presented here are thus an aggregation of these two measures, each equally weighted.

Upon assessing each sub-component separately, it can be seen that Inuit communities typically show lower levels of quantity than of quality. The average Inuit community score for quantity was 0.69 while the sub-component score for quality was 0.75. This specific pattern is different than what is seen in either First Nations or other Canadian communities where quality is usually more of an issue than quantity. Even when looking only at Northern non-Inuit communities (either First Nations or other Canadian communities), we see that while overall scores are lower than in the south, quality typically is more of an issue than quantity.

This pattern highlights the significance of the issues associated with crowding in Inuit communities. The Strategic Research and Analysis Directorate at INAC has partnered with the Inuit Tapiriit Kanatami to produce reports on several main themes linked to Inuit communities. These reports point to the high proportions of multiple family households and the high fecundity levels of Inuit (INAC and ITK, forthcoming).

Chapter 8). In this section of our chapter, we focus specifically on Inuit communities of Northern Canada, which will be assessed using CWB methodology, and then compared with both First Nations communities and other Canadian communities, now defined as non-First Nations and non-Inuit communities.

Methodology

Out of 4,685 communities included in the original CWB database, 51 communities were tagged as Inuit communities.[9,10] These 51 communities have an average size of 1,021 inhabitants, but it should be noted that they present variations in size with the largest showing a population of 7,969 compared to the smallest at 114 in 2001. **Table 7.2** shows the distribution of communities by region along with an indication of the average size. A few of these communities have road access to southern points or even neighbouring villages, but the vast majority of Inuit communities are accessible only by air, which impacts access to goods and services and as well as the cost of living. For most communities, a large majority of the population is Inuit.

The initial scores calculated for Canadian communities as part of the CWB research project were used as is. It is important to note that scores reflect the entire population of a community, regardless of their ethnicity and/or cultural background of its inhabitants.[11] Additional information pertaining to the methodology of the CWB is available in Chapter 6 of this book. While that chapter also provides a lengthy discussion of the limitations of the CWB model, the main issues should be highlighted again here. First, the CWB focuses primarily on the socio-economic aspects of well-being. Limitations of the Canadian Census prevented the incorporation into the model of equally important aspects of well-

Table 7.2: Community Characteristics by Region

Inuit Region	Number of Communities	Average Population	Standard Deviation	Smallest Community	Largest Community	Total Population	Average Proportion of Inuit Population (%)
Labrador	6	1,767	3,057	215	7,969	10,603	76
Nunavik	14	688	517	159	1,932	9,632	93
Nunavut	25	1,063	1,007	163	5,236	26,583	91
Inuvialuit	6	876	1,029	114	2,894	5,254	76
Total	51	1,021	1,303	114	7,969	52,072	86

Source: Statistics Canada, 2001 Census

being such as physical, psychological, and cultural well-being. It is also important to note that the socioeconomic indicators of which the index is comprised may not capture fully the reality of the Inuit communities' economic situation. Many Inuit are still heavily involved in traditional economic pursuits, which, although contributing to their material well-being, are not manifested directly in monetary income or paid employment (Usher, Duhaime, and Searles, 2003).

Community Type Comparisons

For the purpose of this report, Inuit communities are compared to First Nations and other Canadian communities. The distinction between First Nations and other Canadian communities is based on INAC's 2001 geography hierarchy (2002). The INAC listing of communities includes the legal list of Indian reserves and Indian settlements as well as a selection of other CSD types selected from Saskatchewan, Yukon, and Northwest Territories. It is the same as the listing used by the department to report on reserve population counts from the Census.[12] A total of 539 First Nations were available for analysis for the purpose of this study. Other Canadian communities exclude those communities identified as Inuit communities or as First Nations communities, for a total of 4,095 communities. Both First Nations and other Canadian communities were located in all Canadian territories and provinces with the exception of Nunavut which contained Inuit communities only.

The purpose of comparing Inuit communities to these two groupings separately is to avoid inducing bias. As First Nations typically present lower levels of well-being (McHardy and O'Sullivan, 2004) and because they are sufficient to influence overall Canadian scores, a decision was made to present comparisons of Inuit communities to these two sets of communities separately.

Time Series Component

When assessing disparities between communities in terms of well-being, it is important to take time into consideration. Demographic changes, migration to

Figure 7.5: Average Community Well-being Score by Community Type, 2001

Average CWB Score

Inuit (N=51)   First Nations (N=539)   Other (N=4,095)

Figure 7.6: Distribution of Inuit, First Nations, and Other Canadian Communities by Community Well-being Score, 2001

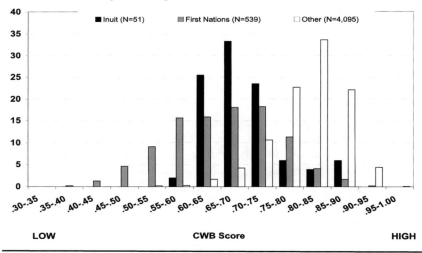

and from communities, and economic developments are just a few of the factors which, over time, may affect well-being either positively or negatively.

In order to reflect such potential changes in the well-being of communities, CWB scores have been calculated for three censuses—1991, 1996, and 2001. This timeseries obviously involves concrete steps to ensure that communities may be compared adequately over time. It is worth mentioning that out of the Inuit communities initially available for analysis in the CWB database, all 51 were also deemed as "consistent geographic entities" over time. This was neither the case for First Nations nor other Canadian communities, several of which could

Figure 7.7: Average Community Well-being Score by Inuit Region, 2001

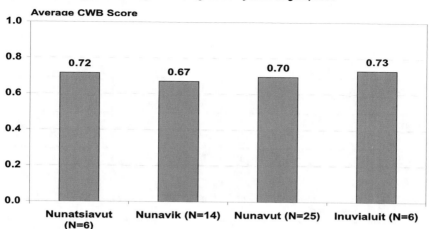

not be tracked over time. For an in-depth description of the steps taken to ensure comparability, as well as details on the resulting set of communities, see Chapter 6 in this book, and O'Sullivan and McHardy, 2004.

Results

Overall Community Well-being Scores

Figure 7.5 indicates that the average CWB score for Inuit communities is slightly higher than that of First Nations, but that both are much lower than the average score for other Canadian communities. This initial finding points to the overall lower level of well-being in Inuit communities and First Nations when compared to other Canadian communities.

Figure 7.6 further illustrates the clear disparities between Inuit, First Nations, and other Canadian communities. Inuit communities are typically distributed towards the middle point of the CWB range. When compared with other Canadian communities, it can also be observed that their CWB scores are higher overall than those of First Nations who are more concentrated towards the bottom of the range of scores. It is also worth mentioning that Inuit communities, while showing significant disparities in their levels of well-being, are more densely concentrated than First Nations, whose range of scores is wider and spreads across more categories. In other words, Inuit communities tend to share more "even levels" of well-being than First Nations, for which the gap between "have" and "have not" communities is wider.

Inuit communities can vary in terms of well-being across regions. As such, looking at the national picture may in fact hide such interregional variations. **Figure 7.7** presents average CWB scores for Inuit communities by region. It can be seen that Nunavik presents the lowest average CWB when compared to other regions.

Table 7.3: Community Well-being Index (CWB): Distribution of Inuit Communities by Inuit Region, 2001

Region	CWB Score Range							Total
	0.55 – 0.60	0.60 – 0.65	0.65 – 0.70	0.70 – 0.75	0.75 – 0.80	0.80 – 0.85	0.85 – 0.90	
Nunatsiavut	0	1	2	1	1	0	1	6
Nunavik	1	6	3	3	1	0	0	14
Nunavut	0	5	10	6	1	2	1	25
Inuvialuit	0	1	2	2	0	0	1	6
Total	1	13	17	12	3	2	3	51

Table 7.4: Average Community Well-being Component Score by Community Type, Canada, 2001

Community Type	Income	Education	Housing	Labour
Inuit	0.57	0.64	0.71	0.80
First Nation	0.47	0.68	0.69	0.69
Other Canadian	0.70	0.76	0.93	0.81

Table 7.5: Descriptive Statistics of the CWB Index Across Time for Inuit Communities (N=51)

Census Year	Minimum CWB Score	Maximum CWB Score	Average CWB Score	Standard Deviation
1991	0.50	0.85	0.63	0.078
1996	0.58	0.84	0.67	0.069
2001	0.57	0.87	0.69	0.068

Table 7.6: Community Well-being Gaps between Community Types, 1991–2001

Gap Between Community	1991	1996	2001
Other Canadian–Inuit	0.14	0.10	0.11
Other Canadian–First Nations	0.19	0.15	0.15
First Nations–Inuit	-0.05	-0.05	-0.04

Table 7.7: Descriptive Statistics of the Evolution of Community Well-being Scores by Community Type, Between 1991 and 2001

Community Type	Minimum Variation	Maximum Variation	Average Variation	Standard Deviation
Inuit	-0.06	0.14	0.06	0.04
First Nation	-0.07	0.29	0.07	0.06
Other Canadian	-0.17	0.26	0.03	0.04

Figure 7.8: Community Well-being Average Component Scores by Inuit Region, 2001

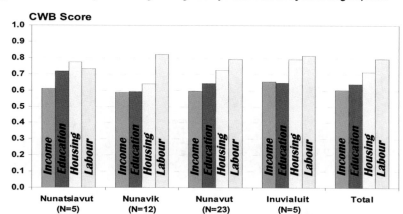

Table 7.3 further breaks down the distribution of Inuit communities by looking at the distribution of CWB scores by Inuit region. While it deals with very small numbers, it can nevertheless be observed that well-being scores are not distributed evenly across regions, with Nunavik showing lower scores. This finding points to the distribution of CWB scores across Inuit communities in Canada. This kind of disparity between lowest and highest communities in terms of their CWB scores was also previously observed to an even higher degree with First Nations communities (Chapter 6; McHardy and O'Sullivan, 2004). While the average CWB score for all 51 Inuit communities is 0.69, the range of scores is actually quite large, going from a low of 0.58 to a high of 0.87.[13]

Component Scores

As variations are outlined between Inuit regions on the overall CWB score, it is interesting to assess which components of the CWB may be responsible for the overall observed differences. **Figure 7.8** shows that while all components show some variations from region to region, education and housing are the two components for which the larger variations are observed. For both of these components, lowest scores are observed in Nunavik which explains the overall lower scores obtained by that region. It is worth mentioning, however, that Nunavik shows the highest score on the labour component of the CWB. Another interesting element is observed for the Labrador communities, which show the highest score on the education component, while also presenting the lowest labour characteristics. This last finding highlights the specific economic and labour market characteristics of this region in contrast to other Inuit regions.

When assessing individual CWB components by community type, interesting differences are highlighted. Differences by component are not systematic between the three community types examined in this report. **Table 7.4** shows that Inuit communities fall about midway between First Nations and other Canadian communities on the income component, slightly behind First Nations in education,

Figure 7.9: CWB Average Scores by Community Type, 1991–2001

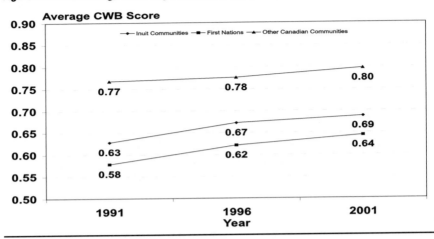

slightly above First Nations in terms of housing, and very close to other Canadian communities on labour force. When looking more closely at these patterns, it can further be seen that First Nation minimum scores on each component are much lower than those of Inuit communities, which tend to be closer to the minimum observed for other Canadian communities.

Community Well-being Time Series

The evolution of the CWB score in Inuit communities between 1991 and 2001 is presented in **Table 7.5** (page 162). It can be seen that while scores progressed during that period, much of the growth is observed between 1991 and 1996. This finding mirrors what was previously found for First Nations (Chapter 6; O'Sullivan and McHardy, 2004).

The increase in well-being of Inuit, First Nations, and other Canadian communities is further compared in **Figure 7.9** (this page) and **Table 7.6** (page 162). An almost perfect parallelism is found between the two types of Aboriginal communities along with a closure of the gaps with Other Canadian communities in the first intercensal period (1991–1996) followed by a somewhat more static gap in the subsequent period (1996–2001).

When looking at the individual evolution of CWB scores for Inuit communities in the 1991–2001 time period, it can be seen that the vast majority (47 communities) have seen some form of increase in their well-being ,while just a few communities (4) have actually experienced a decline, with two of these actually showing a very small decline of only 0.01. **Table 7.7** (page 162) further assesses changes between 1991 and 2001 and shows that the average variation of scores for Inuit communities is comparable to that of First Nations and that both are experiencing higher positive variations than other Canadian communities. It can also be seen that the highest increase in Inuit communities is much smaller than

Figure 7.10: Inuit Communities CWB Distribution Over Time: 1991-2001

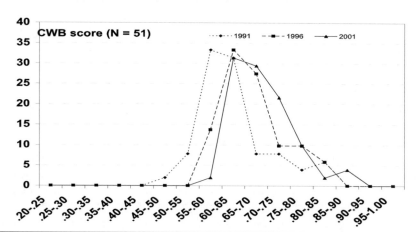

that of both First Nations and other Canadian communities. On the other hand, the largest decline amongst Inuit communities is similar to the largest decline in First Nations, with both showing smaller declines than other Canadian communities.

Over time and in general, the distribution of the CWB scores of Inuit communities present a shift to the right, while retaining the same shape, which can be seen in **Figure 7.10**. This is associated with an "across the board" improvement of well-being in Inuit communities and is consistent with what is observed for both First Nations and other Canadian communities (see Chapter 6; O'Sullivan and McHardy, 2004, for these data).

Discussion

The CWB index provides us with a tool that can be replicated over time. This offers us an additional tool in our attempt to move towards a deeper understanding of the socio-economic conditions in Inuit communities and of their well-being relative to First Nations and to the broader Canadian population. The descriptive statistics contained herein illustrate clearly the marked disparity in socio-economic well-being between Inuit communities and other Canadian communities. This places Inuit communities closer to First Nations than to other Canadian communities in terms of well-being. These statistics also highlight the great disparities that exist between Inuit communities, with some communities enjoying fairly high levels of well-being, while others are still facing difficulties.

This report highlights the relative well-being of Inuit communities with respect to Canada's First Nations and other Canadian communities. We would caution readers to keep in mind that these Inuit communities have characteristics that may influence this direct comparison. First, all Inuit communities are located very far from large urban centres, in isolated northern locations. This is associated with high costs, especially when it comes to goods which have to be "imported" from southern locations. As such, the high cost of living probably has an impact on income, which is incidentally the lowest component score in Inuit communities. We can also observe that there is a widely acknowledged role for the traditional economy that still exists in many communities (Usher, Duhaime, and Searles, 2003). This may soften the impact of cost of living on the overall well-being.

Conclusion

This chapter combines the results of two research projects that we carried out. We hope that they point to a coherent picture of the living conditions of the inhabitants of Canada's northernmost areas. Key socio-economic indicators represented within both the Human Development Index and the Community Well-Being Index clearly illustrate the gap that inhabitants of the North are experiencing today. Results also show the progress accomplished to date, the areas where improvements have occurred, as well as key areas presenting further challenges.

While the projects presented here can be seen as first steps in establishing a better understanding of the dynamics of socio-economic progress within the North, further research is—as usual—required to refine this understanding. Key steps required would be to dig deeper in the distribution of well-being between the Inuit and non-Inuit inhabitants of the North, to include and consider additional elements related to the specific cultural, social, economic, and historical realities of the Inuit, and to assess qualitative elements associated with the core concepts of well-being.

In this chapter, Inuit communities are compared to all First Nations and all other Canadian communities, regardless of size and location. If, as proposed above, the specific geography of Inuit communities has an impact on well-being, it would be interesting to compare Inuit with other northern communities. This work was done by White and Maxim for the First Nations of the south (see Chapter 8) and proved to be very valuable for isolating geographic and related influences. Future research plans are aimed at this very issue and will try to establish a comparable community framework which could help in refining the findings of this study. This comparable research and further analysis aimed at causes and correlates of community well-being are required. Elements such as the cultural composition of communities in terms of Inuit versus other cultural/ethnic identities, isolation, size, and the like would help refine our understanding of the relative well-being of Inuit communities.

Despite their inherent limitations, these two projects contribute to the body of knowledge available on the well-being of Inuit. Limitations in data availability and the tendency of numerous research programs to be focused solely on First Nations population have in the past contributed to the lack of public awareness on key issues associated with Inuit well-being. It is hoped that the focus of research such as the ones presented here can elicit the interest of stakeholders within the policy research area so that a clearer picture can emerge. Along those lines, improvements of available data sources on the Inuit are seen as one of the key in helping researchers and stakeholders in their quest for knowledge.

Endnotes

1 Note that throughout the literature, several concepts such as living conditions, quality of life, life chances, living standards, human development, social progress, and well-being are often used to refer to similar socio-economic concepts (see Cooke, 2005). Within the present chapter, the terms "well-being" and "living conditions" will be used interchangeably to refer to such concepts. Where appropriate, the terms Human Development Index and Community Well-Being Index will be used to refer to specific indicators introduced here.

2 In the Census, the Aboriginal identity population refers to those persons who reported identifying with at least one Aboriginal group, i.e. North American Indian, Métis or Inuit (Eskimo), and/or those who reported being a Treaty Indian or a Registered Indian as defined by the *Indian Act* of Canada and/or who were members of an Indian Band or First Nation.

3 For more information on ITK, visit <**www.itk.ca**>, and for additional information on the history and current situation of Inuit communities, see ITK, 2003.

4 The case of Happy Valley–Goose Bay is worth discussing in more details. While it is technically not within the boundaries if the Nunatsiavut land claim settlement, a large portion of its residents are Inuit. Through discussions with ITK and with the Labrador Inuit Association, it was decided to include Happy Valley–Goose Bay in the list of Labrador Inuit communities.

5 Census subdivision is the general term used by Statistics Canada for municipalities (as determined by provincial and territorial legislations) or their equivalent (Statistics Canada, 2003b).

6 See Wilkins et al., for a detailed list of areas included.

7 Other Canadians is defined here as that portion of Canada's population which is not a registered Indian and is not residing in the Inuit-inhabited areas defined in the context of this research. It does include non-registered Indians, Métis, as well as Inuit residing outside of Inuit-inhabited areas.

8 Change over time is calculating by subtracting the 2001 score from the 1991 score for each component. A positive value thus illustrates an increase in the component score from 1991 to 2001, while a negative value represents a decrease.

9 Two communities from the Kitikmeot region of Nunavut (Bathurst Inlet and Umingmaktok, which are identified by ITK as Inuit communities) were excluded from the analysis, as their population was under the threshold of 65 used in this study.

10 The actual list of communities can be consulted in a previous version of this research posted at: <**www.ainc-inac.gc.ca/pr/ra/cwb/icc/index_e.html**>.

11 Inuit communities are to a large degree inhabited by individuals of Inuit ancestry and/or identity. In this analysis, only four communities had less than 75% of their population self-identifying as Inuit.

12 With two exceptions: Aklavik and Inuvik (in the Northwest Territories), which are both First Nations and Inuit communities, have been tagged here as Inuit communities. This explains why the First Nations total is lower than that presented in other chapters of this book.

13 See Appendix A for a map representing CWB levels of Inuit communities for all regions.

References

Beavon, D., and Cooke, M. 2003. "An Application of the United Nations Human Development Index to Registered Indians in Canada." In White, J.P., Maxim, P., and Beavon, D. n *Aboriginal Conditions*. Vancouver: UBC Press.

Cooke, M. 2005. "The First Nations Community Well-Being Index (CWB): A Conceptual Review." Catalogue No. R2-400/2005E-PDF. Strategic Research and Analysis Division. Ottawa: Indian and Northern Affairs Canada.

Cooke, M., Beavon, D., and McHardy, M. 2004. "Measuring the Well-Being of Aboriginal People: An Application of the United Nations' Human Development Index to Registered Indians in Canada, 1981–2001." Catalogue No. R2-345/2001E-PDF., Strategic Research and Analysis Division. Ottawa: Indian and Northern Affairs Canada.

Cooke, M., and Beavon, D. 2004. "Measuring the Well-being of Canada's Aboriginal Peoples: Application of the UNDP Human Development Index to Canada's Aboriginal People." Technical Appendix. Unpublished report.

Indian and Northern Affairs Canada—Inuit Tapiriit Kanatami, (forthcoming). "The size and type of Inuit households: Changes and trends from 1981–2001." Strategic Research and Analysis Division. Ottawa: Indian and Northern Affairs Canada.

Indian and Northern Affairs Canada. 2002. "2001 Census Linkage Files." Corporate Information Management Directorate, First Nations and Northern Statistics Section. Ottawa: INAC.

Inuit Tapiritt Kanatami. 2003. Inuit Kanatami/Inuit of Canada. Retrieved 12 Jan. 2007. <**www.itk. ca**>.

Nault, F., Chen, J., George, M.V., and Norris, M.J. 1993. "Population Projections of Registered Indians, 1991–2016." Report prepared by the Population Projections Section, Demography Division, Statistics Canada, for Indian and Northern Affairs Canada. Ottawa: INAC.

McHardy, M., and O'Sullivan, E. (2004). "First Nations Community Well-Being in Canada: The Community Well-Being Index (CWB), 2001." Catalogue No. R2-344/2001E., Strategic Research and Analysis Division. Ottawa: Indian and Northern Affairs Canada.

Norris, M.J., Kerr, D., and Nault, F. 1995. "Projections of the Population with Aboriginal Identity in Canada, 1991–2016." Report prepared by the Population Projections Section, Demography Division, Statistics Canada, for the Royal Commission on Aboriginal Peoples. Ottawa: Canada Mortgage and Housing Corporation and the Royal Commission on Aboriginal Peoples.

O'Sullivan, E., and McHardy, M. 2004. "The Community Well-Being (CWB) Index: Disparity in Well-Being Between First Nations and Other Canadian Communities Over Time." Catalogue No. R2-349/2004E. Strategic Research and Analysis Division. Ottawa: Indian and Northern Affairs Canada, Rowe, G., and Norris, M.J. 1985. "Mortality Projections of Registered Indians, 1982 to 1996." Ottawa: Indian and Northern Affairs Canada.

Statistics Canada. 2003a. "2001 Census: Analysis Series Aboriginal Peoples of Canada: A Demographic Profile." Catalogue No. 96F0030XIE2001007, Ottawa: Minister of Industry. 15.

Statistics Canada. 2003b. "2001 Census Handbook. Ottawa, Minister of Industry." Catalogue No. 92-379-XIE. Ottawa: Minister of Industry. 103.

Statistics Canada. 1995. "Life Tables, Canada and Provinces 1990–92." Catalogue. No. 84-537. Ottawa: Statistics Canada.

Statistics Canada. 1998. "Life Expectancy Abridged Life Tables, at Birth and Age 65, by Sex, for Canada, Provinces, Territories, and Health Regions." CANSIM table 102-0016. Ottawa: Statistics Canada.

United Nations Development Programme. 2003. Human Development Report 2003. New York: Oxford University Press.

Usher, P.J., Duhaime, G., and Searles, E., 2003. "The Household as an Economic Unit in Arctic Aboriginal Communities, and Its Measurement by Means of a Comprehensive Survey." Social Indicators Research. 61:175–202.

Wilkins, R., Uppal, S., Finès, P., Senécal, S., Guimond, E., and Dion, R. (submitted for publication in Health Reports). "Life expectancy in the Inuit-inhabited areas of Canada from 1991 to 2001."

Verma, R., Michalowski, M., and Gauvin, R.P. 2003. "Abridged Life Tables for Registered Indians in Canada, 1976–80 to 1996–2000." Paper presented at the annual meeting of the Population Association of America, May 1–3, Minneapolis.

Appendix

Appendix Map 1:   Measuring Well-being in Inuit Communities: The Community Well-being Index (CWB)

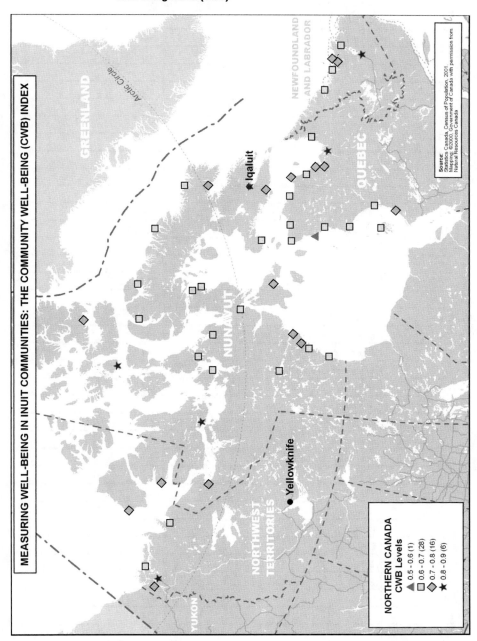

Appendix Table 1: Ranking of Selected Countries and Registered Indian and Reference Populations by Human Development Index, 2001

HDI Rank	Country	HDI Score
Countries with High Human Development		
1	Norway	.944
2	Iceland	.942
3	Sweden	.941
4	Australia	.939
	Reference Population	*.939*
5	Netherlands	.938
6	Belgium	.937
7	United States	.937
8	*Canada*	*.937*
9	Japan	.932
10	Switzerland	.932
13	United Kingdom	.930
16	Austria	.929
17	France	.925
19	Spain	.925
20	New Zealand	.917
23	Portugal	.896
30	Republic of Korea	.879
31	Brunei Darussalam	.872
32	Czech Republic	.861
	Registered Indian off-Reserve	*.856*
33	Malta	.856
34	Argentina	.849
35	Poland	.841
36	Seychelles	.840
37	Bahrain	.839
38	Hungary	.837
39	Slovakia	.836
40	Uruguay	.834
41	Estonia	.833
42	Costa Rica	.832
43	Chile	.831
44	Qatar	.826
45	Lithuania	.824
46	Kuwait	.820
47	Croatia	.818

Appendix Table 1 Continued

HDI Rank	Country	HDI Score
	Registered Indian Population	*.817*
48	United Arab Emirates	.816
49	Bahamas	.812
50	Latvia	.811
51	St. Kitts and Nevis	.808
52	Cuba	.806
53	Belarus	.804
54	Trinidad and Tobago	.802
55	Mexico	.800
Countries with Medium Human Development		
56	Antigua and Barbuda	.798
57	Bulgaria	.795
58	Malaysia	.790
59	Panama	.788
60	Macedonia, TFYR	.784
	Inuit inhabited areas population	*.783*
61	Libyan Arab Jamahirya	.783
62	Mauritius	.779
63	Russian Federation	.779
64	Colombia	.779
65	Brazil	.777
66	Bosnia and Herzegovina	.777
67	Belize	.776
68	Dominica	.776
69	Venezuela	.775
70	Samoa (Western)	.775
71	Saint Lucia	.775
72	Romania	.773
	Registered Indian On-Reserve	*.772*
73	Saudi Arabia	.769
74	Thailand	.768
75	Ukraine	.766
76	Kazakhstan	.765
77	Suriname	.762
78	Jamaica	.757
79	Oman	.755
80	St. Vincent and the Grenadines	.755
81	Fiji	.754

Appendix Table 1 Continued

HDI Rank	Country	HDI Score
82	Peru	.752
83	Lebanon	.752
84	Paraguay	.751
85	Philippines	.751
... 85–102 deleted		
103	Cape Verde	.727
104	China	.721
105	El Salvador	.719
... 106–135 deleted		
135	Lao People's Democratic Republic	.525
136	Bhutan	.511
137	Lesotho	.510
138	Sudan	.503
139	Bangladesh	.502
140	Congo	.502
141	Togo	.501
Countries with Low Human Development		
142	Cameroon	.499
143	Nepal	.499
144	Pakistan	.499
145	Zimbabwe	.496
146	Kenya	.489
147	Uganda	.489
148	Yemen	.470
149	Madagascar	.469
... 150–175 deleted		

Source: Data from HDI table, p. 237-240 from "Human Development Report 2003" by UNDP (2003) by permission of Oxford University Press; Remaining data: Authors' Calculations

8

Community Well-being: A Comparable Communities Analysis

Jerry White and Paul Maxim

Introduction

The purpose of this chapter is to develop a better understanding of the gaps in well-being between First Nation and non-Aboriginal communities throughout Canada. The primary concern of the research is to determine the degree to which the size and location of a community affects its inhabitants' levels of well-being. Well-being is assessed through the Community Well-being Index (CWB), developed by researchers at Indian and Northern Affairs Canada (INAC) to measure the social and economic well-being in Canadian First Nations communities (see Chapter 7). Given that the CWB is a composite indicator, it combines several facets of community well-being into a single index. The analysis uses this CWB and its constituent components (income, education, housing, and labour force activity) as outcome or dependent variables to assess First Nations and non-Aboriginal communities.

The comparison of well-being is accomplished utilizing the Matching Communities 2001 analysis (Maxim and White, 2005) created by of The University of Western Ontario. The analysis provides a pairwise comparison between each First Nation and a matched non-Aboriginal community. This approach provides controls for differences in the type of community (INAC classification), locality, and population size.

For the past several years, INAC's Strategic Research and Analysis Directorate has been researching well-being in First Nations communities. Among other things, the directorate has produced the Community Well-being Index (CWB), which was discussed extensively in Chapter 6. The index uses Census data to assign a well-being score to all Canadian communities,[1] allowing the comparison of reserves[2] to other Canadian communities across time. Initial analyses of the CWB revealed that reserves had lower well-being than other Canadian communities in 2001 (McHardy and O'Sullivan, 2004), but that the gap had narrowed since 1991 (O'Sullivan and McHardy, 2004).

These findings, at first glance, suggest that there is something *about* reserves that inhibits well-being. This is not necessarily the case, however. The relationship between well-being and reserve status may be a spurious one. Reserves tend to have much smaller populations than non-reserves. The average reserve has approximately 500 persons. Larger communities are few and very rarely reach more than 5,000 persons. Reserves are also located disproportionately in remote or Northern areas where access to commodity, labour, and consumer markets is limited. It may be these factors, and not characteristics intrinsic to reserves, behind the lower levels of well-being observed in reserve communities.

To assess this possibility, we paired a selection of reserves with non-reserve communities that are "comparable" on the basis of location and population size, effectively "controlling" for these factors. We then compared the disparity in well-being (CWB) between reserves and all non-reserve communities to the disparity between reserves and their "comparable" non-reserve matches. A significantly smaller disparity between the matched communities would indicate that the lower levels of well-being observed in reserve communities were at least somewhat attributable to their location and population size. No disparity between the matched communities would indicate that being a reserve had absolutely no bearing on a community's well-being.

The Community Well-being Index (CWB)

As discussed in Chapter 6, the CWB is a composite index which includes four facets of well-being including education, labor force activity, income, and housing. Education is measured by the proportion of the population who have grade 9 or higher and the proportion of the population who have achieved at least a high school education. Labour force activity is measured by labour force participation and the employed proportion of the total labour force. Housing is measured by the proportion of the population living in dwellings with no more than one person per room and the proportion of the population reporting that their dwellings did not need major repairs. Finally, income is measured as income per capita.

Cooke (2005) developed a conceptual critique of the CWB index. After assessing the key dimensions of well-being that are included in the CWB, the sources of data and their availability and comparability over time, the sensitivity of the indicators to change, and the weights and scaling assigned to the components in the index calculations, he concluded that the CWB compares favourably to other indices and that "the CWB promises to be a useful indicator of the well-being in Aboriginal communities, and as other composite indices have done, it promises to make a positive contribution to Canadian policy research" (see Chapter 2 in this volume for more discussion).

Creating the Matching Communities

Given that reserves have special circumstances or conditions, any comparison of their characteristics with those of other Canadian communities has reduced validity. The primary aim of this study is to examine the degree to which the lower than average levels of well-being in reserve communities are a function of the size and location of those communities. To do this, we selected a matched sample of non-reserve communities based on proximity and population size.

The list of matching communities was generated in a four-stage process. First, we measured the direct line distance between each reserve[3] community and every non-reserve community in Canada. This distance was then standardized.[4] Second, we recorded and standardized each community's population size. Third, we used a mathematical algorithm to match each reserve with proximate non-reserves of similar population size.[5] We chose the following algorithm, which is based on the mean absolute euclidean distance across the variables for the two communities in question:

$$D = \frac{\sum w_j |\tilde{z}_j - z_j|}{J}$$

Here, D is the distance coefficient between two communities; $\tilde{z}$ is the standard score or z-value for the jth variable of a First Nations CSD; z is the standard score or z-value for the jth variable of a non First Nations CSD; w is a weight attached to the jth variable; and, J is the number of variables under consideration. The FN refers to First Nation so this is a short form for the CSDs (as defined in note 3) that make up the reserve or first nation communities. We created the files for the FN communities by manually looking at each CSD that could have potentially made up the community. We then created the communities using the CSD data (or CSDs).

Finally, from the eight closest matches, we selected the best match based on direct examination. Using this method, we were able to create 495 reserve/non-reserve pairs.[6]

Analysing Disparities Between Reserves and Comparable Communities

First, we measured the disparity in CWB (and its four components) means between reserves[7] and all other Canadian communities. Second, we compared those disparities to those measured between reserves and the 495 similar non-reserves with which they were paired. We also compared the differences in CWB means between reserves and their non-reserve pairs within four gross geographical categories: Urban, Rural, Remote, and Special Access. Details on each of these geographic zones, which are defined and assigned by INAC (2001),[8] are as follows:

- Zone 1 (Urban): A geographic zone where the First Nation is located within 50 km of the nearest service centre with year-round road access.
- Zone 2 (Rural): A geographic zone where the First Nation is located between 50 and 350 km from the nearest service centre with year-round road access.
- Zone 3 (Remote): A geographic zone where the First Nation is located over 350 km from the nearest service centre with year-round road access.
- Zone 4 (Special Access): A geographic zone where the First Nation has

Table 8.1: Comparison of Non-reserve and Reserve Communities

Variable	Non-reserve	Reserve	Difference	S.E. Difference
CWB Score	0.806	0.650	0.156	0.005
Income	0.727	0.499	0.228	0.006
Education	0.760	0.692	0.068	0.006
Housing	0.927	0.712	0.215	0.007
Labour Force Activity	0.808	0.696	0.112	0.005

Note: N=495 for reserve communities; N=4181 for non-reserve communities. All differences are statistically significant at p<.01

Table 8.2: Comparison of Matched Reserve and Non-reserve Communities

Variable	Non-reserve	Reserve	Difference	S.E. Difference
CWB Score	0.805	0.650	0.155	0.005
Income	0.721	0.499	0.222	0.007
Education	0.788	0.692	0.096	0.007
Housing	0.893	0.712	0.181	0.007
Labour Force Activity	0.820	0.696	0.124	0.006

Note: N=495 matches. All differences are statistically significant at p<.01

no year-round road access to a service centre and, as a result, experiences a higher cost of transportation.

Results

Reserve vs. Non-reserve Communities

In the unmatched analyses, where all reserves were compared with all other Canadian communities, reserves scored lower on the CWB index and its components. Based on the data presented in **Table 8.1**, the average CWB score for the 495 reserves included in this study was about 19% lower than the average score for other communities (.650 versus .806). For income, education, housing, and labour force activity, the differences were approximately 31%, 9%, 23%, and 14% respectively, all in favour of the non-reserve communities. These values provide a baseline against which the subsequent analyses can be compared.

Matched Communities

Table 8.2 presents the results of the matched pairs analysis of the CWB index and its components. Overall, the disparities between reserves and their matched non-reserve communities differ little from those derived from the comparison of all reserves to all non-reserve communities. The results are presented graphically in **Figure 8.1**.

Figure 8.1: Matched vs. Unmatched Community Comparisons

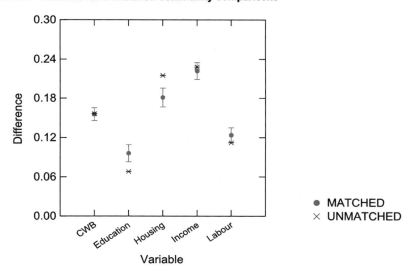

In **Figure 8.1**, the vertical lines represent the results of the matched analyses of the CWB and each of its four components (**Table 8.2** data). Specifically, the lines define the 95% confidence intervals around the difference between the average scores for reserves and the average scores for their non-reserve matches. Each of the lines shares its vertical plane with an H. These Hs represent the results of the unmatched analysis drawn from **Table 8.1**. Where the H falls above the vertical line, we may say that the gap between reserves and non-reserves decreased significantly when we controlled for community location and population size. Where the H falls below the vertical line, we may say that the gap increased significantly when we controlled for community location and population size.

Only the unmatched values for housing and education fell outside the confidence boundaries generated by their respective matched analyses. The unmatched disparity in housing conditions fell about two points (on the 100-point scale) above the upper boundary of the matched confidence interval. This suggests that on the housing sub-index, there is a small tendency toward convergence in the quality of housing when communities are matched on the basis of location and size. Undoubtedly, part of this convergence is due to the greater homogeneity of housing stock in remote areas.

The unmatched disparity in education, on the other hand, fell about two points below the lower boundary of the matched confidence interval. Again, this is not too surprising since more remote Aboriginal communities often suffer a "talent drain" while smaller and more remote non-Aboriginal communities are often "talent magnets." This latter situation is particularly the case for resource-based communities where the demand for highly trained engineers and technicians is great.

Table 8.3: Comparison of Matched Non-reserve and Reserve Communities by Zone

Variable	Non-reserve	Reserve	Difference	Standard Error Difference
Community Well-being				
Zone 1 (Urban)	0.832	0.706	0.126	0.009
Zone 2 (Rural)	0.800	0.640	0.160	0.007
Zone 3 (Remote)	0.745	0.639	0.106	0.022
Zone 4 (Special Access)	0.782	0.583	0.199	0.015
Income				
Zone 1 (Urban)	0.742	0.550	0.192	0.012
Zone 2 (Rural)	0.716	0.468	0.248	0.009
Zone 3 (Remote)	0.660	0.549	0.111	0.034
Zone 4 (Special Access)	0.707	0.480	0.227	0.016
Education				
Zone 1 (Urban)	0.827	0.769	0.058	0.010
Zone 2 (Rural)	0.768	0.702	0.066	0.010
Zone 3 (Remote)	0.735	0.576	0.159	0.043
Zone 4 (Special Access)	0.770	0.537	0.233	0.018
Housing				
Zone 1 (Urban)	0.933	0.782	0.151	0.012
Zone 2 (Rural)	0.900	0.704	0.196	0.011
Zone 3 (Remote)	0.843	0.713	0.130	0.026
Zone 4 (Special Access)	0.821	0.626	0.195	0.027
Labour Force				
Zone 1 (Urban)	0.825	0.721	0.104	0.011
Zone 2 (Rural)	0.817	0.686	0.131	0.009
Zone 3 (Remote)	0.741	0.716	0.025	0.042
Zone 4 (Special Access)	0.832	0.687	0.145	0.015

No statistically significant difference was observed between the matched and unmatched analyses of either the income or labour force activity sub indices, or for the overall CWB index.[9]

Stratifying by Geography

The previous analysis suggests that, even when population size and proximity are controlled, there is no systematic convergence in measured well-being between reserves and non-reserve communities.

Another question that might be asked, however, is whether there are variations in discrepancy between reserves and matched non-reserve communities when gross geography is considered. One might hypothesize, for example, that matched pairs in remote areas are more similar than those in less remote areas.

Figure 8.2: CWB Differences by Zone

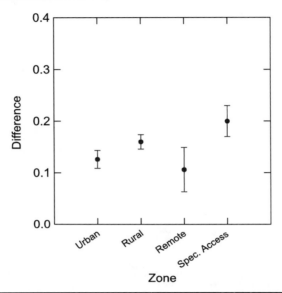

We addressed this question by using the broad, four-category zonal differentiation described earlier. Our results for the CWB and each of its components, broken down by geographic zone, are presented in **Table 8.3**.

The first block in **Table 8.3** presents the results for the CWB. As previously demonstrated in McHardy and O'Sullivan (2004), reserves in and near urban areas had the highest scores, while reserves in the Special Access zone had the lowest scores. The scores calculated for reserves in Zones 2 and 3 fell between these two extremes. Our matched community analysis demonstrates that the relative well-being of reserves and their non-reserve matches were distributed in the same way: the disparity between reserves and their non-reserve matches increased with isolation.

The fact that reserves in Zone 3 had higher scores than reserves in the less remote Zone 2 is somewhat counterintuitive. This anomaly notwithstanding,[10] however, these results indicate that isolation adversely impacts both reserves and non-reserves, but that the effect on reserves is more pronounced. **Figure 8.2** provides 95% confidence intervals for the differences between the two types of communities provided in **Table 8.3**. It demonstrates that the likely disparity in CWB scores between reserves and their non-reserve matches in Zone 1, for example, fell between about 0.11 and 0.14.

The remaining blocks in **Table 8.3** display the distribution of income, education, housing, and labour force participation respectively by geographical zone. Confidence intervals for those results are presented in **Figures 8.3** through **8.6** (pages 180–181. As might be expected with a large number of comparisons, some

Figure 8.3: Income Differences by Zone

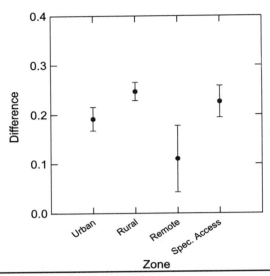

Figure 8.4: Education Differences by Zone

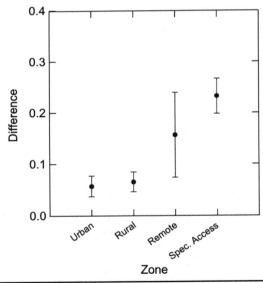

deviations from an overall pattern exist. Generally speaking, though, the results were similar to those calculated for the CWB index. Reserves in Zone 4 tended to have the lowest scores while reserves proximal to urban areas had the highest scores. Scores for reserves in Zones 2 and 3 generally fell between those calculated for reserves in Zones 1 and 4. In most cases, the average score for the 11 reserves in Zone 3 were higher than that of the 200 reserves in Zone 2. The disparity between reserves and non-reserves tends

Figure 8.5: Housing Differences by Zone

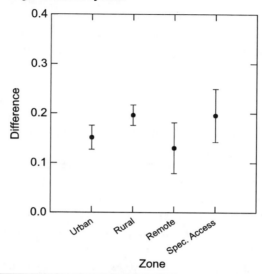

Figure 8.6: Labour Differences by Zone

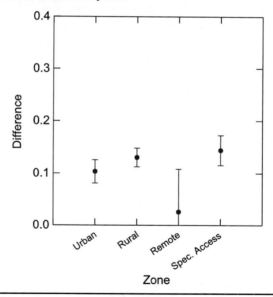

to follow the same pattern. The Zones, ranked from smallest to largest in terms of the reserve/non-reserve disparities therein, are as follows: Zone 1 (Urban), Zone 3 (Remote), Zone 2 (Rural), and Zone 4 (Special Access). Again, the preponderance of reserves in Zone 3 over those in Zone 2 notwithstanding, isolation appears to have a negative effect on well-being in both types of communities, but impacts on reserves more strongly.

Conclusion

The impetus behind this analysis was to ascertain whether the negative relationship between reserve status and community well-being reported by McHardy and O'Sullivan (2004) was spurious. That is, were the lower levels of well-being found on-reserve attributable to the fact that more reserves are remotely situated and sparsely populated, rather than to the fact that they are reserves per se? Overall, our matched analyses, which controlled for differences in location and population size between reserves and non-reserves, produced similar results to analyses that did not control for these factors. Evidently, there is something about reserves, apart from their isolation and small size, that has inhibited their ability to achieve levels of well-being akin to those observed in other Canadian communities. The list of possible factors is virtually endless. Perhaps community well-being on reserves was adversely affected by the legal limitations on reserve land transfer. Perhaps the cultural and social impacts of colonial rule were significant.

We did, however, identify an interaction effect between gross geography and reserve status. Specifically, it seems that the well-being of reserves, both in absolute terms and relative to non-reserves, decreases as isolation increases. Based on the overall CWB scale, as well as on its components, it is evident that reserves near urban areas are more similar to non-reserve communities than those in difficult to access parts of the country. There are some inconsistencies in our findings, however, indicating a need for further research in this area. Of particular interest in this regard are those reserve communities in the Remote (Zone 3) band that often show far more similarity with their matched counterparts than do reserves in other parts of the country.

Endnotes

1 Excluded from analyses were communities with fewer than 65 inhabitants, communities with data quality issues, and communities which did not participate in the Census.

2 INAC's list of reserves, which the designers of the CWB termed "First Nations communities," differed slightly from ours. They categorized both legal and non-legal reserves as First Nations communities, as this definition corresponds to that used by INAC and Statistics Canada to retrieve "on-reserve" figures from the Census of Canada. For reasons that will be expounded later, we chose to categorize non-legal reserves as "other Canadian communities" or non-reserves.

3 As indicated earlier, the original CWB analysis conducted by McHardy and O'Sullivan catego-rized a selection of non-legal reserves as First Nations, or reserve, communities. These communi-ties are uniformly northern and can be of any type. INAC, interested in tracking the progress of communities with informal affiliations with First Nations bands or large Registered Indian popu-lations, classifies non-legal reserves as such on a case-by-case basis. As McHardy and O'Sullivan were interested in how well-being in First Nations compares to that in other communities, their inclusive approach was appropriate. We, however, were interested in whether the causes for the disparity are inherent to First Nations or incidental. As such, it was necessary for us to adopt the stricter definition of reserve. With a few exceptions, legal reserves share the distinction of being governed by the *Indian Act* (a piece of legislation with unique provisions and correspondingly unique effects) or specific self-government agreements. We should also note that the terminology used to refer to reserve communities varies in the literature, and that particular attention should always be paid to how reserves/First Nations/Aboriginal communities, etc. are defined in a given study.

4 All measures were converted to z-scores in order to provide for a common metric across all variables. One cannot reasonably compare measures based on kilometres or miles with size of population.

5 We should note that this method allows a non-reserve community to be selected as a match for more than one reserve community. Statistically, this is known as sampling with replacement and generally provides better parameter estimates (Maxim, 1999). In addition, we weighted the two variables, giving population more influence than geography.

6 It is important to emphasize again that our reserve/non-reserve typology is based on location and not exclusively population characteristics. Not all of the people living on a reserve are necessarily Aboriginal. Many non-Aboriginal spouses and children of band members or status Indians reside in reserve communities. Also, non-Aboriginal people are often employed on-reserve. Some First Nations also rent or lease reserve land to non-Aboriginal persons. Consequently, it is possible that a reserve and its non-reserve match may have the same proportion of Aboriginal inhabit-ants. Indeed, the non-reserve match may have more. This geographically-based classification is appropriate given our interest in the effects on well-being of the special circumstances that exist on legal Indian reserves. Additional research that defines Aboriginal communities in terms of the size of their Aboriginal populations is warranted, but would address different issues than the ones under consideration here.

7 This comparison group was comprised of only the 495 reserves for which we were able to generate matches. Including the 46 additional reserves for which CWB data were available would have confounded our interpretation of the matched pairs: we would not have been able to eliminate the possibility that the absence of the unmatched reserves from the matched pairs analysis was the cause of any differences detected in well-being observed between the complete and paired samples.

8 Where a First Nation band includes more than one reserve, that band is assigned to a remote-ness category based on its most populous site. Consequently, remoteness classifications are not available for reserves not designated as a band's more populous site. In total, remoteness classifi-cations were available for 387 of the 495 (78%) reserves under consideration in this study. It must also be noted that remoteness classifications are not available for non-reserves. Since reserves are matched with non-reserves based, in part, on location, it is likely that most reserve/non-reserve pairs lie within the same remoteness zone. It is possible, however, that a non-reserve may occupy a different zone from the reserve with which it was matched.

9 McHardy and O'Sullivan (2004) found that, although the overall disparity between reserves and

non-reserves was significant in 2001, well-being varied greatly among reserves. As an aside, we examined the differences in CWB scores between individual reserve/non-reserve pairs. In keeping with McHardy and O'Sullivan's findings, we found a great deal of variation among pairs. The disparities between reserves and their non-reserve pairs (measured as non-reserve CWB score minus reserve CWB score) were normally distributed between about -.23 and .44. Still, the predominance of the non-reserve communities was clear: the reserve had a higher score than its non-reserve match in about 7% of the cases only.

10 We chose not to attach too much significance to this anomaly given that the distinction between Zones 2 and 3 is arbitrary, and that only 11 reserves were categorized as Zone 3 reserves. Further research is certainly indicated, however, as there are a number of interesting reasons why remote reserves might achieve higher levels of well-being than rural reserves. A popular explanation is that a road into a remote community indicates the nearby exploitation of natural resources. Such exploitation could, of course, spur economic development.

References

Cooke, M. 2005. "The First Nations Community Well-Being Index (CWB): A Conceptual Review." Ottawa: Department of Sociology, University of Western Ontario/Indian Affairs and Northern Development. < www.ainc-inac.gc.ca/pr/ra/cwb_e.html>

Indian and North Affairs Canada. 2001. "Band Classification Manual." Corporate Information Management Directorate. Ottawa: INAC. <www.ainc-inac.gc.ca/pr/pub/fnnrg/2001/bandc_e.pdf>

Maxim, P. 1999. *Quantitative Research Methods in the Social Sciences*. New York: Oxford University Press.

McHardy, M. and O'Sullivan, E. 2004. "First Nations Community Well-Being in Canada: The Community Well-Being Index (CWB), 2001." Strategic Research and Analysis Directorate. Ottawa: INAC.

O'Sullivan, E. and McHardy, M. . 2004. "The Community Well-Being (CWB) Index: Disparity in Well-Being Between First Nations and Other Canadian Communities Over Time." Catalogue no. R2-349/2004E. Ottawa: INAC,

9

Assessing the Net Effects of Specific Claims Settlements in First Nations Communities in the Context of Community Well-being

Jerry White, Nicholas Spence, and Paul Maxim

Introduction

The historical relationship between the Crown and First Nations people in Canada is one of the most fundamental in Canada society; indeed, it has framed the context in which First Nations have developed across a broad spectrum of dimensions, including cultural, social, economic, and political. In certain instances, the legal obligations of Canada to First Nations people, rooted in historic treaties, the *Indian Act*, and other formal agreements, have failed to be met, with adverse consequences that are sometimes difficult to fully grasp and quantify. The specific claims process is one mechanism that has been designed to address outstanding grievances of First Nations people. Each specific claim addresses the unique historical relationship between the Crown and a specific First Nation (Butt and Hurley, 2006; Indian Affairs Canada, 2006). The scope of the claim can vary from improper management of First Nations funds, to failing to provide sufficient reserve land, to surrendering reserve lands in the absence of consent from a First Nation. Specific claims serve a few key purposes: improving the socio-economic well-being of communities and addressing historic injustices to build trust and foster cohesion between Aboriginal and non-Aboriginal Canadians.[1]

The Problem and Scope of the Study

The purpose of this study is to develop and test a research design that will allow for a temporal assessment of the impact of specific claims and litigation on the overall well-being of First Nations communities. A research design was developed for assessing the impact that the claims and litigation process might have had on well-being as measured by the Community Well-being Index (CWB). The CWB is a composite index developed by the Strategic Research and Analysis Directorate of Indian and Northern Affairs Canada (INAC) to measure selected elements of well-being across communities over time, using readily available indicators from the Canadian Census, as discussed in great detail in Chapter 6.

The project proceeded in five stages:

- **Stage 1**. We determined the quality, comparability, and availability of well-being indicators from Census Canada data over the Census periods of 1981, 1986, 1991, 1996, and 2001.

- **Stage 2**. We gathered specific claims and litigation data from the departmental Specific Claims Branch (SCB) and Litigation Management and Resolution Branch (LMRB) databases from the inception of the databases to date.

- **Stage 3**. We categorized First Nation communities into relevant subcategories within the design, including those having submitted/filed a claim (or claims) that has resulted in a settlement; those with an ongoing claim; those communities that have not submitted/filed a claim; etc.

- **Stage 4**. We produced a research design that allowed for a comparison of those different types of communities to determine whether any temporal differences in well-being indicators are related to claims settlement.

- **Stage 5**. We assessed the design using the CWB with its four components: education, labour force, income, and housing.

Claims and Settlements: The Links to Socio-economic Development

Currently there are some 123 specific claims in negotiation in Canada. From 1973 to September 2006, 275 specific claims have been settled. The indemnity involved in the claims exceeds $5 billion.[2] It appears prima facie that legal settlements bring new resources to a community. Those resources may be in the form of dollars, mineral reserves, land, or access to previously blocked resources such as fish or forestry. New resources in free enterprise models should result in new economic development producing more overall wealth and prosperity. This prosperity, it seems logical to assume, should also result in greater employment and income as well as advancing social conditions and improving well-being. In this study, we examine this empirically, but there are indications in the research literature that these assumptions are not applicable in every case.

Gaming Windfalls in the US

Considerable controversy exists in the US over the economic activities that arose out of the tribal sovereignty rights that spawned both tax-free tobacco sales and gambling halls on reservations. From the high stakes bingos of Florida's Seminole Indians in the 1970s (Kersey, 1992), to the large-scale casino operations of the Capazon and Morongo bands in California, the courts upheld the rights of tribes to establish gaming on reservations—California versus Cabazon and Morongo Bands—(Snipp 1995). These decisions led to the proliferation of gaming as a revenue generator on Indian land.[3] Oregon, for example, has only one tribe without a casino (Darian-Smith 2004). The consequent results are mixed: "Those

Diagram 9.1: Status of Claims by Census Year

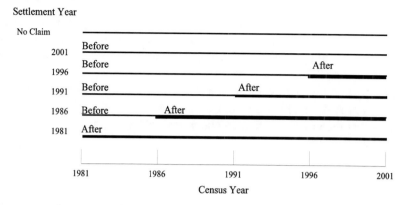

with successful operations are quick to point out the benefits ... better schools and improved public services" (Snipp 1995). However, as Darian-Smith (2004) points out, there are both successful and unsuccessful reservations.

These findings concur with the Harvard study led by Cornell and Kalt (1992). These researchers have been looking at the economic, political, and social development of a sample of Southwest US reservations. They have been trying to isolate the factors that either contribute to or block development. Generally, they reject standard economic theories that point to differential access to financial capital or different endowments of natural resources or human capital. They have compiled much anecdotal evidence that suggests that tribes with superior resources, such as the Crow of Montana, with billions in coal, have drastic social problems but tribes with fewer resources, such as the Cohiti Pueblo, are doing very well. They conclude that the one factor that sets socio-economic success in motion is the development of political institutions or what they call increased political sovereignty (Cornell and Kalt 1992). Whether this assessment is true is unsubstantiated, but for our purposes it is interesting to note that the mere existence of resources seems not to guarantee development and well-being. Having provided a brief overview of the potential contributions of claims to economic development in First Nations communities, we will now proceed with the analysis.

Analysis

Design

Essentially, the design used to measure the impact of specific claims on well-being consists of a series of before/after measures. The date of settlement of a community's first claim is used as the cut-point. Data on the outcome variable is observed before the settlement date and compared with outcome variable data after the settlement date. **Diagram 9.1** illustrates how this creates a step pattern of before and after periods for the different groups of communities. Some communities, of course, have no settlements.

As can be seen from this diagram, communities that had a settlement in 2001 have no "after" observations for comparison. Similarly, communities that settled in 1981 have no "before" observations. Those that settled in 1991 have a ten-year period of before and after observations.

One of the limiting factors underlying this study was our inability to identify the year in which the claim was filed. Consequently, it is difficult to fully assess the impact that the process of filing a claim, regardless of outcome, might have had on the community.

Data

There are two basic sources of data for this study. The first source of data consists of the decennial and quinquennial census estimates generated by Statistics Canada between 1981 and 2001 for the calculation of the CWB. The second source of data consists of specific claims that were either initiated or settled prior to December 31, 2003. Those data were obtained from the Specific Claims Branch of INAC. Both data bases have issues surrounding them; consequently, we will discuss each separately.

Census Data and the CWB

This analysis uses the CWB, which utilizes Census data over the 1981–2001 period[4] to document well-being trends for First Nations communities. The limitations of the Census data in constructing the CWB have been described in great detail elsewhere (Chapter 6), but for the sake of convenience, we will highlight the key issues that are particularly relevant for this study.

Data at the CSD (Census subdivision) level were used to develop CWB scores for First Nations communities. CSD level data are appropriate since this unit of analysis generally corresponds closely with both the legal and conventional definition of a community. Most First Nations communities (reserves) can be identified by a single CSD. One key problem we face involves matching CSDs over sequential Census periods. In order to legitimately compare a community across time, one must be sure that one is assessing the same entity. Fortunately for analysis purposes, most First Nations communities remain geographically stable and the Statistics Canada CSD identifier code remains consistent over the period of investigation. There are, however, numerous exceptions to this rule: new reserves are created; some reserve lands are split and new CSD identifiers are assigned; some areas amalgamate; and, occasionally, some reserves become unpopulated. To take these issues into account the CWB excludes communities deemed "inconsistent entities" across time.

Perhaps the most important issue related to any use of Census data in examining the First Nation population, including the CWB, is *under enumeration* Many communities have been under enumerated in recent Censuses due to political

Diagram 9.2: Range of Claims by Census Year

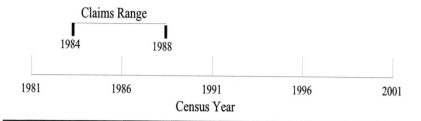

tensions between some communities and the federal government.[5] Consequently, it is common to have data on a community in, for example, 1981, 1991, and 2001 but not in 1986 or 1996. The under enumeration problem remained insurmountable. Its scope is also such that we must impose strong reservations on the results generated by this analysis. As will be discussed in the conclusions, we would strongly suggest that any future analysis take a different approach to assessing the impact of claims and claims settlements on the communities in question.

Thus, CWB scores between 1981 and 2001 are based upon the following criteria:

- The CSD existed in each Census year.
- The CSD did not gain or lose more than 5% of its population.
- The CSD had a CWB score in each Census year.
- The CSD had a population of at least 65 in each Census year.

Claims Data

Data on both opened and settled claims were supplied by the Specific Claims Branch of INAC. The data file contained information on claims by band, filed and settled between 1971 and 2003, inclusive. In order to match the claims data to the CWB data, we aggregated the claims data into five-year intervals. For example, since a Census was conducted in 1986, claims data for the period were aggregated between the years 1984 and 1988 inclusive and identified as a 1986 data point. The overall pattern is illustrated in **Diagram 9.2** where the claims data for the years 1984 to 1988 are aggregated about the 1986 census period. If a community filed or settled a claim within that period, a flag was set within the database.

In some cases, more than one claim was filed or settled within each five-year period. That pattern increased with time, but the flag was based on an "all or nothing" outcome. As a result, three types of communities were identified: those with no claim (either settled or filed); those with a claim filed but not settled; and, those with a settled claim within that period. Some communities also had claims filed or settled across more than one Census period. Where several claims were settled within a five-year period, the aggregate dollar amount of those claims was calculated in constant dollars.

Figure 9.1: Community Well-being Scores for Communities With No Claims: 1981–2001

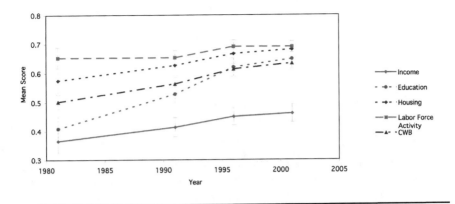

Figure 9.2: Community Well-being Scores for Communities That Have Ever Settled a Claim: 1981–2001

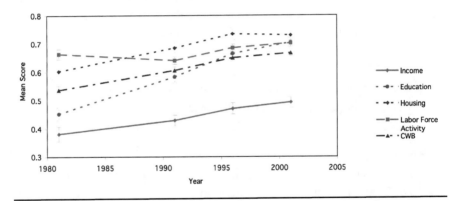

Figure 9.3 Community Well-being Scores for Communities With a Field Claim but No Settlement: 1981–2001

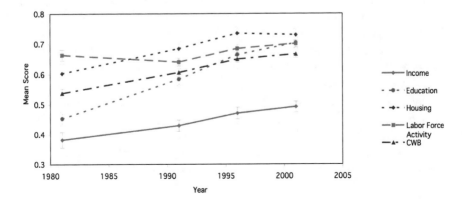

One group of claims that was excluded consisted of those settled at the tribal or council level. The difficulty with claims at the tribal council level is that it is not clear which, if any, of the constituent communities might have been actively involved or might have actively benefited from the claims action.

As indicated in the discussion of the CWB data, matching the claims data to the CWB data proved difficult in some instances due to the under enumeration problem. For several communities, we know that a claim was filed or resolved, but it is impossible to assess the impact of that action within the current framework because the characteristics of the community, as operationalized by the CWB, were not available.

Outcome Indicator: The Community Well-being Index (CWB)

As discussed previously, successful claims settlements by First Nation communities are thought to be one avenue through which well-being could be improved. Choosing appropriate outcome indicators that are sensitive to changes resulting from these settlements is important if one seeks to assess their full impact.

For the past several years, the Strategic Research and Analysis Directorate at INAC has been researching the notion of well-being in First Nations communities. One of the fruits of this endeavour has been the creation of the Community Well-Being Index (CWB). The CWB is a useful tool that captures socio-economic well-being through the use of several relevant indicators. A score is generated for each First Nation community[6] which provides a snapshot of its well-being. CWB scores range between zero and one, with higher numbers indicating greater well-being. The index, which measures four equally weighted components—education, housing, income, and employment—uses Census data to track the well-being of Canadian First Nation communities over time (see Chapter 6). Thus, for the purposes of the research question at hand, this measure provides us with a way to assess the likely impact of claims initiation/settlement on well-being, as defined by this index.

Statistical Analysis

Several approaches were taken to the analysis of the data. Essentially, we looked for two things: aggregate before and after differences, and differences in secular or temporal trends. Simple before/after analyses provide limited information since it is not clear that any difference is due to the settlement "intervention" or to external on-going processes. By comparing groups of communities with staggered settlement dates, however, it is possible to separate out the potential impact of the settlement interventions from other temporal trends.

Applying several standard general linear model procedures (e.g., analysis of variance based on before/after effects, interrupted analysis of covariance) produced similar results. **Figures 9.1, 9.2**, and **9.3** show the overall basic temporal patterns of CWB scores and components for the three different groups—"no claims," "settled

Figure 9.4: Community Well-being Scores for Communities With Claims Settled in 1981: 1981–2001

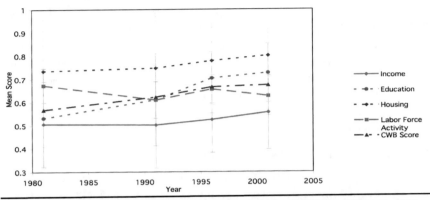

Figure 9.5: Community Well-being Scores for Communities With Claims Settled in 1986: 1981–2001

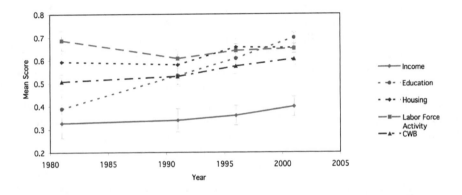

Figure 9.6: Community Well-being Scores for Communities With Claims Settled in 1991: 1981–2001

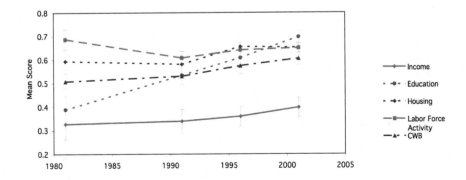

a claim," and "filed a claim but no settlement"—from 1981 to 2001. Overall, the CWB and component scores tend to increase over time; however, across the three different groups there is no significant difference in the magnitude of the changes of each group over the 1981–2001 period, as indicated by the massive overlap in 95% confidence intervals. In other words, every group increased their CWB score by a similar amount over time[7] and there are no systematic differences in the CWB across the different groups.

Figures 9.4 to **9.8** (pages 192 & 194) illustrate the period over period differences from 1981 to 2001 and the 95% confidence intervals for those differences within the group "settled a claim," in terms of CWB and components scores, by year of settlement.[8] As indicated by the overlap in confidence intervals, there are no systematic changes in the outcome variables over time across the groups of communities. For the most part, the difference in CWB and component scores from Census to Census, regardless of the year in which the claim was settled, do not appear to be systematically significant when compared to changes in the groups "no claims" and "filed a claim but no settlement" over the same time periods. In other words, having a settled claim does not seem to increase the CWB scores any more than one observes in the other two groups ("no claims" and "claims but no settlements").

Conclusions and Future Directions

Based on the current analysis, it is not possible to identify a significant linkage between the claims process and the outcome measure used. We offer several explanations for the null findings below and emphasize that they do not necessarily mean that specific claims settlements did not impact on well-being. An alternative methodological approach is recommended given the problems with the existing study.

Validity Issue

The absence of an effect of specific claims settlements on well-being could be a product of the very limited number of potential impact factors that we have been able to examine. While the existing literature and conventional wisdom suggest that the variables we examined are reasonable candidates,[9] there are major bodies of literature that would have us look elsewhere (e.g., The Royal Commission on Aboriginal People, 1996). The CWB may indeed be an insensitive indicator of the benefits accruing to communities from claims. Given its socio-economic focus, changes in the physical, political, psychological, and cultural milieu, as well as the social capital and cohesion of communities, are not examined. There may also be benefits to more tangible measures such as lower rates of suicide or substance abuse. Unfortunately, the Census does not include any of those indicators within its orbit. These issues appear relevant given previous research. For example, in his examination of development outcomes of the Meadow Lake Tribal Council during 1986

Figure 9.7: Community Well-being Scores for Communities With Claims Settled in 1996: 1981–2001

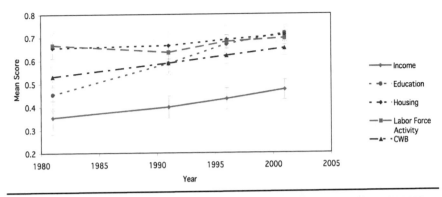

Figure 9.8: Community Well-being Scores for Communities With Claims Settled in 2001: 1981-2001

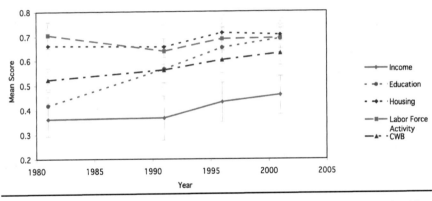

to 1996, Anderson (2002) reveals that the people of the Meadow Lake First Nations in northwestern Saskatchewan were pleased with the increase in employment and business activity resulting from forestry, but many were dissatisfied with the clear cutting process and its effects on their ability to continue traditional practices, as well as the lack of influence with respect to operating decisions. Thus, this would indicate that socio-economic development must be considered in the context of traditional values and control over development activities. Similarly, studies by Anderson and Bone (1999) and Anderson (2002) claim that the First Nations approach to economic development includes the following purposes: improvement of socio-economic circumstances; greater control of activities on their traditional lands; attainment of economic self-sufficiency in support of self government; and the preservation and strengthening of traditional culture, values, and languages, and their application in economic development and business activities. These features of economic development echo the Royal Commission on Aboriginal People (1996). Our indicators are insensitive to much of these notions of socio-economic development. Moreover, the socio-economic indicators of the CWB provides an incomplete snapshot of the situation in First Nation communities, as many Aboriginal people engage in traditional activities such as hunting and fishing, which contributes to well-being but fails to be captured in Census measures.

On another note, perhaps the most important shortcoming of this research on the effects of specific claims on well-being is the inability to test the extent to which they enhance trust and understanding, as well as promote cohesiveness and partnerships, between Aboriginal and non-Aboriginal people of Canada. In fact, the extent to which the resolution of grievances has resulted in the perception of justice being served in the eyes of stakeholders is a central goal of the claims process, but is not captured in this analysis due to a lack of data.

N Size

Another possible reason for the null effects of specific claims on well-being is related to the "n" size of the data. Specifically, even if the measures we used have been influenced by the claims process, we face the problem of small numbers over time. While the aggregate number of claims filed and claims settled is technically sufficient to detect a significant impact, the reduced numbers due to Census under enumeration pose a major obstacle. In technical terms, under enumeration can lead to sample selection bias and to statistical power problems. Sample selection bias would result from those communities not participating in the Census being systematically different on the selected indicators from those communities that remain in the Census process. It is certainly conceivable that the more "successful" or more newly resourced communities might take a more aggressive stand against the census takers and refuse to cooperate. The statistical power problem results from there simply being too few communities to allow us to detect a statistically significant difference. This is particularly problematic when the effects that we are looking for evolve gradually or manifest themselves in a subtle manner.

Utilization of Specific Claims Settlements

The manner in which claims settlements are utilized by a community may play a role in determining whether any effects are observed. It would be worthwhile to see whether any transfers made to the communities were used simply on consumption or were invested in community resources. Distributed settlements where each band member receives x dollars could have a positive impact on the community, but a very diffuse one that is not sensitive to detection by the CWB index. For example, band members might use distributed funds to fix or decorate their homes, buy a new car, or simply spend the funds on food, clothing, and other consumables, which may largely contribute little to increasing income, housing, education, or labour force indicators. On the other hand, communities that retain the aggregate settlement and use it as a source of capital would be more likely to produce a focused outcome by building a better school, stimulating employment, improving the overall quality of band housing, and developing sustainable infrastructure to spawn overall socio-economic development.[10] Tracking how the funds are distributed requires additional research.

Settlement Size and Temporal Issues

We expect that the size of a settlement would largely influence the magnitude of change one would expect to observe in outcome indicators of well-being. In the analysis at hand, the size of the settlements varies considerably. Although some of the more recent settlements go into the several million dollar ranges, many settlements are for a relatively inconsequential amount. Sample selection bias and statistical power problems due to missing data make an analysis of the dollar impact difficult. It is likely that depending upon the amount of the claims settlement and how the capital is used (e.g., dispersed to individuals versus infrastructure to enhance educational attainment) it may be unrealistic to expect any detectable change in the outcome.

In terms of temporality, the resources obtained from the settlement of a specific claim would unlikely result in any instantaneous change in outcome indicators of well-being. In fact, the flow of resources and the returns to long-term strategic investments require time to fully manifest themselves. The exact time period is uncertain, but may be influenced by the existing capacity of the community, including cohesion, geography, demographics, and existing human, social, financial/natural capital.[11, 12] Moreover, the type of investment and outcome expected will dictate the length of time before an effect is observed. Furthermore, it is plausible that there is a threshold effect, where a claim must be of a certain value to have any detectable/significant effect on the outcome variables measured. Given these other factors, delineating the effects of claims on well-being is a complex task on which we are continuing to work diligently.

In sum, we would suggest that the reader be cautious in over interpreting these findings. We feel it is not suggested that specific claims settlements have no effect on well-being. We would say that the data suggests that any community impacts are likely to occur over the long term, and if they are to be positive, it would demand that the settlements be invested into the community in ways that will encourage educational and socio-economic improvements. Further research would be useful to determine how these particular mechanisms might work.

Conclusion

This work sought to test the effects of claims on community well-being, and to develop a way to systematically accomplish this task using socio-economic indicators that are readily available in the Census. Our approach is a cost-effective manner of examining temporal changes, and the generalizability of results is directly of benefit to all stakeholders. As we noted above, the problem we face here is that the results of this work are less than definitive, given the time span of the data and the limited availability of relevant outcomes of the claims settlements.

If future studies were to take place, we would recommend that a detailed case study approach be adopted in conjunction with the aggregate statistical analysis. This approach could mitigate some of the difficulties faced by the aggregate statistical approach taken here, given a case study's holistic and in-depth analytical framework. As well, we would suggest waiting until more time has elapsed so that more post-settlement data would be available. This would allow a finer-tuned assessment of the effect of the settlements on well-being. We realize that using a case study approach creates a tradeoff between specificity and generalizability.[13] However, such a study would allow us to draw some understanding of how settlements are being used in the communities. We could then proceed to see if there are any potential relationships between how settlements are used and their impact on a specific community's well-being. Combining this understanding with a longer time frame might allow us to interpret the aggregate data more finely. On the one hand, from a policy perspective, individual community accounts are limited in terms of what they represent—are the events and conditions of a specific community typical of First Nations communities that have received claims? On the other hand, this approach tends to capture a part of what is missed through survey methodology that only utilizes Census data. As discussed earlier, if socio-economic success must be defined as a multidimensional concept that includes traditional socio-economic indicators as well as governance, cohesion, culture, tradition, and other social processes absent from the Census, it may be essential to use multiple investigation methods to capture these themes.[14, 15, 16]

In closing, the issue of the effects of claims and litigation on the well-being of First Nations people is a crucial one, with significant implications for all stakeholders. While it is troubling that we were unable to find a positive effect of specific claims settlements on well-being, this work is one piece of the puzzle; we have outlined the difficulties in assessing such a complex relationship and offered some key points to consider. We will continue to monitor and examine this relationship using different methodological approaches and shed more light on this cardinal issue.

Endnotes

1   For a detailed account of the history of specific claims and the relationship between the Crown and First Nations, see Butt and Hurley (2006) and the specific claims website at <**www.ainc-inac.gc.ca/ps/clm/index_e.html**>.

2   See the specific claims website for more details: <**www.ainc-inac.gc.ca/ps/clm/scb-eng.asp**>. Also, see White, Maxim, and Spence (2004) for more information on the link between the legal framework of society and the structuring of relations in society, including socio-economic development and overall well-being.

3   It should be noted that there has been legislation passed that limits Indian gaming operations. The *Indian Gaming Regulatory Act* (National Indian Gaming Commission 1988), for example, restricts gaming on reservations to roughly the level of gaming allowed in the state where the reservation is found. Tribes must negotiate with their home state if they want Las Vegas–style (Class III) gaming (Darian-Smith 2004).

4   There are no CWB scores for 1986 because of differences in the manner in which relevant variables were measured in the Census, coupled with the large number of First Nation communities that did not participate.

5   For example, thirty First Nation communities, including about 30,000–35,000 Registered Indians, chose not to participate in the 2001 Census.

6   Excluding communities that did not participate in the Census, had data quality issues, or had populations of less than 65.

7   Accompanying the graphical descriptions of the results presented in the figures are tables with "n" sizes, averages, and standard errors, which can be found in Appendix 1.

8   Accompanying the graphical descriptions of the results presented in the figures are tables with "n" sizes, averages, and standard errors, which can be found in Appendix 2.

9   For a detailed discussion on the CWB, including validity and reliability issues, see Chapters 2 & 6.

10 On the one hand, if the resources are allocated in a diverse manner towards various needs of the community, many small positive changes may occur across each of the outcomes of interest, but no single outcome may improve in a significant manner. On the other hand, where resources are allocated exclusively for improving an outcome of interest, for example educational attainment, we may be more likely to observe a change in the outcome of interest.

11 For example, White, Spence, and Maxim (2005) found that social capital has a positive effect on educational attainment in First Nations communities, but the relationship is an interactive one, contingent upon community norms, cultural openness, and community capacity. Thus, increasing educational attainment from claims settlements using this social capital framework may be the primary objective; however, for this goal to be achieved there is a critical period in which resources will take time to flow in, contributing to the preconditions necessary for maximizing social capital for educational purposes for a specific community. This period may be several years and will likely vary by community, given existing conditions.

12 For an in-depth examination of how these issues relate to economic development, see *Aboriginal Conditions: Research as a Foundation for Public Policy* (White, Maxim, and Beavon, 2002).

13 See Yin (1984) for more on the debate regarding case study research and generalizability.

14 One of the hallmarks of case study methodology is that it is a multiple perspective analysis which gives voice to the powerless (Feagin, Orum, and Sjoberg, 1991). This point is particularly relevant given the historical treatment of First Nations people in Canada.

15 Given the diversity of First Nations people, culturally, historically, and socio-economically (e.g., Young, 2003; Waldram, Herring, and Young, 1995), as well as the specific historical relationship between the Crown and each First Nation with a grievance, it may in fact be absolutely necessary to use the case study approach to truly understand the (non) effects of specific claims.

16 For an in depth examination of case study methodology, see Feagin, Orum, and Sjoberg (1991), Stoke (1995) and Yin (1984; 1994).

References

Anderson, R.B. 2002. "Entrepreneurship and Aboriginal Canadians: A Case Study in Economic Development." *Journal of Developmental Entrepreneurship.* 7(1):45–65.

Anderson, R.B. and Bone, R. 1999. "First Nations Economic Development: The Meadow Lake Tribal Council." *Journal of Aboriginal Economic Development.* 1(1):13–34.

Butt, E. and Hurley, M.C. 2006. Specific Claims in Canada. Ottawa: Library of Parliament.

Cornell, S. and Kalt, J.P. 1992. "Reloading the Dice: Improving the Chances for Economic Development on American Indian Reservations." In S. Cornell and J.P. Kalt. (Eds.). *What Can Tribes Do? Strategies and Institutions in American Indian Economic Development.* Los Angeles: American Indian Studies Center, University of California

Darian-Smith, E. 2004. *The New Capitalists: Law, Politics and Identity Surrounding Casino Gaming on native American Land.* Belmont CA: Thompson-Wadsworth.

Feagin, J., Orum, A., and Sjoberg, G. 1991. *A Case for Case Study.* Chapel Hill: University of North Carolina Press.

Indian Affairs Canada. 2006. Specific Claims.<**www.ainc-inac.gc.ca/ps/clm/scb-eng.asp**>. Accessed 17 July 2006.

Kersey, H. 1992. "Seminoles and Miccosukees: A Century in Retrospective." In J.A. Paredes. (Ed.). *Indians of the Southeastern United States in the Late 20th Century,.* Alabama: University of Alabama Press. 102–119.

National Indian Gaming Commission. 1988. *Indian Gaming Regulatory Act.* <**www.nigc.gov/ LawsRegulations/IndianGamingRegulatoryAct/tabid/605/Default.aspx**>. Accessed 17 July 2006.

Royal Commission on Aboriginal Peoples. 1996. *The Report on Aboriginal People.* Ottawa: Government of Canada.

Snipp, C.M. 1995. "American Indian Economic Development." In E. Castle. (Eds.). *The Changing American Countryside: Rural People and Places.* Lawrence: University of Kansas Press. 303–317.

Stake, R. 1995. The Art of Case Research. Newbury Park: Sage Publications.

Waldram, J., Herring, A., and Young, T. 1995. *Aboriginal Health in Canada: Historical, Cultural, and Epidemiological Perspectives.* Toronto: University of Toronto Press.

White, J., Spence, N., and Maxim, P. 2005. "Social capital and educational attainment among Aboriginal peoples: Canada, Australia and New Zealand." In *Policy Research Initiative Social Capital Project Series, Social Capital in Action: Thematic Studies.* Ottawa: Policy Research Initiative, Government of Canada. 66–81.

White, J.P., Maxim, P., and Spence, N. 2004. *Permission to Develop.* Toronto: Thompson Educational Publishing.

White, J.P., Maxim, P., and Beavon, D. 2002. *Aboriginal Conditions: Research as a Foundation for Public Policy.* Vancouver: UBC Press.

Yin, R. 1984. *Case Study Research: Design and Methods.* Beverly Hills, CA: Sage Publications.

Yin, R. 1994. *Case Study Research: Design and Methods,* Second Edition. Thousand Oaks, CA: Sage Publications.

Young, T.K. 2003. "Review of research on Aboriginal populations in Canada: relevance to their health needs." BMJ. 327: 419–422.

Appendix 1

Appendix 1A: Community Well-being and Component Scores for Communities with No Claims: 1981–2001

Income					
Year	Average	Standard Error	95% Confidence Interval		n
1981	0.3660	0.0201	0.3266	0.4053	62
1986	-	-			-
1991	0.4140	0.0167	0.3813	0.4467	72
1996	0.4507	0.0151	0.4200	0.4802	76
2001	0.4619	0.0156	0.4312	0.4926	78

Housing					
Year	Average	Standard Error	95% Confidence Interval		n
1981	0.5750	0.0241	0.5278	0.6223	62
1986	-	-			-
1991	0.6267	0.0175	0.5924	0.6609	72
1996	0.6666	0.0149	0.6374	0.6958	76
2001	0.6806	0.0153	0.6506	0.7106	78

CWB Score					
Year	Average	Standard Error	95% Confidence Interval		n
1981	0.5021	0.0123	0.4780	0.5263	62
1986	-	-			-
1991	0.5631	0.0109	0.5417	0.5845	72
1996	0.6138	0.0092	0.5957	0.6318	76
2001	0.6334	0.0093	0.6152	0.6515	78

Education					
Year	Average	Standard Error	95% Confidence Interval		n
1981	0.4091	0.0221	0.3657	0.4525	62
1986	-	-			-
1991	0.5284	0.0184	0.4923	0.5645	72
1996	0.6204	0.0163	0.5884	0.6524	76
2001	0.6483	0.0188	0.6115	0.6851	78

Labour Force Activity					
Year	Average	Standard Error	95% Confidence Interval		n
1981	0.6528	0.0178	0.6179	0.6878	62
1986	-	-			-
1991	0.6534	0.0121	0.6296	0.6771	72
1996	0.6907	0.0112	0.6687	0.7126	76
2001	0.6903	0.0098	0.6711	0.7095	78

Appendix 1B: Community Well-being and Component Scores for those Communities That Have Ever Settled a Claim

Income					
Year	Average	Standard Error	95% Confidence Interval		n
1981	0.3508	0.0210	0.3096	0.3919	58
1986	-	-			-
1991	0.3811	0.0174	0.3471	0.4152	62
1996	0.4139	0.0161	0.3823	0.4456	72
2001	0.4465	0.0157	0.4156	0.4774	75

Housing					
Year	Average	Standard Error	95% Confidence Interval		n
1981	0.6255	0.0232	0.5801	0.6710	58
1986	-	-			
1991	0.6309	0.0231	0.5856	0.6763	62
1996	0.6846	0.0177	0.6499	0.7193	72
2001	0.6835	0.0176	0.6490	0.7180	75

CWB Score					
Year	Average	Standard Error	95% Confidence Interval		n
1981	0.5184	0.0124	0.4940	0.5428	58
1986	-	-			-
1991	0.5619	0.0123	0.5378	0.5860	62
1996	0.5999	0.0117	0.5769	0.6230	72
2001	0.6282	0.0102	0.6083	0.6481	75

Education					
Year	Average	Standard Error	95% Confidence Interval		n
1981	0.4209	0.0217	0.3784	0.4635	58
1986	-	-			-
1991	0.5575	0.0180	0.5222	0.5929	62
1996	0.6364	0.0148	0.6074	0.6655	72
2001	0.6980	0.0118	0.6749	0.7212	75

Labour Force Activity					
Year	Average	Standard Error	95% Confidence Interval		n
1981	0.6778	0.0154	0.6477	0.7080	58
1986	-	-			-
1991	0.6251	0.0104	0.6046	0.6456	62
1996	0.6661	0.0102	0.6462	0.6861	72
2001	0.6720	0.0092	0.6539	0.6901	75

Appendix 1C: Community Well-being and Component Scores for Those Communities with a Filed Claim but no Settlement: 1981–2001

Income					
Year	Average	Standard Error	95% Confidence Interval		n
1981	0.3823	0.0132	0.3564	0.4082	137
1986	-	-			-
1991	0.4295	0.0096	0.4107	0.4904	156
1996	0.4708	0.0100	0.4512	0.4904	162
2001	0.4921	0.0094	0.4736	0.5106	175

Housing					
Year	Average	Standard Error	95% Confidence Interval		n
1981	0.6033	0.0164	0.5710	0.6355	137
1986	-	-			
1991	0.6849	0.0115	0.6624	0.7073	156
1996	0.7350	0.0108	0.7138	0.7561	162
2001	0.7297	0.0101	0.7099	0.7494	175

CWB Score					
Year	Average	Standard Error	95% Confidence Interval		n
1981	0.5378	0.0074	0.5233	0.5522	137
1986	-	-			-
1991	0.6058	0.0063	0.5934	0.6182	156
1996	0.6496	0.0057	0.6383	0.6608	162
2001	0.6662	0.0056	0.6552	0.6771	175

Education					
Year	Average	Standard Error	95% Confidence Interval		n
1981	0.4532	0.0113	0.4311	0.4753	137
1986	-	-			-
1991	0.5837	0.0105	0.5630	0.6043	156
1996	0.6647	0.0097	0.6457	0.6837	162
2001	0.7036	0.0090	0.6861	0.7212	175

Labour Force Activity					
Year	Average	Standard Error	95% Confidence Interval		n
1981	0.6638	0.0092	0.6458	0.6819	137
1986	-	-			-
1991	0.6407	0.0067	0.6275	0.6538	156
1996	0.6851	0.0064	0.6725	0.6977	162
2001	0.7012	0.0058	0.6898	0.7126	175

Appendix 2

Appendix 2A: Community Well-being and Component Scores for those Communities With Claims Settled in 1981: 1981–2001

		Income			
Year	Average	Standard Error	95% Confidence Interval		n
1981	0.5068	0.0939	0.3228	0.6909	5
1986	-	-			-
1991	0.5024	0.0951	0.3160	0.6887	5
1996	0.5253	0.0729	0.3824	0.6682	6
2001	0.5565	0.0814	0.3969	0.7160	5

		Housing			
Year	Average	Standard Error	95% Confidence Interval		n
1981	0.7365	0.1268	0.4879	0.9851	5
1986	-	-			
1991	0.7483	0.1245	0.5043	0.9922	5
1996	0.7791	0.0926	0.5976	0.9607	6
2001	0.8016	0.1004	0.6047	0.9984	5

		CWB Score			
Year	Average	Standard Error	95% Confidence Interval		n
1981	0.5684	0.0812	0.4092	0.7275	5
1986	-	-			-
1991	0.6231	0.0707	0.4845	0.7616	5
1996	0.6661	0.0576	0.5532	0.7790	6
2001	0.6739	0.0544	0.5671	0.7806	5

		Education			
Year	Average	Standard Error	95% Confidence Interval		n
1981	0.5333	0.1096	0.3184	0.7482	5
1986	-	-			-
1991	0.6111	0.1013	0.4125	0.8096	5
1996	0.7036	0.0584	0.5892	0.8180	6
2001	0.7266	0.0644	0.6003	0.8528	5

		Labour Force Activity			
Year	Average	Standard Error	95% Confidence Interval		n
1981	0.6738	0.0371	0.6011	0.7465	5
1986	-	-			-
1991	0.6103	0.0402	0.5315	0.6892	5
1996	0.6564	0.313	0.5951	0.7176	6
2001	0.6266	0.0426	0.5437	0.7094	5

Appendix 2B: Community Well-being and Component Scores for those Communities With Claims Settled in 1986: 1981–2001

Income					
Year	Average	Standard Error	95% Confidence Interval		n
1981	0.4073	0.0973	0.2165	0.5980	4
1986	-	-			-
1991	0.4465	0.0402	0.3677	0.5253	5
1996	0.4603	0.0457	0.3707	0.5499	4
2001	0.4753	0.0255	0.4253	0.5253	4

Housing					
Year	Average	Standard Error	95% Confidence Interval		n
1981	0.6511	0.1380	0.3807	0.9216	4
1986	-	-			
1991	0.6573	0.0632	0.5334	0.7812	5
1996	0.7223	0.0322	0.6593	0.7854	4
2001	0.6318	0.0510	0.5319	0.7317	4

CWB Score					
Year	Average	Standard Error	95% Confidence Interval		n
1981	0.5693	0.0752	0.4218	0.7168	4
1986	-	-			-
1991	0.5995	0.0538	0.4940	0.7049	5
1996	0.6509	0.0332	0.5858	0.7160	4
2001	0.6486	0.0305	0.5889	0.7084	4

Education					
Year	Average	Standard Error	95% Confidence Interval		n
1981	0.4283	0.1196	0.1938	0.6627	4
1986	-	-			-
1991	0.6097	0.0931	0.4272	0.7922	5
1996	0.6511	0.0993	0.4564	0.8458	4
2001	0.7126	0.0701	0.5753	0.8499	4

Labour Force Activity					
Year	Average	Standard Error	95% Confidence Interval		n
1981	0.7227	0.0520	0.6208	0.8246	4
1986	-	-			-
1991	0.6843	0.0350	0.6157	0.7529	5
1996	0.6985	0.0144	0.6704	0.7267	4
2001	0.7245	0.0178	0.6897	0.7593	4

Appendix 2C: Community Well-being and Component Scores for Those Communities with Claims Settled in 1991: 1981–2001

Year	Average	Standard Error	95% Confidence Interval		n
Income					
1981	0.3273	0.0331	0.2625	0.3921	24
1986	-	-			-
1991	0.3392	0.0255	0.2893	0.3891	26
1996	0.3599	0.0215	0.3177	0.4020	29
2001	0.3980	0.0212	0.3565	0.4395	32
Housing					
1981	0.5932	0.0337	0.5271	0.6593	24
1986	-	-			-
1991	0.5801	0.0334	0.5146	0.6456	26
1996	0.6557	0.0250	0.6067	0.7046	29
2001	0.6517	0.0255	0.6018	0.7016	32
CWB Score					
1981	0.5075	0.0163	0.4754	0.5395	24
1986	-	-			-
1991	0.5301	0.0180	0.4947	0.5654	26
1996	0.5739	0.0173	0.5400	0.6078	29
2001	0.6046	0.0255	0.6018	0.7016	32
Education					
1981	0.3888	0.0319	0.3263	0.4513	24
1986	-	-			-
1991	0.5334	0.0239	0.4866	0.5801	26
1996	0.6073	0.0221	0.5640	0.6506	29
2001	0.6963	0.0128	0.6713	0.7214	32
Labour Force Activity					
1981	0.6865	0.0218	0.6438	0.7293	24
1986	-	-			-
1991	0.6071	0.0148	0.5781	0.6361	26
1996	0.6408	0.0146	0.6121	0.6695	29
2001	0.6495	0.0102	0.6295	0.6696	32

Appendix 2D: Community Well-being and Component Scores for Those Communities with Claims Settled in 1996: 1981–2001

Income					
Year	Average	Standard Error	95% Confidence Interval		n
1981	0.3546	0.0372	0.2817	0.4275	21
1986	-	-			-
1991	0.3991	0.0247	0.3508	0.4474	25
1996	0.4343	0.0234	0.3885	0.4801	28
2001	0.4740	0.0217	0.4315	0.5166	28

Housing					
Year	Average	Standard Error	95% Confidence Interval		n
1981	0.6548	0.0395	0.5774	0.7321	21
1986	-	-			
1991	0.6642	0.0353	0.5951	0.7334	25
1996	0.6890	0.0303	0.6295	0.7485	28
2001	0.7091	0.0288	0.6528	0.7655	28

CWB Score					
Year	Average	Standard Error	95% Confidence Interval		n
1981	0.5310	0.0220	0.4879	0.5741	21
1986	-	-			-
1991	0.5892	0.0185	0.5529	0.6256	25
1996	0.6211	0.0182	0.5853	0.6568	28
2001	0.6519	0.0161	0.6204	0.6834	28

Education					
Year	Average	Standard Error	95% Confidence Interval		n
1981	0.4539	0.0337	0.3878	0.5200	21
1986	-	-			-
1991	0.5870	0.0249	0.5383	0.6358	25
1996	0.6697	0.0182	0.6339	0.7054	28
2001	0.7166	0.0179	0.6815	0.7516	28

Labour Force Activity					
Year	Average	Standard Error	95% Confidence Interval		n
1981	0.6665	0.0289	0.6098	0.7232	21
1986	-	-			-
1991	0.6359	0.0147	0.6071	0.6646	25
1996	0.6805	0.0149	0.6513	0.7097	28
2001	0.6958	0.0149	0.6666	0.7250	28

Appendix 2E: Community Well-being and Component Scores for Those Communities with Claims Settled in 2001: 1981–2001

Income					
Year	Average	Standard Error	95% Confidence Interval		n
1981	0.3620	0.0349	0.2935	0.4305	15
1986	-	-			-
1991	0.3676	0.0457	0.2780	0.4573	14
1996	0.4313	0.0410	0.3509	0.5118	17
2001	0.4593	0.0400	0.3809	0.5377	18

Housing					
Year	Average	Standard Error	95% Confidence Interval		n
1981	0.6621	0.0353	0.5929	0.7314	15
1986	-	-			
1991	0.6552	0.0457	0.5655	0.7448	14
1996	0.7134	0.0356	0.6436	0.7831	17
2001	0.7037	0.0342	0.6368	0.7707	18

CWB Score					
Year	Average	Standard Error	95% Confidence Interval		n
1981	0.5230	0.0236	0.4767	0.5693	15
1986	-	-			-
1991	0.5620	0.0260	0.5110	0.6129	14
1996	0.6021	0.0268	0.5496	0.6546	17
2001	0.6293	0.0247	0.5809	0.6776	18

Education					
Year	Average	Standard Error	95% Confidence Interval		n
1981	0.4182	0.0347	0.3503	0.4861	15
1986	-	-			-
1991	0.5659	0.0365	0.4943	0.6374	14
1996	0.6514	0.0330	0.5867	0.7161	17
2001	0.6883	0.0307	0.6282	0.7483	18

Labour Force Activity					
Year	Average	Standard Error	95% Confidence Interval		n
1981	0.7051	0.0274	0.6515	0.7588	15
1986	-	-			-
1991	0.6378	0.0269	0.5850	0.6905	14
1996	0.6877	0.0245	0.6397	0.7358	17
2001	0.6901	0.0216	0.6478	0.7323	18

10

Well-being in First Nations Communities: A Comparison of Objective and Subjective Dimensions

Susan Wingert*

Introduction

There has been a growing recognition that public policy should promote well-being as opposed to merely addressing social problems. However, well-being is an elusive concept. What constitutes well-being and the mechanisms underlying it has generated substantial theoretical and empirical work, but little consensus. To date, definitions have been broad and abstract. In 2004, at the Royal Society Discussion Meeting, well-being was defined as "a positive and sustainable state that allows individuals, groups, or nations to thrive and flourish" (Huppert, Baylis, & Keverne, 2004, p. 1331). Despite these fuzzy definitions, this line of research has begun to shed light on how well-being is produced. Public policy itself is an important determinant of a society's well-being (Huppert & Baylis, 2004). In particular, there is evidence to suggest that public policy influences individuals through multiple channels (Helliwell, 2003). As a result, a policy may have a positive effect on well-being via one channel and a negative one via another, which can help to explain why expected outcomes are not always evident. Understanding these possible multiple outcomes can lead to the development of better policies.

One approach to the study of well-being has been the development of composite indicators (Cooke, 2005). Since well-being is not directly measurable, researchers have combined key determinants of well-being that are shared across social groups (Dasgupta, 1999). This method enables researchers and policy makers to make comparisons across groups and locations, and over time. In addition, these indicators provide a way of evaluating policies and their alternatives (Dasgupta, 1999).

In this chapter we use one such measure: the Community Well-being Index (CWB). This index provides a simple and understandable objective measure of basic socioeconomic dimensions of well-being, including education, labour force participation, income, and housing.[1] These dimensions have been recognized as key non-medical determinants of health and well-being (First Nations Inuit Health Branch, 2005). Furthermore, many in Aboriginal communities have stressed the importance of these issues. For example, many Aboriginal people, as well as other researchers, argue that education is needed to fully participate in Canadian society and achieve self-governance (Abele, 2004; Silver & Mallet, 2002, see also White et al., 2003 and 2007). As Abele (2004) noted, Aboriginal peoples have been affected by many of the macro-level changes in society that have restructured labour markets, increased income inequality, and changed educational needs. As a result, there is a shared interest in creating a society that supports the well-being of its citizens; however, Aboriginal peoples may approach the issue from a different cultural and historical perspective.

The CWB has been used to compare conditions across First Nations, and between First Nations and non-First Nations communities (see Chapter 8). As critics have noted, it does not include measures of the cultural dimension (Ten Fingers, 2005). There are several issues that make the inclusion of culture in indices difficult. First, there is no pan-Aboriginal culture. There is tremendous cultural diversity across First Nations and other Aboriginal groups. In order to add a cultural dimension, we need to find a measure that is equally valid across different cultural groups. A second, and related challenge, is finding a way of quantifying culture that is still meaningful. Obviously, culture is best understood qualitatively, but indices require quantitative data. Language may be a good candidate since it is a primary vehicle for cultural transmission (First Nations Inuit Health Branch, 2005). Norris (1998) and Norris and MacCon (2003), for example, classified Aboriginal languages as extinct, near extinction, endangered, viable with a small population base, and viable with a large population base. This approach provides a way of quantifying a proxy measure of cultural vitality. An additional challenge, if we are interested in seeing how First Nations compare to other groups, is finding an equivalent measure of culture for those other groups. Finally, there is limited data available that would enable such intra- or inter-group comparisons (Cooke, 2005). As data become available, it will be possible to see if culture adds sufficient explanatory power to justify its inclusion in the CWB.

Qualitative research conducted by or in partnership with First Nations is drawing attention to local understandings of well-being and the processes that link culture and well-being (see for example Ten Fingers, 2005). It will be exciting to see, as both lines of research develop, whether they compliment or contradict one another. The reconciliation of these two different perspectives on well-being will likely bring about important advancements in terms of theory, method, and knowledge.

In the study of well-being, there has been growing recognition that measures of objective conditions only provide part of the picture (Biswas-Diener, Diener, & Tamir, 2004; Kahn & Juster, 2002). Individuals interpret their own objective conditions and create their own subjective understandings and evaluations. Subjective well-being refers to an individual's own personal assessment (McBride, 2001). Research has identified three distinct dimensions of subjective well-being: positive affect, negative affect, and life satisfaction (Biswas-Diener et al., 2004). Since the former two are reactive to short-term changes in external circumstances, most of the research in the field has focused on life satisfaction (Helliwell, 2003).

Existing research has demonstrated that the relationship between objective conditions and subjective evaluations of well-being is complex. In this chapter, we examine the relationship between objective measures of community well-being and the subjective assessments of residents who live in those First Nations. We are interested in determining whether there are patterns in residents' responses depending on whether they live in a below average, average, or above average CWB community. We will address three research questions: 1) What do residents of First Nations communities identify as the top priorities for their communities and do they vary across CWB levels? 2) Is there an association between residents' subjective assessments of their community and its CWB score? 3) Is there a relationship between community well-being, as measured by the CWB, and subjective dimensions of individual well-being? Correspondence with subjective data provides support for the CWB as a proxy measure of community well-being. Where there are discrepancies, we are challenged to find explanations that will advance our understanding about the interplay between external conditions and the assessments of individuals.

Review of Well-being Literature

It is generally agreed that well-being has the following five characteristics. First, it is more than the absence of negative outcomes (Diener, Suh, Lucas, & Smith, 1999; Huppert et al., 2004). Well-being implies a high level or large number of positive outcomes relative to negative ones. Second, it is multifaceted and includes psychological, physical, social, and economic states (Diener et al., 1999; Huppert et al., 2004). Third, processes that produce well-being take place at the individual, community, national, and international levels (Helliwell, 2003). Fourth, well-being has objective and subjective dimensions, which may not be concordant (Diener et al., 1999). Subjective dimensions of well-being are relative and influenced by culture (Diener et al., 1999; Oishi, Diener, Lucas, & Suh, 1999). In other words, to whom we compare ourselves influences how well we think we are and what is most salient to our assessments depends on what our culture tells us is important. Finally, well-being is produced through interaction between individual agency, and structural and cultural constraints (Thoits, 2006). Individuals exercise personal agency in order to seek out opportunities to improve their well-being, avoid or mitigate situations that are deleterious, and cope with or compensate for negative circumstances beyond their control. However, individuals do not have carte blanche. Structured social relations make certain choices and actions difficult or impossible by differentially distributing stressors, resources, demands, obligations, expectations, etc.

Well-being is related to, but not synonymous with, economic prosperity (Diener et al., 1999). Most studies find only a modest correlation between personal income, and various measures of subjective well-being (e.g., happiness, life satisfaction)

(Diener & Biswas-Diener, 2002; Diener et al., 1999). When relative income norms increase, subjective well-being tends to decrease (McBride, 2001). On the one hand, having a low personal income substantially increases the risk of negative outcomes such as unhappiness, distress, and disorder (Diener & Biswas-Diener, 2002). In addition, concentrated disadvantage in neighbourhoods is associated with a wide range of negative outcomes including higher mortality rates, poorer health, crime, accidental injury, and suicide (Sampson, Morenoff, & Gannon-Rowley, 2002). On the other hand, there are strong positive correlations between national wealth and mean subjective well-being probably due to the indirect benefits of living in a wealthy nation (e.g., better infrastructure, clean drinking water, government funded education, etc.) (Diener & Biswas-Diener, 2002; Diener et al., 1999). Helliwell (2003) called these spill-over effects. Research has also shown that meeting basic needs predicts subjective well-being across cultures; however, higher order goals vary by culture (Oishi et al., 1999). The relatively high rates of poverty in the Aboriginal population suggest that basic needs are not being met in many communities (Abele, 2004). Research has also found evidence of diminishing returns at both the individual and national levels; that is, increases in wealth have a larger effect on subjective well-being among low-income individuals and citizens of poor nations, but level off as wealth increases (Diener & Biswas-Diener, 2002).

There are small, but significant correlations between an individual's education level and subjective well-being (Diener et al., 1999; Witter, Okun, Stock, & Haring, 1984). Consistent with findings on income, the effects of education are stronger among individuals with low incomes and those living in poorer nations (Diener et al., 1999). Helliwell (2003) found a strong positive effect between the average level of education in a nation and life satisfaction. He concluded that, for the most part, education affects well-being indirectly through increases in "participation, health, perceived trust, and higher incomes" (p. 351). Indeed, part of the effect is due to overlap with income and occupation; however, education may have benefits beyond higher income and a better job. A study by Steverink, Westerhof, and Bode (2001) showed that physical decline, continuous growth, and social loss were particularly relevant to the subjective well-being of adults past middle age. Individuals with higher income and education, along with better self-rated health and lower levels of loneliness, reported less physical decline and social loss and higher levels of continuous growth. In their analysis of distress in the off-reserve Aboriginal population, Wingert and White (2006) found that individuals with higher levels of education had a stronger sense of mastery, which contributed to lower levels of distress. Individuals with high levels of mastery may be better able to create conditions that are beneficial for well-being. However, education may have a negative effect on subjective well-being when it leads to goals that cannot be achieved (Diener et al., 1999). For example, if an individual cannot translate higher education into tangible benefits, such as a high paying job that uses his or her skills, higher levels of distress may occur. This may be the case on reserves with limited economic opportunities.

Work has received less attention in the subjective well-being literature. Kahn and Juster (2002) stated:

> Work is a source of income, which in turn determines housing, neighbourhood, and the many other aspects of life that are in some degree monetized. A person's employment demands a significant part of his or her time and energy. For most people it is also a source of friendships, and for many it provides a means of utilizing valued skills and abilities. For all these reasons, work (employment) ranks high among the determinants of overall life satisfaction. (pp. 634-635)

Research has shown a connection between unemployment and negative mental health outcomes (Avison, 2001). In addition to health, employment opportunities and income have been associated with neighbourhood stability, pessimism, viability, and social functioning (Christakopoulou, Dawson, & Gari, 2001).

Existing research suggests that many of the dimensions of community well-being that the CWB captures are associated with a wide range of outcomes that directly or indirectly affect the subjective well-being of individuals. In the next section, we compare what residents at different CWB levels say about their communities and their own well-being.

Method

The analyses are based on two waves of a panel telephone survey by EKOS Research Associates, Inc. between February and June 2005. The sampling frame was derived by identifying postal codes from the ten provinces associated with Census subdivisions that contain a reserve or Band office. This exhaustive list of postal codes was used to find telephone numbers from all telephone books from those areas. Telephone numbers were selected at random.

Survey respondents met three eligibility criteria: 1) they were a member of an Indian band or First Nation; 2) aged 16 or older; and 3) resided on a reserve in Canada for at least part of the year preceding the survey. Survey respondents were asked to name their First Nation community, which was matched to its corresponding CWB score.[2] CWB scores were missing for respondents who did not provide the name of their community. These cases were excluded, leaving a final sample of 2,065 individuals. There were 785 individuals who completed wave 1 only, 745 in wave 2 only, 513 in both waves, and 22 missing cases. Weights for each wave were calculated based on age, gender, and region for the First Nations population living on-reserve, according to Statistics Canada figures.

Sample Description by CWB

The CWB scores, which range between 0.42 and 0.90, were divided into three groups. The "average" group had scores that were within one standard deviation

Figure 10.1: Percentage of Respondents in CWB Categories

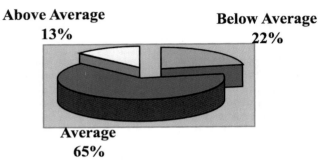

Figure 10.2: Age Structure by CWB

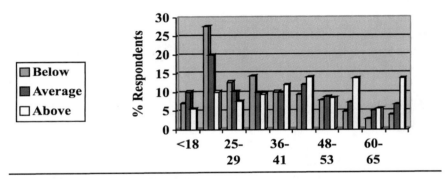

Figure 10.3: Highest Level of Education by CWB

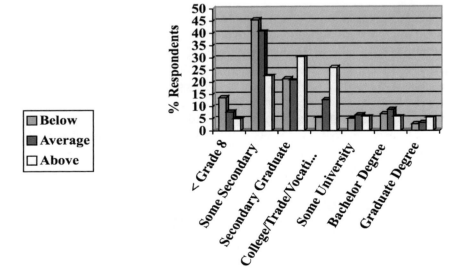

above or below the mean. Scores that were more than one standard deviation below the mean were labelled "below average," and more than one standard deviation above was "above average." **Figure 10.1** shows the percentage of respondents in each CWB category. As one would expect, close to two-thirds were in the average range.

Looking at the age structure of the sample, according to the Kruskal-Wallis test, there are significant differences in median age between CWB categories in both wave 1[3] and wave 2.[4] **Figure 10.2** shows the percentage of respondents in each CWB by age category averaged across both waves of data. A series of Mann-Whitney tests with Bonferroni adjustments were used to compare each pair of CWB categories for significant differences. Compared to below-average communities, average[5] and above average[6] communities had significantly higher mean ranks, which indicates an older population. Above-average communities had a significantly higher mean rank relative to average communities.[7] We would expect that below-average communities have higher birth and death rates, which contribute to a population that is younger on average.

In wave 1 and wave 2, respondents were asked to indicate their highest level of education. Given that two components of the CWB are based on educational attainment, functional literacy (proportion of the community population over the age of 15 with at least a grade 9 education), and high school plus (proportion of the community population that has at least a high school diploma) (McHardy & O'Sullivan, 2004), we would expect to find significant differences in respondents' educational attainment across CWB groupings if this sample is representative of the population at each community level. **Figure 10.3** shows the percentage of respondents by CWB level in each educational category. In general, we can see that respondents in below-average communities are overrepresented in the less than secondary categories while above-average communities have a higher percentage of residents in the secondary graduate, college, trade, vocational, and graduate degree categories. Interestingly, more residents in average communities had some university or a bachelor's degree compared to the other two categories. Results confirmed that there are differences in median educational level.[8] These differences were significant between respondents in below-average and average communities with average communities having a higher mean rank.[9] Compared to average communities, above-average communities had a higher mean rank.[10] Finally, the difference between below- and above-average communities was also statistically significant.[11] Therefore, we can conclude that there is no response bias based on education in this sample because the pattern mirrors the CWB, which is based on population data from the Census.

The CWB also uses a measure of income per capita in the community. Here we examine whether there are differences in household income (waves 1 & 2) across the three CWB groups. **Figure 10.4** (page 216) shows the income distribution of the sample by CWB averaged across both waves of data. The distribution is as expected, with below-average communities having a higher proportion of individ-

Figure 10.4: Household Income by CWB

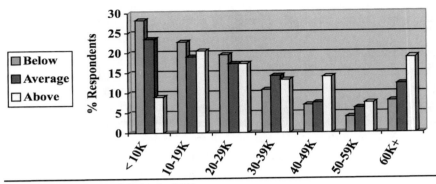

Figure 10.5: Employment Status by CWB

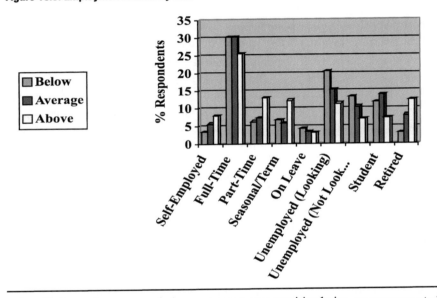

uals with lower incomes and above-average communities being overrepresented at the upper end of the scale. Furthermore, we verified that there were statistically significant differences in the expected direction across the three groups.[12] Average communities have a higher median income compared to below-average communities.[13] Above-average communities had higher household incomes compared to average communities.[14] Finally, residents in below-average communities had significantly lower household incomes than those in above-average communities.[15] Again, it is important to note that given that the CWB includes income measures, if our sample is representative, this is an expected outcome.

The CWB measure of labour force activity captures the percentage of the adult population that is in the labour force and the percentage that are employed. In both waves of the EKOS survey, respondents were asked whether they were self-employed, employed full-time, part-time, seasonally, in a term position, on leave (sick, disability, maternity, or parental), unemployed looking for work, unemployed not looking for work, a student, or retired. **Figure 10.5** shows the percentage of respondents in each CWB category (averaged across the two waves) in each employment category. According to the chi-square test, there was a statistically significant association between CWB level and employment status for both waves.[16] Adjusted residuals tell us where there are statistically significant differences between the observed and expected frequencies. We find that a higher proportion of respondents in below-average communities were unemployed looking for work[17] and unemployed not looking for work.[18] On the other hand, fewer people in these same communities were retired,[19] self-employed,[20] or working part-time.[21] Average communities had fewer seasonal or term[22] employees and a higher number of students.[23] There were fewer full-time workers,[24] unemployed but looking,[25] and students[26] in above-average communities; yet, there were more part-time,[27] seasonal and term,[28] and retired[29] persons than expected. This more detailed measure confirms that more residents in below-average communities are affected by unemployment than in average and above-average communities; however, in terms of employment, there are some unexpected findings. For example, we might have expected average communities to have a higher proportion of residents who are working, but in less stable forms of employment such as seasonal, term, or part-time, which might explain why they have lower average incomes compared to those in above-average communities. However, above-average communities are characterized by these types of employment. The older average age in above-average communities may help to explain why a lower percentage of residents were students and a higher proportion was retired. It may also be that economic opportunities in and around above-average communities allow residents to work part-time or seasonally while pursuing higher education.

In wave 1, respondents who indicated that they were employed were asked whether they were employed on-reserve, off-reserve, or both, as well as their occupational category (labourer; semi-skilled; skilled trade; sales, service, or clerical; professional or management; or administrative). When we look at where respondents were employed, the vast majority across CWB levels were employed on-reserve (**Figure 10.6** — page 218). However, analyses showed a significant association between CWB and employment location.[30] A higher proportion of residents in below-average communities were employed on-reserve while fewer were employed off-reserve. The opposite relationship was found for above-average communities. There was no association between CWB and occupational category. It appears that part of the advantage of above-average communities may be proximity to other centres, which become a source of economic opportunities.

In waves 1 and 2, respondents were asked what language they first learned as a child and still understand (meaning that if a child learned an Aboriginal language but subsequently lost it, it wouldn't count). In order to ensure adequate cell sizes, responses were recoded into English or French, and Aboriginal

Figure 10.6: Employment Location by CWB

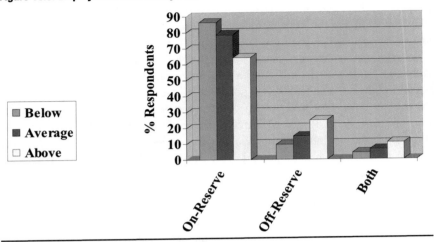

Figure 10.7: Language First Learned by CWB

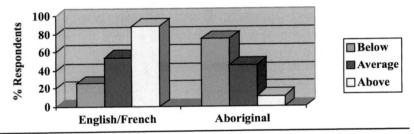

languages. Results are presented in **Figure 10.7**. We can clearly see there is an association between first language and CWB.[31] Respondents in below average CWB communities were much more likely to have learned an Aboriginal language[32] as their first language while those in average[33] and above-average[34] communities were more likely to have learned English or French. In wave 1, respondents were asked to rate on a five-point scale how important it was to keep, learn, or relearn their Aboriginal language. There were no differences by CWB level, with the vast majority in all three groups reporting it was very important. Respondents in wave 2 were asked whether they had participated in any traditional or cultural activities over the past 12 months. There was a significant association with CWB[35] with respondents in below-average communities being less likely to have participated.[36]

Based on the data available here, it appears there is a complex relationship between culture and CWB. With respect to first language, we may be seeing a spurious relationship because Cree, one of the most prevalent Aboriginal languages, is concentrated across the prairie provinces, which also have a disproportionate number of below average CWB communities (McHardy & O'Sullivan, 2004).

However, there may indeed be a relationship between first language and economic integration, which means those without proficiency in English or French may be more likely to experience economic disadvantage. It is also unusual that the vast majority of residents in below-average communities cite an Aboriginal language as their mother tongue, but were less likely to have participated in traditional activities. This finding runs counter to the language as a vehicle for culture argument. Boldt (1993) asserted much of the cultural revitalization among Aboriginal peoples has been in an expressive-ritualistic form as opposed to reasserting traditional values and norms that are encoded in language. If language is indeed a vehicle for culture, traditional livelihoods may be an integral part of life in below-average communities. However, respondents may not think of traditional ways of living as traditional activities, which may be conceptualized as specific events. However, it is also possible that there is a disconnect between language and cultural activities. It may be that communities with more resources are able to provide organized, large scale, and more formalized traditional activities for their residents. It may also be the case that while the majority of residents in average and above-average communities learn English or French first, some may subsequently acquire their traditional language and enjoy the best of both worlds.

Results

In wave 1, respondents were asked what areas of their First Nations community most urgently needed attention to improve the lives of residents. They were not read a list of choices and could give up to three answers. **Figure 10.8** (page 220) shows the percentage of respondents who said each category was a priority for their community, by CWB level. The results provide support for the contention that the CWB taps into key dimensions of well-being. More or better housing, education, and jobs were among the top three priorities. Fewer respondents living in below-average communities said that healthcare was a priority.[37] On the other hand, significantly more residents in these communities listed infrastructure.[38] Residents in average communities were more likely to say housing needed urgent improvement.[39]

Survey respondents were also asked what the Government of Canada's priority for First Nations should be (**Figure 10.9** — page 220). Respondents were not read a list of choices and were asked to give one answer. Living conditions in the community, education, and health and social services were the top three responses. When we compare responses across CWB levels, we also find a significant relationship.[40] A higher proportion of residents in below-average communities said that living conditions should be a government priority.[41] On the other hand, residents of above-average communities were much less likely to cite living conditions.[42] Governance, rights, and funding were seen as the priority by many more residents in above-average communities.[43]

Figure 10.8: Areas Needing Urgent Improvement by CWB

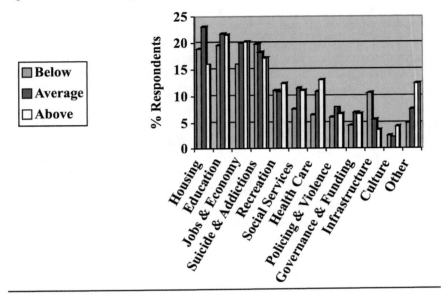

Figure 10.9: Government of Canada's Priorities for First Nations by CWB

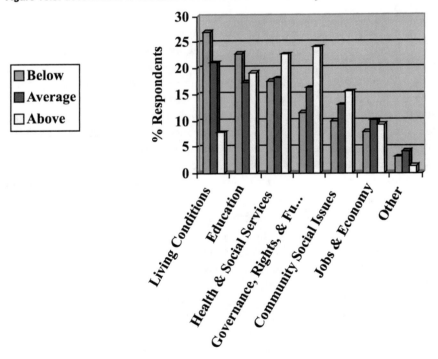

When we compare these responses with those about community priorities, we see that jobs and the economy is a community priority, but not one on which the federal government should focus. On the other hand, issues of governance, rights, and funding are a lower priority for First Nations communities, but are areas where Federal Government involvement was seen as important. On the one hand, residents in below-average communities tended to see living conditions and infrastructure, including water, as priorities. On the other hand, residents in above-average communities were more likely to focus on issues at the centre of the Aboriginal rights movement, including land claims, self-government, funding for reserves, and government accountability.

Next, we wanted to know whether there were differences in respondents' subjective assessments of their communities across CWB levels. In other words, do residents' own opinions mirror the objective information from the CWB score? Respondents were asked to rate on a five-point scale (1 = very bad and 5 = excellent) education (kindergarten through grade 12), health care (amount and quality), safety, housing (amount and quality), drinking water, social support from friends and family, jobs and the economy in their community. The availability of social support and health care showed no significant differences. It may be that since these variables are less connected to socio-economic conditions that they are distributed randomly across CWB levels. However, there were significant differences with respect to education,[44] safety,[45] quality of housing,[46] drinking water,[47] jobs,[48] and economy.[49] **Figure 10.10** (page 222) shows the mean ranks for the statistically significant variables with higher scores, indicating higher ratings on average compared to the other groups.

Below-average and average communities differed significantly on the quality of housing available[50] with respondents in average communities giving higher ratings. Respondents from above-average communities rated safety,[51] quality of housing,[52] quality of drinking water,[53] amount and quality of jobs,[54] and the community economy[55] higher than those living in average communities. When below- and above-average communities were compared, there were significant differences across all six variables.[56] With the exception of education, residents in above-average communities gave more favourable ratings. It is interesting that residents in below-average communities reported that the quality of education was better compared to those in above-average communities. It may be that residents in above-average communities have higher expectations with regard to education and as a result, provide less favourable ratings. Other studies have found a similar pattern. White, Spence, and Maxim (2005) reported that among Aboriginals in Australia, children, families, and communities took more interest in schooling in regions where education could lead to employment. It is also possible that initiatives to improve educational quality have been targeted toward the communities with the greatest need.

On a five-point scale (1 = strongly disagree and 5 = strongly agree), respondents were asked to indicate how well their community was run, whether they

Figure 10.10: Ratings of Community Areas by CWB

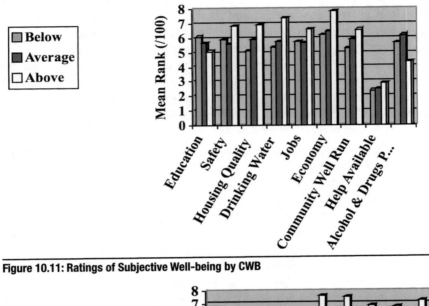

Figure 10.11: Ratings of Subjective Well-being by CWB

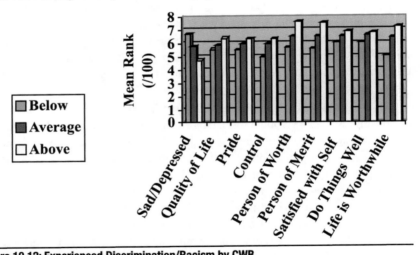

Figure 10.12: Experienced Discrimination/Racism by CWB

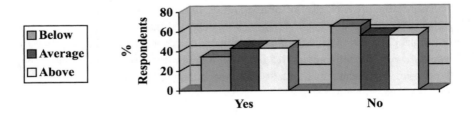

had any say in how their community was run, and the extent to which they got the help they needed in their community (**Figure 10.10**). There were significant differences between CWB levels in ratings for getting help in the community[57] and how well the community was run[58] (**Figure 10.10**). Differences were significant between below-average and average,[59] average and above-average,[60] and below- and above-average[61] for ratings of how well the community was run. It appears, not surprisingly, that residents in above-average communities gave higher marks compared to the other two groups. There was a statistically significant difference between respondents' ratings in below-average and above-average communities with respect to getting help.[62] Other research has found a positive relationship between socio-economic status and social support (Wingert & White, 2006).

Respondents were also asked to rate how big a problem domestic violence, and drugs and alcohol were in their community (1 = no problem at all and 5 = a very big problem). There were no significant differences with respect to domestic violence, but there was a relationship between CWB and drugs and alcohol[63] (**Figure 10.10**). Residents in average communities had the highest mean rank, which means drugs and alcohol were seen as a bigger problem in these communities. Pairwise comparisons indicated that ratings for drug and alcohol were significantly different between average and above-average,[64] and below- and above-average communities.[65] In both cases, above-average communities had a lower mean rank indicating drugs and alcohol were seen as less of a problem. These analyses do not allow us to look at the causal direction of this relationship. It may be that increases in well-being lead to reductions in substance abuse or the prevalence of these problems may erode community well-being over time. In addition, both processes may be at work. It is clear that even though the CWB does not directly measure many elements of community life, we generally find more positive assessments as we move up the CWB ladder.

Our third research question asks whether there is a relationship between CWB level and residents' assessments of their own personal well-being. In wave 1, respondents were asked to rate their quality of life (1 = very bad and 5 = very good). In addition, they were asked how strongly they disagreed or agreed with the statements: I often feel sad and depressed; I can meet most of the challenges that come my way; I have a lot to be proud of; and I have control over what happens to me. We found that there were statistically significant differences across CWB groups for quality of life,[66] sadness and depression,[67] pride,[68] and control[69] (**Figure 10.11**). Only "confidence in one's ability to meet challenges" showed no difference. Between below-average and average communities, there were differences in feelings of sadness and depression,[70] pride,[71] and control.[72] People in below-average communities more strongly agreed that they often felt sad and depressed and that they felt much less pride and control. Between average and above-average communities, only feeling sad and depressed was statistically significant[73] with people in average communities experiencing more sadness and depression. When we compare below and above-average communities, all of the variables are statistically significant.[74] Respondents in below-average communities more strongly agreed they often felt sad and depressed, while those in above-average communities felt more pride, control, and that they had a good quality of life.

In wave 2, respondents were asked how strongly they agreed or disagreed that they were a person of worth, person of merit, satisfied with themselves, do things as well as most, and that life was worthwhile. Significant differences emerged between CWB categories on all of these variables[75] (**Figure 10.11** — page 222). The differences in mean rank were significant between respondents in below-average and average communities for person of worth,[76] person of merit,[77] doing things well,[78] and life is worthwhile.[79] Respondents in average communities had relatively higher scores across the board. The respondents from above-average CWB communities felt more self-worth,[80] merit,[81] and that life was worthwhile[82] compared to respondents from average communities. Finally, compared to respondents in below-average communities, those in above-average communities had much more positive assessments of themselves and their lives.[83]

Research has shown that experiencing discrimination or racism can be deleterious to well-being (Whitbeck, McMorris, Hoyt, Stubben, & LaFramboise, 2002). In wave 2, respondents were asked whether they had experienced discrimination or racism in the past two years because of their Aboriginal heritage. **Figure 10.12** (page 222) shows responses to this question as a percentage within each CWB level. Over half of respondents in each category indicated that they had not experienced discrimination or racism. However, there was an association between CWB level and having a negative experience related to ethnicity.[84] Those in below-average communities had a lower frequency of experiencing discrimination or racism.[85] On the other hand, those in average communities had a significantly higher rate.[86] The association was not statistically significant for above-average communities. McHardy and O'Sullivan (2004) examined average CWB scores by geographic zone classification (urban, rural, remote, and special access). Special access communities had the lowest average CWB score (.60), followed by rural (.65), remote (.68), and urban (.71). It may be that residents in low CWB communities experience less racism and discrimination because they have less contact with non-Aboriginal communities. On the other hand, if respondents in below-average communities have a stronger connection to culture, there may be a buffering effect that may mitigate the negative effects of discrimination, which makes the experience less memorable.

Finally, we looked at a measure of health. Respondents in wave 2 were asked if they had a physical or mental condition that impaired their daily functioning. The results were not statistically significant. It may be that this measure of health is too narrowly defined to detect differences. Less than one-third of respondents indicated that they had a functional impairment. Self-rated health may be a more sensitive measure.

Conclusions

This chapter has aimed to expand our knowledge of well-being in First Nations communities by looking at how subjective assessments relate to objective conditions. A central issue is whether the CWB taps into dimensions of well-being that community residents deem important or if it imposes a view that is markedly discrepant from local perspectives. The first research question asked whether community priorities vary by CWB level. Here, it was evident that the CWB captures key issues for community residents across all three levels, since housing, education, jobs, and the economy were the most commonly cited. Health and social services are lower priorities for below-average community residents. What warrants further investigation is whether residents are happy with the level of service or there are more pressing issues in the community. It appears that one of those pressing issues is basic living conditions and infrastructure, which were more likely to be a top priority for residents in below-average communities. Given that other research has found the most dramatic gains in subjective well-being when improvements are made in the poorest areas and among the poorest people, it seems that addressing basic needs and community capacity in the communities with the lowest CWB scores would be the most efficacious use of resources. Responses about community versus government priorities seem to suggest that respondents saw community building as the responsibility of local governments while the federal government's role was to assist communities less able to achieve or maintain adequate living conditions, as well as providing high quality education, social services, and ensuring Aboriginal rights are protected.

Next, we looked at whether subjective assessments mirrored the information provided by the CWB. In general we find the expected pattern, with above-average community respondents providing more favourable assessments (with the exception of education). Further investigation is needed to uncover whether the quality of education is relatively poor in high CWB communities or whether there are higher expectations. Another issue is whether average communities have the highest drug and alcohol abuse rates or whether residents in these communities are simply more aware of or bothered by the current level. It may be that widespread recognition of the problem is necessary to motivate the community to address the problem. In addition, compared to below-average communities, average ones may have the resources needed to provide treatment and support. It is also not clear whether rates of domestic violence are randomly distributed across CWB levels or whether there is less recognition of the problem where it is prevalent. It may be that drug and alcohol use more often takes place in a group setting or public place, making it more visible, while domestic violence is more likely to occur in private, rendering it less visible. The spill over effects of drugs and alcohol may also be more disruptive to other community members compared to domestic violence.

Finally, we looked at how CWB levels related to assessments of personal well-being. The pattern was quite clear with respondents in higher CWB categories reporting more positive perceptions of themselves and their lives. These findings are in line with the large body of research connecting socio-economic conditions and psychological well-being (for review, see Yu & Williams, 1999). Here, we see that the CWB corresponds with a range of individual outcomes that it does not directly measure. This finding supports the contention that the CWB measures key determinants of community well-being that are in turn associated with dimensions of personal well-being.

Perhaps the most intriguing questions are raised around the relationship between CWB and culture. Aboriginal peoples have emphasized that their culture is central to their individual and collective well-being. There is widespread acceptance for the contention that the history of cultural oppression and marginalization is a major contributing factor to present levels of inequality. Relatively few studies have examined the role of culture in the production of well-being, but studies examining mental health outcomes have found positive effects. For example, Whitbeck et al. (2002) found that among American Indians living on reservations, engaging in traditional practices was protective against the deleterious effects of discrimination. Studies have reported lower levels of psychological distress among individuals who spend more time in the bush (Kirmayer, Boothroyd, Tanner, Adelson, & Robinson, 2000). Culture ranked very low on the list of community priorities. Again, there is no way of knowing why fewer respondents cited it as a priority. There are a number of possibilities. It may be that respondents are satisfied with the availability of cultural activities in their communities or it may be that other initiatives are believed to have a wider or more profound impact on the lives of residents. It may also be that since cultural activities generally do not require the cooperation of government, communities have more direct control over provision. The context in which cultural activities occur may also matter. The positive effects of culture may be off-set by the negative effects of socio-economic deprivation. For example, the relatively high rates of Aboriginal languages as a mother tongue in below-average communities do not seem to translate into positive self-perceptions and affect, or life satisfaction. As Kirmayer, Brass, and Tait (2000) argued, "attempts to recover power and maintain cultural traditions must contend with the political, economic, and cultural realities of consumer capitalism, technocratic control, and globalization" (p. 616).

We predicted that there would be a complex relationship between objective measures of community well-being and subjective assessments. Certainly, research examining the processes and mechanisms connecting the two will undoubtedly uncover tremendous complexity. However, these analyses show definite patterning. Generally, residents in communities with better socio-economic conditions were focused on community building, as opposed to meeting basic needs, and had more positive assessments of their communities, themselves, and their lives. These analyses support the contention that there is concordance between the CWB and other dimensions of well-being.

Endnotes

* The author would like to acknowledge and thank Susan Galley, senior vice president of quantitative research, and her team at EKOS Research Associates, Inc. who collected and prepared the data. Susan and Elliot Gauthier provided valuable technical advice during the preparation of this chapter. Also thanks to Jerry White who worked with the author on the development of the analysis .

1 In this chapter, communities have been grouped by score into three broad categories: below average, average, and above average.

2 CWB scores have been calculated by researchers at Indian and Northern Affairs Canada (INAC) and the University of Western Ontario (UWO) for all communities in Canada that were completely enumerated in the 2001 Census (McHardy & O'Sullivan, 2004).

3 $H = 40.61$, $p < .001$

4 $H = 33.54$, $p < .001$

5 Wave 1 $Z = 3.69$, $p < .001$; wave 2 n.s.

6 Wave 1 $Z = 6.29$, $p < .001$; wave 2 $Z = 5.97$, $p < .001$

7 Wave 1 $Z = 4.42$, $p < .001$; wave 2 $Z = 4.77$, $p < .001$

8 Wave 1 $H = 39.91$, $p < .001$; wave 2 $H = 29.25$, $p < .001$

9 Wave 1 $Z = 4.49$, $p < .001$; wave 2 $Z = 3.12$, $p < .01$

10 Wave 1 $Z = 3.42$, $p < .01$; wave 2 $Z = 3.55$, $p < .001$

11 Wave 1 $Z = 6.17$, $p < .001$; wave 2 $Z = 5.48$, $p < .001$

12 Wave 1 $H = 22.32$, $p < .001$; wave 2 $H = 26.42$, $p < .001$

13 Wave 1 $Z = 2.53$, $p < .02$; wave 2 $Z = 2.40$, $p < .02$

14 Wave 1 $Z = 3.43$, $p < .01$; wave 2 $Z = 3.84$, $p < .02$

15 Wave 1 $Z = 4.72$, $p < .001$; wave 2 $Z = 5.18$, $p < .001$

16 Wave 1 $\chi^2 = 36.39$, $p < .01$; wave 2 $\chi^2 = 74.70$, $p < .001$

17 Wave 1 adjusted residual = 2.8, $p < .01$, wave 2 adjusted residual = 2.1, $p < .05$

18 Wave 1 adjusted residual = n.s.; wave 2 adjusted residual = 2.3, $p < .05$

19 Wave 1 adjusted residual = -3.3, $p < .001$; wave 2 adjusted residual = -2.9, $p < .01$

20 Wave 1 adjusted residual = n.s.; wave 2 adjusted residual = -1.9, $p < .1$

21 Wave 1 adjusted residual = n.s.; wave 2 adjusted residual = -1.9, $p < .1$

22 Wave 1 adjusted residual = n.s.; wave 2 adjusted residual = -2.6, $p < .01$

23 Wave 1 adjusted residual = n.s.; wave 2 adjusted residual = 2.9, $p < .01$

24 Wave 1 adjusted residual = n.s.; wave 2 adjusted residual = -2.4, $p < .05$

25 Wave 1 adjusted residual = n.s.; wave 2 adjusted residual = -2.4, $p < .05$

26 Wave 1 adjusted residual = -2.2, $p < .05$; wave 2 adjusted residual = -2.1, $p < .05$

27 Wave 1 adjusted residual = 1.8, $p < .1$; wave 2 adjusted residual = 3.5, $p < .001$

28 Wave 1 adjusted residual = n.s; wave 2 adjusted residual = 4.2, $p < .001$

29 Wave 1 adjusted residual = 1.9, $p < .05$; wave 2 adjusted residual = 3.1, $p < .01$

30 $\chi^2 = 14.82$, $p < .01$

31 wave 1 $\chi^2 = 180.16$, $p < .001$; wave 2 $\chi^2 = 154.07$, $p < .001$

32 Wave 1 adjusted residual = 10.9, $p < .001$; wave 2 adjusted residual = -9.2, $p < .001$

33 Wave 1 adjusted residual = 2.6, $p < .01$; wave 2 adjusted residual = n.s.

34 Wave 1 adjusted residual = 9.9, $p < .001$; wave 2 adjusted residual = 10.1, $p < .001$

35 $\chi^2 = 5.66$, $p < .1$

36 Adjusted residual = -2.2, $p < .05$

37 $\chi^2 = 6.23$, $p < .05$

38 $\chi^2 = 11.85$, p < .01

39 $\chi^2 = 5.41$, p < .10

40 $\chi^2 = 32.00$, p < .001

41 Adjusted residual = 2.5, p < .05

42 Adjusted residual = -4.0, p < .001

43 Adjusted residual = 2.6, p < .01

44 H = 8.59, p < .05

45 H = 16.42, p < .001

46 H = 27.44, p < .001

47 H = 35.13, p < .001

48 H = 9.20, p < .05

49 H = 26.16, p < .001

50 Z = 3.34, p < .01

51 Z = 3.96, p < .001

52 Z = 3.318, p < .01

53 Z = 5.27, p < .001

54 Z = 3.04, p < .01

55 Z = 4.75, p < .001

56 Education Z = 2.97, p < .01; safety Z = 2.77, p < .01; housing Z = 5.18, p < .001; drinking water Z = 5.773, p < .001; jobs Z = 2.4, p < .02, and the economy Z = 4.53, p < .001

57 H = 4.96, p < .10

58 H = 14.88, p < .01

59 Z = 2.73, p < .01

60 Z = 2.11, p <.02

61 Z = 3.75, p < .001

62 Z = 2.19, p < .02

63 H = 40.31, p < .001

64 Z = 6.34, p < .001

65 Z = 3.78, p < .001

66 H = 5.67, p < .10

67 H = 32.75, p < .001

68 H = 9.34, p < .01

69 H = 21.02, p < .001

70 Z = 3.80, p < .001

71 Z = 2.196, p < .02

72 Z = 4.11, p < .001

73 Z = 3.504, p < .001

74 sad/depressed Z = 5.54, p < .001; quality of life Z = 2.32, p < .02; pride Z = 2.93, p < .01; control Z = 3.85, p < .001

75 person of worth H = 33.67, p < .001; person of merit H = 32.32, p < .001; satisfied with self H = 6.97, p < .05; do things well H = 7.82, p < .05; and life is worthwhile H = 64.96, P < .001

76 Z = 3.157, p <.01

77 Z = 3.71, p < .001

78 Z = 2.37, p < .02

79 Z = 6.25, p < .001

80 $Z = 4.07$, $p < .001$

81 $Z = 3.557$, $p < .001$

82 $Z = 3.59$, $p < .001$

83 person of worth $Z = 5.78$, $p < .001$; person of merit $Z = 5.38$, $p < .001$; satisfied with self $Z = 2.44$, $p < .02$; do things well $Z = 2.48$, $p < .02$; and life is worthwhile $Z = 7.27$, $p < .001$

84 $\chi^2 = 7.04$, $p < .05$

85 Adjusted residual $= -2.7$, $p < .01$

86 Adjusted residual $= 1.9$, $p < .05$

References

Abele, F. 2004. *Urgent need, serious opportunity: Towards a new model for Canada's Aboriginal peoples*. Ottawa: Canadian Policy Research Networks Inc.

Avison, W.R. 2001. "Unemployment and its consequences for mental health." In V.W. Marshall, W. Heinz, H. Krueger, and A. Verma (Eds.). *Restructuring Work and the Life Course*. Toronto: University of Toronto Press. 177–200.

Biswas-Diener, R., Diener, E., & Tamir, M. 2004. "The psychology of subjective well-being." *Daedaus*. 133(2):18–25.

Boldt, M. 1993. *Surviving as Indians: The challenge of self-government*. Toronto: University of Toronto Press.

Christakopoulou, S., Dawson, J., & Gari, A. (2001). "The community well-being questionnaire: Theoretical context and initial assessment of its reliability and validity." *Social Indicators Research*. 56(3): 319–349.

Cooke, M. 2005. "The First Nations Community Well-being Index (CWB): A conceptual review." Strategic Research and Analysis Directorate Ottawa: Indian and Northern Affairs Canada.

Dasgupta, P. 1999. "Valuation and evaluation: Measuring the quality of life and evaluating policy." Stockholm: The Beijer Institute of Ecological Economics.

Diener, E., & Biswas-Diener, R. 2002. "Will money increase subjective well-being? A literature review and guide to needed research." *Social Indicators Research*. 57:119–169.

Diener, E., Suh, E.M., Lucas, R.E., & Smith, H.L. 1999. "Subjective well-being: Three decades of progress." *Psychological Bulletin*. 125(2):276–302.

First Nations Inuit Health Branch. 2005. "A statistical profile on the health of First Nations in Canada." Ottawa: Health Canada.

Helliwell, J.F. 2003. "How's life? Combining individual and national variables to explain subjective well-being." *Economic Modelling*. 20:331–360.

Huppert, F.A., & Baylis, N. 2004. "Well-being: Towards an integration of psychology, neurobiology and social science." *Philosophical Transactions of the Royal Society B*. 359(1449): 1147–1451.

Huppert, F.A., Baylis, N., & Keverne, B. 2004. "Introduction: Why do we need a science of well-being." *Philosophical Transactions of the Royal Society B*. 359(1449): 1331–1332.

Kahn, R.L., & Juster, F.T. 2002. "Well-being: Concepts and measures." *Journal of Social Issues*. 58(4): 627–644.

Kirmayer, L., Boothroyd, L.J., Tanner, A., Adelson, N., & Robinson, E. 2000. "Psychological distress among the Cree of James Bay." *Transcultural psychiatry*. 37(1):35–56.

Kirmayer, L., Brass, G.M., & Tait, C.L. (2000). "The mental health of aboriginal peoples: Transformations of identity and community." *The Canadian Journal of Psychiatry*. 45: 607–616.

McBride, M. 2001. "Relative income effects on subjective well-being in the cross-section." *Journal of Economic Behavior and Organization*. 45:251–278.

McHardy, M., & O'Sullivan, E. 2004. "First Nations community well-being in Canada: The Community Well-being Index (CWB), 2001." Strategic Research and Analysis Directorate. Ottawa: Indian and Northern Affairs Canada.

Norris, M.J. 1998. "Canada's Aboriginal languages." *Canadian Social Trends*. Winter: 8–16.

Norris, M. J., & MacCon, K. 2003. "Aboriginal language transmission and maintenance in families: Results of an intergenerational and gender-based analysis for Canada, 1996." In J.P. White, P. Maxim, & D. Beavon (Eds.). *Aboriginal Conditions: The Research Foundation of Public Policy.* Vancouver: UBC Press. 164–196.

Oishi, S., Diener, E.F., Lucas, R.E., & Suh, E.M. 1999. "Cross-cultural variations in predictors of life satisfaction: Perspectives from needs and values." *Personality and Social Psychology Bulletin.* 25(8): 980–990.

Sampson, R.J., Morenoff, J.D., & Gannon-Rowley, T. (2002). "Assessing 'neighborhood effects': Social processes and new directions in research." *Annual Review of Sociology.* 28: 443–478.

Silver, J., & Mallet, K. (2002). *Aboriginal education in Winnipeg inner city high schools.* Winnipeg: Canadian Centre for Policy Alternatives—Manitoba.

Steverink, N., Westerhof, G.J., & Bode, C. 2001. "The personal experience of aging, individual resources, and subjective well-being." *Journals of Gerontology, Series B: Psychological Sciences and Social Sciences.* 56B(6): P364–P373.

Ten Fingers, K. (2005). "Rejecting, revitalizing, and reclaiming: First Nations work to set the direction of research and policy development." *Canadian Journal of Public Health.* 96: S60–S63.

Thoits, P. (2006). "Personal agency in the stress process." *Journal of Health and Social Behavior.* 47(4): 309–323.

Whitbeck, L. B., McMorris, B. J., Hoyt, D. R., Stubben, J. D., & LaFramboise, T. (2002). "Perceived discrimination, traditional practices, and depressive symptoms among American Indians in the Upper Midwest." *Journal of Health and Social Behavior.* 43(4):400–418.

White, J.P., Wingert, S., and Beavon, D. (Eds.). 2007. *Aboriginal Policy Research: Moving Forward Making a Difference. Volume III.* Toronto: Thompson Educational Publishing.

White, J.P., Maxim, P., and Beavon, D. (Eds.) 2004. *Aboriginal Policy Research: Setting the Agenda for Change, Volume 1.* Toronto: Thompson Educational Publishing.

White, J.P., Spence, N., & Maxim, P. (2005). "Impacts of social capital on educational attainment in Aboriginal communities: Lessons from Australia, Canada, and New Zealand." Ottawa: Policy Research Initiative.

Wingert, S.K., & White, J.P. 2006. "The social distribution of distress in the off-reserve Aboriginal population." Paper presented at the The Tenth International Conference on Social Stress Research.

White, J., Beavon, D. & Maxim, P. 2003. *Aboriginal Conditions: The Research Foundations of Public Policy.* Vancouver: UBC Press.

Witter, R.A., Okun, M.A., Stock, W.A., & Haring, M.J. 1984. "Education and subjective well-being: A meta-analysis." *Educational Evaluation and Policy Analysis.* 6(2):165–173.

Yu, Y., & Williams, D.R. (1999). "Socio-economic status and mental health." In C.S. Aneshensel & J.C. Phelan (Eds.). *Handbook of the sociology of mental health.* New York: Plenum Publishers. 151–166.

Notes on Contributors

Dan Beavon

Dan Beavon is the director of the Research and Analysis Directorate at INAC. He has worked in policy research for 20 years and has dozens of publications to his credit. He manages an Aboriginal research program on a variety of issues, increasing the amount and quality of strategic information available to the policy process. Much of his work involves complex horizontal and sensitive issues requiring partnerships with other federal departments, academics, and First Nations organizations.

Martin Cooke

Martin Cooke is an Assistant Professor jointly appointed in the departments of Sociology and Health Studies, and Gerontology at the University of Waterloo, where he has taught in the Master of Public Health program since 2005. His research interests are in social policy and the life course and social demography of Aboriginal populations. Current research projects include examinations of retirement, the labour market experiences of older workers, and the dynamics of social assistance receipt. He is currently the principle investigator of a SSHRC-funded study of the health and social conditions of Aboriginal Peoples across the life course.

Éric Guimond

Éric Guimond is of Micmac and French descent and a specialist in Aboriginal demography. His educational background includes demography, community health, physical education, and Aboriginal studies. He also possesses university research and teaching experience with expertise in projection models of population and Aboriginal groups. He is completing PhD studies (University of Montreal) on the topic of ethnic mobility of Aboriginal populations in Canada. Currently, Éric is engaged in the projects relating to First Nation housing, Inuit social conditions, and the development of knowledge transfer mechanisms between research and policy. Éric is a senior research manager at the Strategic Research and Analysis Directorate at Indian and Northern Affairs Canada.

Kate Hano

Kate Hano is currently a PhD candidate in the Department of Geography at the University of Waterloo, specializing in tourism. She holds an MA in sociology and is currently studying the accessibility of the physical environment for people with disability, in relation to travel and recreation. Her research interests include inequality, health and disability, as well as social network analysis.

Paul Maxim

Paul Maxim became Associate Vice President for Research at Wilfrid Laurier University in July 2006. Prior to that he was with the Department of Sociology at the University of Western Ontario. His primary research interests are in demographic processes and the socio-economic participation of Aboriginal people in Canadian society. He is the author of numerous articles and books including *Quantitative Research Methods in the Social Sciences* (1999) and his most recent book, released by UBC Press in September 2003, *Aboriginal Conditions: Research as a Foundation for Public Policy*, co-edited with Jerry White and Dan Beavon.

Mindy McHardy

Mindy has been working with First Nations data sources since joining INAC in 1996. She holds a degree in sociology from the University of Lethbridge and is a specialist in census data, survey research, the socioeconomic conditions of First Nations and Northern data sources. Early in her career, Mindy worked for Statistics Canada and as a Survey Research Consultant. Her contributions have been recognized with INAC Circle of Excellence Awards in 2000 and 2002. Since joining SRAD in 2001, Mindy has engaged in a number of projects investigating the well-being of First Nations. She is the lead researcher and manager of the Community Well-Being Index (CWB) project. She also represents the directorate on interdepartmental committees with respect to indicator development, data dissemination, and research ethics.

Frances Mitrou

Francis Mitrou was survey manager for the Western Australian Aboriginal Child Health Survey (WAACHS). Francis joined the Australian Bureau of Statistics in 1994, and has been outposted to the Institute for Child Health Research since 2000. Francis was one of the key data analysts and played a major role in the writing of each of the four volumes of WAACHS results. Francis has had long-term involvement in large-scale population surveys, including census management work and other major data collection and analysis projects involving Aboriginal communities. Francis is currently involved in the development of the 2008 Western Australian Child Development Study.

David Lawrence

David Lawrence is Senior Statistician in the Centre for Developmental Health at Curtin University of Technology. David joined the Centre in 2001 after completing a major record linkage study of the physical health of people with mental illness. David commenced his career in the Australian Bureau of Statistics and has extensive experience in the conduct and analysis of large-scale population based health surveys. Since 2002 David has been heavily involved in the Western Australian Aboriginal Child Health Survey (WAACHS). David is currently involved in the development of the 2008 Western Australian Child Development Study.

Erin O'Sullivan

Erin O'Sullivan has worked at SRAD/INAC since 2001, devoting most of her time to researching well-being in First Nations communities. Erin obtained her Bachelor's and Master's degrees in sociology from the Univeristy of Western Ontario. She is currently pursuing her PhD in sociology at McMaster University, where her work on well-being among Canada's Aboriginal people continues.

Sacha Senécal

Sacha Senécal was born in the Mohawk community of Kahnawake. He holds a PhD in social psychology (UQAM, 1999). During his studies, he specialized in the areas of statistics and research design. He has academic research and teaching experience in the fields of psychology, research methods, and quantitative analysis. Sacha is currently a Senior Strategic Research Manager at Indian and Northern Affairs Canada. His main research interests revolve around social issues within Aboriginal populations of Canada with a particular interest in the topics of well-being, health, education, and labour. Sacha currently resides in Cantley (QC), shares his life with Sophie, and is the proud father of Amélie and Xavier who constantly remind him that life isn't just about work.

Nicholas Spence

Nicholas Spence holds a PhD in sociology from the University of Western Ontario. He has worked for the federal government, and he is currently completing a Post doctoral fellowship at the University of Western Ontario. Nicholas is a member of the Aboriginal Policy Research Consortium (International). His research expertise includes statistics and quantitative research methods, inequality/stratification, health, and education. Nicholas has published several articles on Aboriginal policy and coauthored the book *Permission to Develop: Aboriginal Treaties, Case Law, and Regulations* also published by Thompson Educational Publising, Inc.

Sharanjit Uppal

Sharanjit Uppal has a PhD in Economics from University of Manitoba. He is currently a researcher with the Health Information and Research Division, Statistics Canada. His areas of specialization are Labour Economics and Population Health. His recent work has appeared in *Social Science and Medicine, International Journal of Manpower, Applied Economics, Health Reports*, and *Education Matters*.

Jerry White

Jerry White was Chair of the Department of Sociology at the University of Western Ontario until June of 2006. He is currently Professor and Senior Adviser to the Vice President (Provost), and the Director of the Aboriginal Policy Research Consortium (International). Jerry was the co-chair of the 2006 Aboriginal Policy Research Conference (with Dan Beavon and Peter Dinsdale), and a member of the Board of Governors for UWO. He has written and co-written 11 books and numerous articles on health care, and Aboriginal policy, the most recent being *Aboriginal Conditions* (UBC Press) and *Permission to Develop* (TEP). He is co-editor of the *Aboriginal Policy Research* series.

Susan Wingert

Susan Wingert is a PhD candidate in the Department of Sociology at the University of Western Ontario. She is also a research associate with the Aboriginal Policy Research Consortium. Her research interests include social inequality, race/ethnicity, culture, and mental health. Currently, her research examines social determinants of mental health in the off-reserve population.

0 1341 1321947 8